A GIFT FOR

FROM

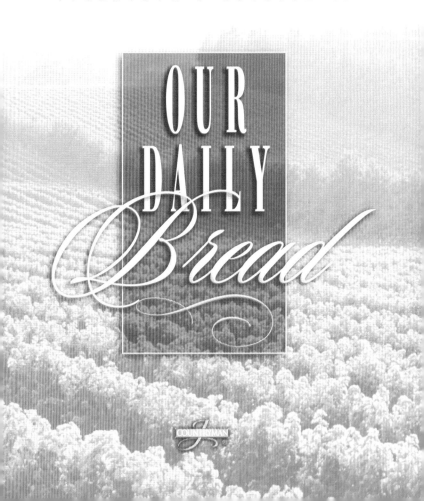

COLLECTOR'S EDITION II

OUR
DAILY
Bread

Published by the J. Countryman division of the Thomas Nelson Book Group,
Nashville, Tennessee 37214.

This book is based upon selections from Our Daily Bread,
Copyright ©1985 to 2001 by RBC Ministries, and is published by
special arrangement with and permission of Discovery House Publishers,
3000 Kraft Avenue, SE, Grand Rapids, Michigan, 49512. All rights reserved.

Compiled and edited by Terri Gibbs.
Project Manager: Michelle Orr

www.thomasnelson.com
www.jcountryman.com

Designed by LeftCoast Design, Portland, Oregon.

ISBN: 1-4041-0184-5

Printed and bound in China

Writers

Henry G. Bosch
(1914–1995)

J. David Branon

Dennis J. De Haan

M. R. De Haan, M.D.
(1891–1965)

Martin R. De Haan II

Richard W. De Haan
(1923–2002)

David C. Egner

Paul R. Van Gorder

Vernon C. Grounds

David C. McCasland

Haddon W. Robinson

David H. Roper

Herbert Vander Lugt

Joanie E. Yoder

FATHER, THANK YOU FOR YOUR SPIRIT,

FILL US WITH HIS LOVE AND POWER;

CHANGE US INTO CHRIST'S OWN IMAGE

DAY BY DAY AND HOUR BY HOUR.

ANONYMOUS

January

Whatever you do, do it heartily, as to the Lord.

COLOSSIANS 3:23

The name Stradivarius is synonymous with fine violins. This is true because Antonius Stradivarius insisted that no instrument constructed in his shop be sold until it was as near perfection as human care and skill could make it. Stradivarius observed, "God needs violins to send His music into the world, and if any violins are defective God's music will be spoiled." His work philosophy was summed up in one sentence: "Other men will make other violins, but no man shall make a better one."

Antonius Stradivarius expected his workers to do their very best in producing violins. How much more should we as Christians strive for excellence in the work assigned to us! Although Paul's words in our text were addressed to servants, they apply to all of us. He said, "Whatever you do, do it heartily, as to the Lord and not to men, knowing that from the Lord you will receive the reward of the inheritance; for you serve the Lord Christ" (Col. 3:23–24).

May it always be said of us that we have done our very best!
—R. W. D.

GOD DOESN'T ASK YOU TO BE THE BEST—JUST TO DO YOUR BEST.

In God is my salvation and my glory;
the rock of my strength, and my refuge, is in God.

PSALM 62:7

A century ago an ocean liner sank off the southwest coast of England, taking many people down with it. A 16-year-old galley boy, who was tossed up along the rugged shore, survived by clinging to a rock all night long. When he was finally rescued, he was asked, "Didn't you shake as you were clinging all night to that rock?" The boy replied, "Yes, of course. But the rock never shook once."

The ancient Israelites learned from their experiences in the desert that rocks were more than masses of stone. A rock could serve as shelter from a sudden storm. It could provide a cool shadow from oppressive heat. It was a stronghold and a place of safety from enemies (Ps. 61:2–3; 62:1–2; Isa. 32:2).

Just as the Hebrews found the rock of their salvation in the Lord who brought them up out of Egypt, so we find our rock of salvation in the One who through His Son delivered us from bondage to sin. When storms of trouble threaten to overwhelm us, we can cling to Him in faith, thankful that our Rock is our unshakable refuge. —V. C. G.

THE ROCK OF AGES IS OUR REFUGE AND STRENGTH.

*I am . . . rejoicing to see your good order
and the steadfastness of your faith in Christ.*

COLOSSIANS 2:5

Deception has always been part of military strategy. The British put it to good use during World War II in North Africa against German forces led by General Erwin Rommel. They constructed pasteboard look-alikes of tanks and airplanes to deceive the Germans. From the air this fake equipment looked real enough to fool reconnaissance personnel, and it could easily be moved.

Followers of Christ today are in a similar battle. How do we defend ourselves against deceivers? Paul used military terms in his comments to the Colossians that can help us to know what to do. First, he commended them for their "good order," which refers to being battle-ready, disciplined soldiers. Second, he spoke of the "steadfastness" of their faith in Christ, which refers to having a solid front. They had an unshaken commitment to their Lord and the advance of His kingdom.

Don't be fooled by Satan's lies. Know the truth of God's Word, and be battle-ready through a disciplined life and an unswerving commitment to Jesus Christ. —D. C. E.

GOD'S TRUTH IS THE BEST PROTECTION AGAINST SATAN'S LIES.

How unsearchable are His judgments
and His ways past finding out!

ROMANS 11:33

How often God delights to astonish us by the wonder of His ways! Our limited understanding of Him can be likened to a fly crawling on one of the great pillars of St. Paul's Cathedral in London. What does that tiny insect know about the architect's magnificent design? It sees only the little space of stone on which it moves. The beautiful carvings and ornamental work seem like towering mountains and deep valleys that only impede progress and obscure the view.

We as Christians often see only our immediate circumstances and perceive but a glimmer of God's marvelous purpose. The obstacles that block our vision and get in the way of our plans are actually part of the beautiful designs of divine grace.

Our heavenly Father knows exactly what He is doing. Although His ways are unsearchable, He assures us that all will work out for our good if we trust Him. —H. G. B.

GOD MAY CONCEAL THE PURPOSE OF HIS WAYS,
BUT HIS WAYS ARE NOT WITHOUT PURPOSE.

Do not be conformed to this world.

ROMANS 12:2

Two university students in Moorhead, Minnesota, painted a mural on the wall outside their dormitory room. According to *USA Today*, it showed a school of fish all swimming in the same direction except for a single fish heading the opposite way.

The one fish was intended to be the age-old symbol for Christ. Printed on the picture were the words, "Go against the flow." University officials, arguing that the mural might offend non-Christians, ordered the students to paint over it.

As we follow Jesus, our motives, values, and habits are bound to be different from those who are not Christians. When we are marching to the beat of a different drummer, of course we will be out of step with people around us. This takes conviction, courage, and courtesy. But by God's enabling grace we can be disturbingly different—and effectively different too. —V. C. G.

WHEN WE WALK WITH THE LORD,
WE'LL BE OUT OF STEP WITH THE WORLD.

I said, "I will confess my transgressions to the Lord,
"and You forgave the iniquity of my sin.

PSALM 32:5

There's a story about a boy whose father pounded a nail in the barn door every time the boy did something wrong. Soon there were many nails. Then one day the boy accepted Christ as Savior and began living for Him. To impress upon his son the wonder of being forgiven, the father took him to the barn and pulled out every nail from the door. "That is what it means to have all your sins forgiven," he said. "They are gone forever."

The boy was deeply impressed. Then looking at the door, he asked, "But Father, how can I get rid of the holes?" "I'm sorry," said the father, "but they will remain."

Even though we may have to live with the consequences of sin, we who have trusted in Christ as the sacrifice for our sins can rejoice in His complete forgiveness. —D. J. D.

ALTHOUGH GOD HEALS THE WOUNDS OF SIN,
SCARS MAY REMAIN.

There are differences of ministries, but the same Lord.

1 CORINTHIANS 12:5

Champion figure skater Paul Wylie is a *cum laude* Harvard graduate and a born-again Christian. His mother always wanted him to be a minister, but he has decided to study law. He believes he does not possess the gifts required to pastoral ministry. But he insists—and rightly so—that whether he's performing on the ice or reading in the library of Harvard Law School, he can serve his Savior Jesus Christ.

"I think that every Christian is called to be a minister in his place of work," he says, "So I try to be a minister wherever I am. When people come up to me and ask questions, I tell them the truth."

Whether we are figure skaters, law students, homemakers, mechanics, nurses, bankers, or have some other job, we can serve Jesus Christ. The New Testament doesn't assign the task of ministry only to those who are officially recognized as pastors. First Corinthians 12 indicates that every believer is spiritually equipped for some kind of service (v.7). —V. C. G.

NO MATTER HOW SMALL IT MAY SEEM,
YOUR WORK FOR CHRIST HAS GREAT VALUE.

Let your "Yes" be "Yes," and your "No," "No."
For whatever is more than these is from the evil one.

MATTHEW 5:37

In 1878, a merchant in Bozeman, Montana, extended to Andrew Garcia what was called "jawbone credit." Without putting anything into writing, he gave Garcia $300 worth of supplies for a hunting and trapping expedition. The trapper promised to return and pay his debt with hides and pelts from his expedition.

While Garcia was away, hostile Indians moved into the area around Bozeman. Weather conditions got bad. Fellow trappers told him to forget about returning to Bozeman, but Garcia wouldn't hear of it. After a series of harrowing experiences, he returned to the merchant with hides and pelts to pay his debt. He kept his word.

God, too, makes vows, but He always keeps His word. If He didn't, we would have no basis for hope. Let's thank Him for being a God of integrity and resolve that we will be people whose word can be trusted. —H. V. L.

PEOPLE WHO TRUST GOD'S WORD
SHOULD BE PEOPLE WHO CAN BE TRUSTED.

Jesus Christ . . . has abolished death and brought life
and immortality to light through the gospel.

2 TIMOTHY 1:10

At the southern tip of Africa, a cape jutting out into the ocean once caused sailors great anxiety. Many who attempted to sail around it were lost in the swirling seas. Because adverse weather conditions so often prevailed there, the region was named the Cape of Storms. A Portuguese captain determined to find a safe route through those treacherous waters so his countrymen could reach Cathay and the riches of the East Indies in safety. He succeeded, and the area was renamed the Cape of Good Hope.

We all face a great storm called death. But our Lord has already traveled through it safely and has provided a way for us to do the same. By His crucifixion and resurrection, Christ abolished eternal death for every believer and has permanently established our fellowship with Him in heaven.

Now all who know Christ as Savior can face life's final voyage with confidence. Even though the sea may be rough, we will experience no terror as we pass through the "cape of good hope" and into heaven's harbor. The Master Helmsman Himself has assured our safe passage. —H. G. B.

CHRIST HAS CHARTED A SAFE COURSE
THROUGH THE DARK WATERS OF DEATH.

If Christ is not risen, your faith is futile;
you are still in your sins!

1 CORINTHIANS 15:17

In the early part of this century, a group of lawyers met in England to discuss the biblical accounts of Jesus' resurrection. They wanted to see if enough information was available to make a case that would hold up in a court of law. They concluded that Christ's resurrection was one of the most well-established facts of history!

In his book *Countdown*, G. B. Hardy offers thought-provoking questions about the resurrection: "There are but two essential requirements: (1) Has anyone cheated death and proved it? (2) Is it available to me? Here is the complete record: Confucius' tomb—occupied. Buddha's tomb—occupied. Muhammad's tomb—occupied. Jesus' tomb—empty! Argue as you will, there is no point in following a loser."

Historical evidence and countless changed lives testify that the resurrection of Jesus is a fact, not a fable! Have you put your hope in the risen Christ? —D. C. E.

CHRIST'S RESURRECTION IS A FACTOR IN SALVATION
BECAUSE IT IS A FACT OF HISTORY.

We then who are strong ought to
bear with the scruples of the weak.

ROMANS 15:1

Each fall we are visited by flocks of migrating geese who stop off at a meadow near our home. For several weeks those birds fly in long, wavy V-formations over our house, honking as they go. But then, as winter approaches, they are off again on their long flight south.

A student of mine furthered my education and my appreciation for these visitors from the north. I learned that geese fly at speeds of 40 to 50 miles per hour. They travel in formation because as each bird flaps its wings, it creates an updraft for the bird behind it. They can travel 70 percent farther in a group than they could if they flew alone.

Christians are like that in a way. When we have a common purpose, we are propelled by the thrust of others who share those same goals. We can get a lot farther together than we can alone.

Geese also honk at one another. They are not critics but encouragers. Those in the rear sound off to exhort those up front to stay on course and maintain their speed. We too move ahead much more easily if there is someone behind us encouraging us to stay on track and keep going. —H. W. R.

WE CAN GO A LOT FARTHER TOGETHER THAN WE CAN ALONE.

Moses wrote this song the same day,
and taught it to the children of Israel.

DEUTERONOMY 31:22

A college student was troubled by sinful thoughts. Even though he regularly read his Bible and prayed, he continued to struggle, so he sought help from a Christian counselor. "What kind of music do you listen to?" asked the counselor. The student said it was secular rock. The counselor then commented, "Think of your mind as a big sheet of paper. Each song you hear is a match burning the edges. You ask God to heal the burn, and He begins applying the salve of His word. But you keep adding matches. Listen to Christian music and see what happens." The student did, and the truth set to music began to heal his mind.

God combines music's power with truth to draw His people closer to Himself. In Deuteronomy 32, Moses taught a new generation of Israelites a long song of 43 verses. The song's purpose was twofold: It would show the Israelites that God had a right to their love, and it would call them back to Himself when they had come to the end of their own strength (vv. 36–39).

Never underestimate the power of music. —D. J. D.

IF THERE'S NO HARMONY IN YOUR LIFE, TRY CHANGING YOUR TUNE.

He counts the number of the stars;
He calls them all by name.

PSALM 147:4

Christian astronomer David Block tells us that the Milky Way contains 100 billion stars—and that is just one small part of the vast heavens of which our planet is but a tiny speck. Considering the utter insignificance of our earth, it is hard to believe that the Creator of the cosmos cares about what happens to the human family.

The astonishing truth is that God does care. Long before the invention of telescopes, David asked, "When I consider Your heavens, . . . what is man that You are mindful of him?" (Ps. 8:3–4). And not only does God care, He cares for everyone as if we each were the sole object of His loving attention. Psalm 147:3–4 contrasts the star-studded sky with the hurts of a single soul: "He heals the brokenhearted and binds up their wounds. He counts the number of the stars; He calls them all by name."

The wisdom and the power that sustain the whole cosmos are focused on every believer. What a source of confidence and strength!
—V. C. G.

HE WHO HOLDS THE STARS IN SPACE
WILL SURELY UPHOLD HIS SAINTS ON EARTH.

There are many members, yet one body.

1 CORINTHIANS 12:20

What does the word *Yankee* mean to you? Robert W. Mayer, in a *Wall Street Journal* article, writes, "To people in other parts of the world it simply means someone from the United States; to people in the United States it means someone from north of the Mason-Dixon Line; to us Northerners it means someone from New England; to New Englanders it means someone from Vermont; to Vermonters it means someone from the Green Mountains."

The term *Christian* has taken on a wide range of meaning too. Some have even equated being a Christian with being an American. That's far too wide! But we who believe in Jesus Christ often make the definition too narrow. We describe as "real Christians" only those men and women who believe and worship exactly as we do.

Certainly sound doctrine is vital! There is no room for disagreement over the fundamentals of the faith. But a "real Christian" is anyone who relies on God's grace and puts his trust in Christ alone as his only hope of salvation. —H. W. R.

DON'T REJECT ANYONE WHOM GOD HAS ACCEPTED.

Satisfy us early with Your mercy,
that we may rejoice and be glad all our days!

PSALM 90:14

When Grandma Moses was 100, she was still painting. George Bernard Shaw wrote a play at 94. Arthur Rubinstein gave a great recital at Carnegie Hall when he was 89. And at 82, Winston Churchill wrote *A History of the English-Speaking Peoples.*

The Bible tells of many godly people who didn't let the advancing years stop them—Caleb and Moses, for instance. At 80, Caleb was one of the men sent to spy out the land of Canaan, and later he was allowed to enter the Promised Land (Num. 14:24; 26:65). And Moses continued to lead the people of Israel faithfully until he was 120 (Ps. 92:14).

As long as we have strength, we need to dedicate ourselves to the Lord's service. Then, no matter what our age, we can "rejoice and be glad." —J. D. B.

TO STAY YOUTHFUL, STAY USEFUL.

Whom He foreknew, He also predestined
to be conformed to the image of His Son.

ROMANS 8:29

*W*omen in nearly record numbers, we're told, were drawn in envy to the picture of a well-known movie actress on the cover of a popular magazine. She had been portrayed as possessing flawless beauty. But the editors of another magazine published a follow-up story telling about a photo company that had billed the first magazine $1,525 for their work on the picture "to clean up complexion, soften eye line, soften smile line, add color to lips, trim chin, . . . adjust color, and add hair on the top of the head." So however beautiful she actually is, she needed something—quite a little it seems—to hide the blemishes that would quickly destroy her image of "ideal loveliness."

What a picture of the human spiritual condition! Every one of us is flawed when compared with the moral excellence of Christ (Rom. 3:23). No matter how good we may appear, we need more than a religious touch-up to conceal our sins. We desperately need the soul-cleansing, atoning blood of Jesus Christ. —V. C. G.

THE MOST BEAUTIFUL PEOPLE
ARE THOSE WHO REMIND US OF CHRIST.

Take up the whole armor of God,
that you may be able to withstand in the evil day.

EPHESIANS 6:13

A story from the Korean War illustrates the truth of that verse. As enemy forces advanced, Baker Company was cut off from the rest of their unit. For several hours no word was heard, even though headquarters repeatedly tried to communicate with the missing troops. Finally a faint signal was received. Straining to hear, the corpsman asked, "Baker Company, do you read me?" "This is Baker Company," came the reply. "What is your situation?" asked the corpsman. "The enemy is to the east of us, the enemy is to the west of us, the enemy is to the north of us, the enemy is to the south of us." Then with a brief pause, the sergeant from Baker Company said with determination, "The enemy is not going to get away from us now!" Although surrounded and out-numbered, he was thinking of victory, not defeat.

As believers in Jesus Christ, we are engaged in spiritual warfare with unseen wicked forces. To overcome our enemy in the power of the Holy Spirit, we must remain resolute in our confidence in God and determine never to accept defeat. —D. J. D.

TO DEFEAT SATAN, SURRENDER TO CHRIST.

All things work together for good . . .
to those who are the called according to His purpose.

ROMANS 8:28

When a cowboy applied for an insurance policy, the agent asked, "Have you ever had any accidents?" After a moments reflection, the applicant responded, "Nope, but a bronc did kick in two of my ribs last summer, and a couple of years ago a rattlesnake bit me on the ankle."

"Wouldn't you call those accidents?" replied the puzzled agent. "Naw," the cowboy said, "they did it on purpose!"

That story reminds me of the biblical truth that there are no accidents in the lives of God's children. What seems like a tragedy from the human standpoint can actually be a providential means of blessing.

Does everything seem to be going against you? These apparent misfortunes are not accidents. The Lord allows such things for a blessed purpose. So, patiently trust Him. Someday you will praise Him for it all!
—R. W. D.

GOD TRANSFORMS TRIALS INTO TRIUMPHS.

*Having then gifts differing according to the grace that is given to us,
let us use them.*

ROMANS 12:6

A concert violinist had a brother who was a bricklayer.
One day a woman began talking to the bricklayer about how
wonderful it was for him to be in the same family as the noted musician.
But then, not wanting to insult the bricklayer, she added, "Of course, we
don't all have the same talents, and even in the same family some just
seem to have more ability than others."

The bricklayer replied, "You're telling me! That violinist brother of
mine doesn't know a thing about laying bricks. And if he wasn't able to
make some money playing that fiddle of his, he couldn't hire a guy with
know-how like mine to build his house. If he had to build a house
himself, he'd be ruined."

In the church, God has gifted us in different ways, too. Our
responsibility is to exercise the spiritual gifts that He has given us. When
we do, we build each other up in the faith, and there is harmony in the
body of Christ.—H. W. R.

THERE ARE NO UNIMPORTANT MEMBERS IN THE BODY OF CHRIST.

My heart's desire and prayer to God . . .
is that they may be saved.

ROMANS 10:1

On the east side of London, pipes for a large drain were being laid in a trench. Suddenly the dirt walls collapsed, and several workmen were buried. Amid the great excitement and confusion a crowd gathered. Many bystanders watched as several people tried to rescue the victims.

A woman came over to one onlooker, put her hand gently on his shoulder, and said, "Bill, did you know your brother is down there?" The color drained from his cheeks, then he sprang into action. Throwing aside his coat and leaping into the trench, he grabbed a shovel and worked frantically until the trapped men were finally set free.

What a lesson for all of us! Masses of humanity are trapped in sin and must be rescued. Although we may express with our words a deep concern over their lost condition, our actions may instead be saying, "Am I my brother's keeper?" (Gen. 4:9). But God will never accept that attitude. Join the rescue effort. Your brother is down there! —H. G. B.

TO BE YOUR BROTHER'S KEEPER MEANS
YOU'LL BE YOUR BROTHER'S SEEKER.

Do not worry about tomorrow.

MATTHEW 6:34

The story is told of a man who raised chickens. Among them was a rooster whose occasional crowing greatly annoyed a neighbor. Early one morning the disgruntled neighbor called the farmer and complained, "That miserable bird of yours keeps me up all night!"

"I don't understand," came the reply. "He hardly ever crows; but if he does, it's never more than two or three times."

"That isn't my problem," retorted the neighbor. "It's not how often he crows that irritates me! What keeps me awake is not knowing when he might crow!"

Many of us are like that man. We worry about the difficulties and distressing circumstances that could arise tomorrow. Rather than living a day at a time and rejoicing in the Lord's sufficiency for the present, we become anxious by borrowing trouble from the future. Friend, stop foolishly "waiting for the rooster"! —R. W. D.

WORRYING IS PAYING INTEREST ON TROUBLES THAT MAY NEVER COME DUE!

We know that the law is good if one uses it lawfully.

1 TIMOTHY 1:8

The Computer Ethics Institute has proposed ten commandments for computer users. The laws include:

- Thou shalt not use a computer to harm other people.
- Thou shalt not snoop around in other people's computer files.
- Thou shalt not copy or use proprietary software for which you have not paid.

Many of us have had enough contact with computers to see the need for such rules. We may also realize, however, that merely publishing laws will not change human nature. Even the Law of Moses, which these principles imitate, was never able to change anyone's heart.

The Law's highest purpose is to show us God's perfect standards and our need for Christ. No one else has paid the price for our forgiveness. Christ doesn't change us by teaching us to keep the Law (Gal. 3:1–5). He transforms us by giving us a new heart. —M. R. D. II

A CHANGED LIFE IS THE RESULT OF A CHANGED HEART.

As for me, I will walk in my integrity.

PSALM 26:11

In June of 1994, 62,000 men gathered at the Hoosier Dome in Indianapolis for an event called Promise Keepers. One goal of the conference was to challenge men to demonstrate integrity by adhering to the principles for godly living set forth in the Bible. According to one report, the men started meeting that goal right away.

During a break, the hallways were jammed with men. One hungry guy who was stuck by a food stand bought a hot dog, but the mustard was clear across the concourse. Undaunted, he handed the dog to the next man and requested, "Mustard." Off it went.

The woman who sold the snacks laughed and said, "Honey, you aren't going to see that hot dog again." "Yes, he will," someone replied. "These guys are Christians." Sure enough, the hot dog made it back—with mustard.

David vowed to walk in integrity (Ps. 26:11). But he could do so only because he trusted the Lord to help him (vv.1–2). We should do the same. Let's surprise people with our integrity—even with something as trivial as a hot dog. —J. D. B.

INTEGRITY IS CHRISTLIKE CHARACTER IN WORK-CLOTHES.

The worlds were framed by the word of God.

HEBREWS 11:3

As part of a marketing campaign to attract subscribers, National Geographic magazine produced a remarkable brochure called *Ten Pictures You'll Never Forget.* Included in the pamphlet were photos such as astronaut Buzz Aldrin on the moon, Mount St. Helens erupting, a Brazilian jaguar sprawled across a tree branch, and a cherubic Russian schoolgirl signaling her age.

As I gaze at this brochure, I'm reminded that these ten unforgettable scenes are possible only because of ten unforgettable words: "In the beginning God created the heavens and the earth" (Gen. 1:1).

In this age of sophisticated sciences, we can be influenced to miss this key point because so much of what we read assumes a godless origin of this world. We need to remind ourselves that God made the moon, mountains, jaguars, and little girls. Just ten words. Don't forget them. They are the foundation of all the beauty and majesty of the universe.

—J. D. B.

ALL OF CREATION BEARS GOD'S AUTOGRAPH.

What is our hope, or joy, or crown of rejoicing?
Is it not even you?

1 THESSALONIANS 2:19

A missionary was once asked about his salary. The inquirer knew it couldn't be much, and he wanted to know why anyone would give so generously of himself to help total strangers, yet be paid so little.

The missionary pulled out a letter and read these words: "If it weren't for you, I wouldn't know Jesus Christ as my Savior. Every morning I kneel in prayer, thanking God for everything you've done for me."

"That's my pay!" exclaimed the dedicated servant of the Lord.

The apostle Paul must have had something similar in mind when he wrote to those he had brought to the Savior, "What is our hope, or joy, or crown of rejoicing? Is it not even you?" (1 Thess. 2:19).

In a day when there is so much emphasis on acquiring material wealth, how refreshing it is to hear of Christians whose greatest reward is to see people accept Christ and grow in spiritual maturity. —R. W. D.

WORK FOR THE LORD—
HIS RETIREMENT PLAN IS OUT OF THIS WORLD.

[Wisdom cries out,] whoever listens to me will dwell safely.

PROVERBS 1:33

In the jungles of eastern Sri Lanka, fifteen soldiers of a government commando unit were saved by two dogs adopted as mascots. According to a news report, the soldiers were completing a ten-mile hike when their dogs sensed danger. Running ahead toward a water hole where the unit planned to rest, the dogs suddenly began barking and circling the area. The troops searched carefully and found twelve buried grenades attached to a taut wire trigger.

The soldiers escaped serious injury and even death because they listened to those barking dogs. Sometimes we are apt to give less credibility and attention to more faithful protectors. How many times have we resented a father's warnings or a mother's advice? How often have we grown tired of pastoral pleadings or a fellow believer's caution?

Yet, how wise and loving is our God! He sends His messengers to whisper, to plead, and sometimes to howl about hidden dangers that can harm our physical and spiritual lives. Let's be wise and listen to the warnings! —M. R. D. II

IF YOU WANT TO BE WISE, LISTEN TO WISE PEOPLE.

Whoever desires, let him take the water of life freely.

REVELATION 22:17

A minister was preaching on Revelation 22:17. The day was hot and some people had trouble paying attention. The heat bothered the pastor too, so from time to time he would take a drink of water. After each sip he would say, "Whoever desires, let him take the water of life freely."

In the audience was a little boy who was very thirsty. Each time the preacher lifted the sparkling glass of water to his lips, the boy's thirst increased. Finally he decided that if the pastor said once more, "Whoever desires, let him take the water of life freely," he would go to the front and take a drink for himself.

Just then the inviting words rang out once more. Resolutely the little fellow left his seat and walked up to the pulpit. The audience watched in astonishment as he picked up the glass and took a deep swallow. Then with a kind "Thank you, pastor!" he returned to his seat. The preacher was moved and used the incident to make a spiritual point. God gives the invitation to drink of the Living Water by faith, but it does us no good unless we accept it. —H. G. B.

**UNLESS ONE DRINKS OF THE "WATER OF LIFE,"
HE WILL THIRST FOREVER!**

Sing to the LORD, bless His name;
proclaim the good news of His salvation from day to day.

PSALM 96:2

ost people are interested in news, but only if it's fresh. We read today's newspaper, not yesterday's. Ratings for news programs would drop out of sight if they covered only last year's or last month's events.

That same need to remain fresh and up-to-date applies to our recognition of the good things God does for us. He wants us to acknowledge that His mercy and compassion are "new every morning" (Lam. 3:22–23).

The Lord is still doing great things today. Look around you at His handiwork. See how His power and wisdom are revealed in nature and in man. Then sing a new song of praise to the God behind it all. Don't treat the good news of His power as if it stopped a long time ago. —M. R. D. II

EACH NEW DAY GIVES US NEW REASONS TO SING GOD'S PRAISE.

Christ Jesus . . . made Himself of no reputation,
taking the form of a bondservant.

PHILIPPIANS 2:5, 7

"Money is power." That principle drives most cultures of the world. People scramble for wealth, often at the price of personal integrity, in order to gain the power to live where and how they want, drive the kind of vehicle they want, and get whatever else they want.

In a culture that worships money, believers in Jesus Christ are in danger of doing the same. Some use their money to control their family, or they may threaten to stop giving to their church if they don't get their way.

How unlike Jesus! He had power over disease, and He used it to heal the sick. He had power over the sea, and He used it to remove fear. He had power to create, and He fed thousands. He had power over sin, and He forgave sinners. He had power over His own life, yet He willingly gave up His life to save all who would call upon Him (Rom. 10:13). Jesus possessed all power, but He used it to serve others. —D. C. E.

THE MORE WE SERVE CHRIST, THE LESS WE WILL SERVE SELF.

You have dealt well with Your servant, O LORD,
according to Your Word.

PSALM 119:65

I'll always remember the Bible teacher who held up his well-worn Bible and said, "Every believer should wreck a copy of the Bible every ten years." In other words, we should use our Bibles so much that they gradually wear out. His challenge also reminds me of the saying: "A Bible that's falling apart is usually owned by someone who isn't!" This certainly became true for me.

I'm not proud of the years when my Bible was considerably under-used. But one day I sensed God reminding me that His Word is full of truth that works. From that point on, I desired to put those truths into action in my life. Little by little, as I read it, digested it, and underlined key phrases, my Bible began falling apart instead of me!

In the margin of many pages in D. L. Moody's Bible, he wrote the letters T and P, meaning "Tried and Proved." He had put into practice passages from God's Word, proving that they work. You too can try and prove God's wonder-working Word. —J. E. Y.

THE BIBLE IS MEANT TO BE BREAD FOR DAILY USE,
NOT CAKE FOR SPECIAL OCCASIONS.

No longer do I call you servants, . . . but I have called you friends.

JOHN 15:15

*S*ocrates once asked a simple old man what he was most thankful for. The man replied, "That being such as I am, I have had the friends I have had."

Our English word *friend* comes from the same root as the word *freedom*. A genuine friend sets us free to be who and what we are. We can pour out our doubts and talk freely about the wolves howling at the door of our life.

A faithful friend also affirms our worth. Queen Victoria said of William Gladstone, "When I am with him, I feel I am with one of the most important leaders in the world." But of Benjamin Disraeli she said, "He makes me feel as if I am one of the most important leaders of the world."

Christians have an inside track on making and being friends because we are part of one family. We have Christ in common—and He is the truest Friend anyone can have.—H. W. R.

OUR BEST FRIENDS DRAW US CLOSER TO CHRIST.

February

Where envy and self-seeking exist,
confusion and every evil thing are there.

JAMES 3:16

Two ships collided in the Black Sea in 1986, hurling hundreds of passengers into the icy waters and causing a tragic loss of life. News of the disaster was further darkened when an investigation revealed that the accident was caused by human stubbornness. Each captain was aware of the other ship's presence and both could have taken evasive action to avert the collision. But neither wanted to yield to the other. By the time they saw the error of their ways, it was too late.

Havoc and loss can be created in human relationships for similar reasons. We prefer to blame the world's problems on religious or political differences. But James said the root problem is "bitter envy and self-seeking in your hearts" (3:14), which stems from pride.

How can we keep selfish ambition and pride from turning into major disasters? We must draw on "the wisdom that is from above"— wisdom that is "pure, then peaceable, gentle, willing to yield, full of mercy and good fruits" (James 3:17). That will mark the beginning of harmony—not havoc. —M. R. D. II

SOME TROUBLES COME FROM WANTING OUR OWN WAY;
OTHERS COME FROM GETTING IT.

You will keep him in perfect peace,
whose mind is stayed on You, because he trusts in You.

ISAIAH 26:3

We spend approximately 30 percent of our lives sleeping—or trying to sleep. Today there are more than 300 sleep disorder clinics in the United States. There are also 90 million Americans who snore, and they (or the people who share a room with them) spend about $200 million a year on anti-snoring remedies.

Think of it! Nearly a third of our entire lives sleeping! Yet how much do we plan and prepare spiritually for those important hours of sleep?

For many years, a friend of mine has followed a simple guideline he refers to as HWLW, which stands for "His Word the Last Word." Every night, just before turning out the light, he reads a passage from the Bible or meditates on a verse he has memorized. Before he goes to sleep, he wants the last word he thinks about to be from God—not the evening news or the weather.

Why don't we all try it? "His Word the Last Word"—spiritual preparation for a peaceful night's sleep! —D. C. M.

BEFORE YOU TURN OUT THE LIGHT,
TURN TO THE LIGHT OF GOD'S WORD.

Oh, give thanks to the LORD! Call upon His name;
make known His deeds among the peoples!

PSALM 105:1

A little boy said, "Salt is what spoils potatoes when it is left out." Using the same kind of negative definition, we can say, "Gratitude is what spoils life when it is left out."

Some of the most grateful people I know have few material possessions and little money in their bank accounts. A character in one of Charles Dickens' stories remarks, "My not knowing at one meal where I shall get the next is a great help to thankfulness."

Riches, on the other hand, may be a handicap. A wealthy woman told her doctor that she was frustrated by a restless desire to accumulate more and more things. He replied, "These are the usual symptoms of too much ease in the home and too little gratitude in the heart."

No matter what your circumstances, count your blessings. The salt of gratitude helps to make all of life taste better. —H. V. L.

A GOOD ATTITUDE BEGINS WITH GRATITUDE TO GOD.

Nation shall not lift up sword against nation,
neither shall they learn war anymore.

ISAIAH 2:4

*P*resident Woodrow Wilson was a staunch idealist whose hope for world peace was deeply embedded in his thinking. Therefore, when he declared war on Germany in 1917, his decision cut to his very heart. It is said that when he returned to the White House, he put his head down on a table and sobbed.

World War I was seen by many as "the war to end all wars." Wilson himself became the leading advocate for the League of Nations, which he hoped would ensure peace. But World War II and many subsequent wars have dashed such hopes.

So the question remains: Can this world ever know true peace? The Bible answers, "Yes!" When individuals trust Jesus as their Savior, they are reconciled to God and are motivated to be peacemakers in their own world of relationships—even with their enemies. God's peace in believers' hearts is a present reality, and the Lord's return to earth is the world's only hope for lasting peace. And it will come! —D. J. D.

ONLY THE PRINCE OF PEACE CAN BRING LASTING PEACE.

We are members of His body, of His flesh and of His bones.

EPHESIANS 5:30

Since ascending to heaven, Christ no longer has a body on earth except ours. In other words, He has no hands, legs, or feet on earth except for the members of His body, the church.

There's a story of a little child who was put to bed in a dark room. She was fearful of being left alone, so her mother brought her a doll. This didn't satisfy her and she begged her mother to stay. The mother reminded her that she had the doll and God, and needn't be afraid. Soon the child began crying. When the mother returned to her side, she sobbed, "Oh, Mommy, I want someone with skin on!"

We're all like that child at times. In our loneliness and suffering, Christ doesn't condemn us for wanting "someone with skin on" to be with us and to care for us. Therefore He sends us out to be His body to one another and to the world, and to go about doing good. Remember this: Right now Jesus has no body on earth but ours! —J. E. Y.

**GOD WORKS THROUGH US
TO MEET THE NEEDS OF THOSE AROUND US.**

*God has chosen the weak things of the world
to put to shame the . . . mighty.*

1 CORINTHIANS 1:27

A renowned violinist announced before a concert that he would play one of the world's most expensive violins. His first composition was played flawlessly, and the audience was thrilled at the performance. After taking his bows, he suddenly smashed the instrument, completely demolishing it. The audience was horrified—that is, until the violinist explained that he had been playing a cheap violin.

Then, picking up the expensive instrument, the virtuoso began to draw the bow across the strings. The sound was beautiful, but most of the people couldn't tell any difference between the music from the expensive violin and the cheap one. The quality of the instrument was secondary to the skill of the violinist.

It's something like that in our service for the Lord. The apostle Paul said that "God has chosen the foolish things of the world to put to shame the wise" (1 Cor. 1:27). Like that cheap violin, we can be instruments in the Master's hands to magnify the Lord and bring blessing to others. —R. W. D.

**GOD CAN USE ORDINARY INSTRUMENTS
TO PRODUCE A CONCERT OF PRAISE.**

When Jesus had received the sour wine,
He said, "It is finished!"

JOHN 19:30

*C*ould you improve on a masterpiece? Imagine that you are walking through the Louvre museum in Paris. As you approach the *Mona Lisa* by Leonardo da Vinci, would you think about taking a palette and brushes and touching up the painting? Maybe put some more color in her cheeks? Perhaps change her nose a little?

"That's ridiculous!" you say. For nearly 500 years the *Mona Lisa* has been considered one of the greatest artistic works of all time. How absurd to think we could add anything to this masterpiece!

Yet that's what many people try to do with Christ's masterpiece—salvation. They think they must improve on it with some work of their own. But that masterpiece was completed when Jesus said, "It is finished," while hanging on the cross (John 19:30). Then He proved that His work of redemption was done when He rose from the dead.

Receive God's gift of salvation. Jesus paid it all. The masterpiece is complete. —J. D. B.

SALVATION IS A GIFT TO BE RECEIVED—
NOT A GOAL TO BE ACHIEVED.

*When the king heard the words of the Book of the Law,
. . . he tore his clothes.*

2 KINGS 22:11

A five-year-old boy recognized himself on a TV show about missing children. He had thought he was where he was supposed to be. But when he saw himself on television, he realized that he was separated from the one to whom he rightfully belonged. He told his babysitter, who then called the authorities. Before long, he was in the arms of his mother.

This reminded me of King Josiah. He had assumed that he and his nation were spiritually where they were supposed to be. But when the long-lost Law of God was read, the king realized that he and his people had been disobedient to God and were separated from Him. Josiah tore his clothes (signifying his own repentance) and made a public covenant "to follow the Lord and to keep His commandments" (2 Kings 23:3). As a result, the nation repented and returned to the God to whom they belonged.

The Bible is God's personal message to us. He gave it to us so that we could see ourselves reflected in it, recognize our sin, and confess, "Hey, that's me!" Then as we repent, we can be "reunited" with Him.—M. R. D. II

**WE MUST ADJUST OURSELVES TO THE BIBLE—
NEVER THE BIBLE TO OURSELVES.**

If anyone is in Christ, . . . old things have passed away;
behold, all things have become new.

2 CORINTHIANS 5:17

A woman who restores valuable paintings says many works of art that seem hopelessly damaged can be saved by an expert. Rebecca McLain has brought color and life back to dulled oil paintings by carefully removing dirt and discolored varnish. But she has also seen the damage done when people attempt to clean their own soiled art with oven cleaner or abrasive powders. Her advice? If you value the art, take it to an expert in restoration.

The same need exists in lives soiled by sin. Our efforts at ridding ourselves of the guilt and defilement of sinful actions and attitudes often end in frustration and despair. In our attempts to get rid of guilt, we sometimes blame others. Or we simply give up, thinking that we cannot be any different.

When it comes to cleansing the canvas of our souls, we cannot do it ourselves. But Jesus our redeemer is the expert who can restore the most damaged and discouraged person. Call on Him today for expert restoration. —D. C. M.

ONLY GOD CAN TRANSFORM A SIN-STAINED SOUL
INTO A MASTERPIECE OF GRACE.

*Look among the nations and watch—
be utterly astounded!*

HABAKKUK 1:5

As the year 1999 came to a close, great leaders of the century were remembered, including Prime Minister Winston Churchill and President Franklin Roosevelt. During World War II, they led Great Britain and the United States to defeat Nazism and Fascism.

Did you know that both men nearly lost their lives before the war began? In December 1931, Churchill was struck by a car as he crossed Fifth Avenue in New York City. In Miami in December 1933, an assassin's bullet barely missed Roosevelt and killed the man standing beside him.

Both leaders could have died, but they survived. Why? I believe God wanted these two men alive to lead their respective nations to victory over the enemy.

When Habakkuk complained that it didn't seem right for God to use wicked Babylon to discipline Israel, the Lord assured the prophet that this did not mean evil would triumph .We, too, can be sure that our times are in God's hands. No matter what may happen in this world, God still rules! —D. C. E.

GOD'S SOVEREIGNTY OVERRULES ANY CALAMITY.

*Be ready, for the Son of Man is coming
at an hour you do not expect.*

MATTHEW 24:44

In 1947, scientists created the Doomsday Clock to symbolically show how close they believe the world is to a nuclear holocaust. In 1953, after the US tested a hydrogen bomb, the hands were set at two minutes before midnight. Since then they have been pushed back and forth thirteen times. The clock's safest setting was in 1991, after the US and Russia signed an arms-reduction treaty. The time was then set at seventeen minutes before midnight. But in May 1999, after India and Pakistan set off nuclear blasts, the hands were advanced to 11:51.

God has a "clock" too. Over the centuries, prophecy buffs have tried to "set the hands" by predicting the "midnight hour" of Christ's return. But their date-settings have failed and left many people disillusioned.

When Jesus spoke of His return, it was to remind us to "be ready" (Matt. 24:44). We are to be faithfully serving Him (v. 45) by faithfully serving the needs of others. Let's leave the hands of God's clock in His hands. —D. J. D.

CHRIST IS COMING—PERHAPS TODAY!

Forgive us our sins,
for we also forgive everyone who is indebted to us.

LUKE 11:4

Under the cover of a dark Philippine night, three teenagers broke into a van owned by a Christian woman. The trio stole some clearly identifiable items and later sold them on the street. Soon the police were notified about the sale of the stolen goods, and the boys were arrested.

So what did the woman do? Seek revenge against the young thieves? No, she visited them in jail, started a Bible study with them, and led each of them to faith in Christ! Then she asked for permission for them to be let out of jail under guard each Sunday to go to church with her.

When someone does something against us, it's easy to think it's okay to get back at our oppressors. After all, we suffered genuine trauma and real loss. Somebody ought to pay! But Christ teaches a better way than revenge. We are to follow the pattern of forgiveness that God has shown to us. Our ability to forgive is a clear test of faith. When we extend forgiveness to others, we demonstrate that we are God's children.
—J. D. B.

THE BEST WAY TO GET EVEN IS TO FORGIVE.

Come to Me, all you who labor and are heavy laden,
and I will give you rest.

MATTHEW 11:28

When guests at The Houstonian Hotel in Houston, Texas, enter the main lobby on a searingly hot summer day, they are often surprised to see flames dancing in a huge stone fireplace. If it's scorching outside and the air conditioning is humming away, why have a fire burning inside? Because people like to gather around a fire. The gas logs don't produce much heat, but there's something warm, inviting, and relaxing about the flickering light. It seems to say, "Pull up a chair, sit down, and rest awhile."

As I read the Bible, I often sense that weary, anxious people were drawn to Jesus Christ in much the same way that travelers today are drawn toward the fireplace in that Texas hotel.

A Christian who loves Jesus is sometimes said to be "on fire for the Lord." What a great way to describe the warm, inviting presence of Christ that radiates from the lives of His children before the eyes of weary people in a troubled world! —D. C. M.

A CHRISTIAN ON FIRE FOR GOD
WILL DRAW OTHERS TO THE LIGHT.

Every tongue should confess that Jesus Christ is Lord.

PHILIPPIANS 2:11

When Britain's Queen Elizabeth was a child, her parents held a garden party at Buckingham Palace, but a rainstorm forced the party to move indoors. Elizabeth and her younger sister wandered into the room where the guests had gathered and were politely bombarded by questions. During a pause in the conversations, Elizabeth pointed toward a nearby wall and a painting of Jesus on the cross. She remarked, "That's the man my papa says is really king."

How right she was to recognize that the Savior who died for us now reigns over us as "the King of kings and Lord of lords" (1 Tim. 6:15). Having risen from the dead, His kingship will one day be universally acknowledged as every knee bows to Him.

Today, you can choose to bow before Him and worship Him as both your Savior and your King! —V. C. G.

**IF YOU ADORE CHRIST AS YOUR SAVIOR,
YOU WON'T IGNORE HIM AS YOUR LORD.**

Blessed be the LORD, for He has shown me
His marvelous kindness in a strong city!

PSALM 31:21

While I was doing some research for a writing project, I interviewed twenty-four people who had been prisoners during World War II. Although they had not been tortured or mistreated, they had suffered hunger, cold, separation, loss of privacy, and a gnawing uncertainty of what lay ahead. None of them spoke of their liberation without tears.

I asked them, "How did your prison experience affect your life?" All of them said that during their time of confinement God had taught them lessons that had prepared them for their life's work. But when I asked if they would have gone to the prison camp voluntarily, each one answered, "No!"

Most of us would not choose difficult circumstances to help us learn to trust God. So, in His perfect wisdom He often will lead us into situations that can strengthen our faith. God uses life's "prison" experiences to teach us spiritual lessons we could learn in no other way. We can therefore praise Him and trust Him in any circumstance. —D. C. M.

GOD USES OUR DOWN TIMES TO BUILD US UP.

He who follows Me shall not walk in darkness,
but have the light of life.

JOHN 8:12

Scholar and historian Will Durant wrote eleven volumes titled *The Story of Civilization*. Across the pages of that monumental work moves a procession of the world's outstanding persons—rulers, philosophers, military heroes, artists, scientists, and explorers.

When someone spends his life studying history and keeping company with the most influential men and women of all time, his appraisal of famous people is worthy of respect. And in Durant's opinion, Jesus of Nazareth stands out above all others.

From a human standpoint, Jesus was a young Jew who was crucified as a criminal in first-century Israel. He never commanded an army, ruled a nation, wrote a book, or did any of the other things that are regarded as significant achievements. Yet that young Jew had the audacity to declare, "I am the light of the world" (John 8:12). And twenty centuries later, people are still following His light and being delivered "from the power of darkness" (Col. 1:13). —V. C. G.

**WALK IN THE LIGHT OF THE SON, AND YOU WILL NOT STUMBLE
IN THE DARKNESS OF THE WORLD.**

He who believes in Me has everlasting life.

JOHN 6:47

A missionary in Africa experienced great difficulty in trying to translate the Gospel of John into the local dialect. He faced the problem of finding a word for *believe*. When he came to that particular word, he always had to leave a blank space.

Then one day a runner came panting into the camp, having traveled a great distance with a very important message. After blurting out his story, he fell exhausted into a hammock nearby. He muttered a brief phrase that seemed to express both his great weariness and his contentment at finding such a delightful place of relaxation. The missionary, never having heard these words before, asked a bystander what the runner had said. "Oh, he is saying, 'I'm at the end of myself, therefore I am resting all of my weight here!'" The missionary exclaimed, "Praise God! That is the very expression I need for the word *believe*!"

To believe correctly, you must first admit that you are a sinner and that you cannot do anything to save yourself. Then cast yourself wholly on Christ for salvation. —H. G. B.

FAITH IS SIMPLY TAKING GOD AT HIS WORD.

Shall the one who contends with the Almighty correct Him?

JOB 40:2

During an afternoon baseball game when American League umpire Bill Guthrie was working behind the plate, the catcher for the visiting team repeatedly protested his calls.

According to a story that appeared in the *St. Louis Post Dispatch*, Guthrie endured this for three innings. But in the fourth inning, when the catcher started to complain, Guthrie stopped him. "Son," he said gently, "you've been a big help to me calling balls and strikes, and I appreciate it. But I think I've got the hang of it now. So I'm going to ask you to go to the clubhouse and show them how to take a shower."

Job also had been complaining about calls he didn't think were fair. In his case, the umpire was God. After listening to Job's objections, the Lord finally spoke out of a violent storm. God was gentle with Job, but He was also firm and direct. The Lord asked him the kind of questions that bring finite man back to his original size. The patriarch listened, gave up his complaining, and found peace in surrendering to God. —M. R. D. II

**SOME PEOPLE SPEND MOST OF THEIR LIFE
AT THE COMPLAINT COUNTER.**

When I see the blood, I will pass over you.

EXODUS 12:13

In his book *The Great Boer War*, Sir Arthur Conan Doyle tells of a small detachment of British troops that was surprised by an overwhelming enemy force. The British retreated under heavy fire, and their wounded lay where they faced certain death.

One of their corporals realized they had to come immediately under the protection of a Red Cross flag if they were to survive. So they used blood from their own wounds to make a large red cross on a piece of white cloth. When the enemy saw that grim flag, they held their fire, and the British were able to move their wounded to a safe place.

Just as the death angel withheld judgment when he saw blood on the doorposts in Egypt, so too God spares all who come under the blood of Christ. He can forgive sins because His wrath was poured out on Jesus, who took our place at Calvary (1 John 2:2). —D. J. D.

TO ESCAPE SIN'S CURSE, COME UNDER THE CROSS.

FEBRUARY 20

But now Christ is risen from the dead.

1 CORINTHIANS 15:20

Konrad Adenauer, former chancellor of West Germany, once told evangelist Billy Graham, "If Jesus Christ is alive, then there is hope for the world. If not, I don't see the slightest glimmer of hope on the horizon." Then he added, "I believe Christ's resurrection to be one of the best-attested facts of history."

Christ's resurrection and ours go together. Establish one, and the other is sure.

When Socrates lay dying, his friends asked, "Shall we live again?" He could only say, "I hope so." In contrast, the night before Sir Walter Raleigh was beheaded, he wrote in his Bible, "From this earth, this grave, this dust, my God shall raise me up."

We who trust Christ don't have to say, "I hope so." Jesus' resurrection gives us a sure hope for our coming resurrection. —D. J. D.

**CHRIST'S EMPTY TOMB GIVES US
FULL ASSURANCE OF HEAVEN.**

You will cast all our sins into the depths of the sea.

MICAH 7:19

In 1799, a British patrol ship ordered an American vessel into Port Royal for inspection. The British suspected that the American ship had contraband aboard. But before reaching the harbor, the captain ordered that the smuggled goods and the cargo list be tossed into the sea.

At the trial it appeared that no one would be convicted because a falsified list was presented with no evidence of contraband. The proceedings took a dramatic turn, however, when Lieutenant Michael Fitton of the British ship *Ferret* produced the genuine papers listing the illegal goods. Earlier, his crew had harpooned a shark and discovered them in its stomach!

This amazing story immediately brought to mind today's text. Speaking to the Lord about Israel's transgressions, the prophet Micah said, "You will cast all our sins into the depths of the sea." When God forgives, our sins are gone forever. Unlike that ship's papers, they will never be retrieved and brought against us. They are forgiven—forever!
—R. W. D.

**OLD SINS CAST LONG SHADOWS
BUT FORGIVENESS DRIVES THEM AWAY.**

*I press toward the goal for the prize
of the upward call of God.*

PHILIPPIANS 3:14

A man came to the studio of British artist Gabriel Rosetti (1828–1882) with samples of his drawings and asked for a candid opinion of their quality. Looking them over, Rosetti saw that they had little value, and in a kind way he let his visitor know that he lacked any real talent.

The man then took from under his coat another set of sketches, saying that they were the work of a young student. The master artist immediately recognized that they displayed a remarkable talent. He predicted that without a doubt the youth would soon distinguish himself. With a look of regret, the man said, "Sir, I was that student. I failed to persevere in my work because my teacher seemed so demanding. You are right in your estimation of my latest drawings. As I feared, they are of little or no value."

There is a spiritual lesson in that sad incident. Once we have received salvation, we must not drift along but "press toward the goal for the prize of the upward call of God" (Phil. 3:14). There are lofty goals to reach! Let's keep pressing on! —H. G. B.

WHEN NOTHING IS GAINED, SOMETHING IS LOST.

Son, you are always with me,
and all that I have is yours.

LUKE 15:31

A sociologist was writing a book about the difficulties of growing up in a large family, so he interviewed the mother of 13 children. After several basic questions, he asked, "Do you think all children deserve the full, impartial love and attention of a mother?" "Of course," said the mother. "Well, which of your children do you love the most?" he asked, hoping to catch her in a contradiction. She answered, "The one who is sick until he gets well, and the one who is away until he gets home."

That mother's response reminds me of the shepherd who left ninety-nine sheep to seek the one that was lost (Luke 15:4), the woman who searched for the one coin (v. 8), and the father who threw a party when his wayward son returned (vv. 22–24). The religious leaders of Jesus' day resented the way He gave so much attention to sinners (vv. 1–2). So He told those stories to emphasize God's love for people who are lost in sin. God has more than enough love to go around.
—M. R. D. II

GOD LOVES EVERY ONE AS IF THERE WERE BUT ONE TO LOVE.

*Your Father who sees in secret
will Himself reward you openly.*

MATTHEW 6:4

The novelist Dr. A. J. Cronin was once a practicing physician in a small Welsh mining village. He worked with a nurse who for twenty years had given her patients loving attention and care. Dr. Cronin was greatly impressed with her ability and considered her an exemplary member of her profession.

When he learned how small her salary was, he said, "Nurse, why don't you make them pay you more? It's ridiculous that you should work for so little." She replied that she was getting enough to meet her needs. "But you deserve more," the doctor replied. "God knows you're worth it." The nurse was silent for a moment. Then, with a smile on her face she exclaimed, "Dr. Cronin, if God knows I'm worth it, that's all that matters!"

Are you discouraged today—unrecognized, or unappreciated? Then remember these reassuring words: "God is not unjust to forget your work and labor of love which you have shown toward His name" (Heb. 6:10). He overlooks nothing that is done in His name. —R. W. D.

**REWARD IN ETERNITY DOES NOT DEPEND
ON RECOGNITION IN LIFE.**

*I plead with you . . . that you be
perfectly joined together in the same mind.*

1 CORINTHIANS 1:10

Along the western coast of Ireland, fishermen use a round-bottomed keelless craft known as a *currach*. This boat has a tarred canvas over a wooden frame. Because of its unique construction, it is vulnerable to sharp rocks or floating objects, and it requires the oarsmen to cooperate completely, rowing in perfect unison.

Out of this need for unity has come the Irish expression, "You will have to pull with the crew." Or, as another Irish proverb states, "There is not strength without unity."

What is true for Irish fishermen is especially true for believers in Jesus Christ. Unity is so important to the success of the cause of Christ that Paul pleaded with the believers in Corinth to eliminate division and to work as one. In our ministry efforts, are we striving to work together in harmony? If not, let's ask God to give us the spirit of unity so that we will always "pull with the crew." —J. D. B.

**A CHURCH WITH ONE HEART AND ONE MIND
IS A WONDERFUL CHURCH.**

For to me, to live is Christ,
and to die is gain.

PHILIPPIANS 1:21

A bank in Binghamton, New York, had some flowers sent to a competitor who had recently moved into a new building. There was a mix-up at the flower shop, and the card sent with the arrangement read, "With our deepest sympathy."

The florist, who was greatly embarrassed, apologized. But he was even more embarrassed when he realized that the card intended for the bank was attached to a floral arrangement sent to a funeral home in honor of a deceased person. That card read, "Congratulations on your new location!"

A sentiment like that is entirely appropriate for Christians, because they do move to a wonderful new location when they die. They go to be with Christ. The sorrows and heartaches of earth are past forever. Near the end of his life, Paul said that to be with Christ is "far better" than to remain on earth (Phil. 1:23). To every believer who dies, therefore, it would be appropriate to say, "Congratulations on your new location!"
—R. W. D.

DON'T DRIVE YOUR STAKES TOO DEEP—
WE'RE MOVING IN THE MORNING.

There is a way that seems right to a man,
but its end is the way of death.

PROVERBS 14:12

When the crowd is running the wrong way, it's hard to be the oddball who runs the right way. Most of the participants in the NCAA 10,000-meter cross-country race in Riverside, California, thought Mike Delcavo was heading the wrong way. He kept waving for the other 127 runners to follow him, but only four believed he had taken the right turn—the turn that all the other competitors had missed.

When he was asked about the reaction to his mid-course decision not to let the crowd determine his direction, Mike responded, "They thought it was funny that I went the right way."

First-century pagans reacted the same way to the changed lifestyle of their Christian neighbors. The apostle Peter said, "They think it strange that you do not run with them in the same flood of dissipation, speaking evil of you" (1 Pet. 4:4). Non-Christians still think that followers of Jesus Christ are going in the wrong direction. But actually, believers are headed for the victor's crown and a heavenly home (2 Tim. 4:7–8). —V. C. G.

IT'S BETTER TO BE RIGHT THAN POPULAR.

*Let your light so shine before men, that they may see
your good works and glorify your Father in heaven.*

MATTHEW 5:16

Roddy Roderique had served seventeen years of a life-sentence
and was appealing for an early release before the high court in
Montreal. His pastor, Charles Seidenspinner, was testifying on his behalf.

"Why should this man be released?" asked the Crown Attorney.

"Because God has come into his life, and changed him, and will
hold him steady," replied the pastor.

"What do you mean 'God has come into his life?'" asked the
judge. He listened thoughtfully as the pastor shared in detail how Christ
transforms a life. The judge then asked a loaded question: "Suppose this
man is released. Would you want him for a neighbor?"

"Your Honor," said the pastor, "that would be wonderful! Some
of my neighbors need to hear the same message that changed his life."
Roddy was released, and today he's living for the Lord and is active in
his church. —D. J. D.

**JESUS CAN CHANGE THE FOULEST SINNERS
INTO THE FINEST SAINTS.**

March

Be doers of the Word, and not hearers only.

JAMES 1:22

On one occasion while Sir Henry Brackenbury (1837–1914) was a military attaché in Paris, he was talking with the distinguished French statesman Leon Gambetta. "In these days," said Gambetta, "there are only two things a soldier needs to know. He must know how to march, and he must know how to shoot!"

The Englishman quickly responded, "I beg your pardon, Excellency, but you have forgotten the most important thing of all!"

"What's that?" asked Gambetta.

Brackenbury replied, "He must know how to obey!"

This truth also applies to followers of Jesus Christ. It's not enough for us to know the facts about Christianity so that we can look like a soldier of Christ. What's most important is that we accept the Word of God by faith and then obey it. —R. W. D.

ONE DAY OBEYING GOD'S WORD
IS WORTH YEARS OF SIMPLY STUDYING IT.

You shall be perfect,
just as your Father in heaven is perfect.

MATTHEW 5:48

When Charles Stuart Rolls was walking through his factory in its early days, he overheard a lathe operator say, "Oh, that'll do," as he tossed a part into a basket. The part looked all right to the casual observer, but Mr. Rolls expected his workmen to use a micrometer and be satisfied with nothing less than precision accuracy. So when Mr. Rolls heard that comment, he reprimanded the man, "That may do for anyone else, but it will not do for Rolls-Royce."

God is satisfied with nothing less than perfection. Divine specifications do not allow for any flaws. Jesus brought this out in Matthew 5:21–48. First He said to His listeners, "You have heard"—that's the human standard. Then He said, "But I say to you"—that's God's standard. He highlighted the perfection by which God's children should stand out from the crowd on six of life's most crucial issues: anger, sexual purity, marital fidelity, honesty in speech, nonretaliation, and treatment of enemies.

May we never be satisfied with less than the best! —D. J. D.

IF WE'RE STRIVING FOR PERFECTION,
WE'RE HEADED IN THE RIGHT DIRECTION.

MARCH 3

Great peace have those who love Your law,
and nothing causes them to stumble.

PSALM 119:165

Two men had been out deep-sea fishing when night began to fall. As they headed back toward land, the more experienced seaman got sleepy and turned the helm over to his friend. The veteran sailor pointed out the North Star and said, "Just keep the boat going in that direction."

The man had not been at his task very long before he too fell asleep. When he awoke he was thoroughly confused. He shook his friend frantically and shouted, "Wake up and show me another star! I've run clean past that first one!"

Many people today are looking for something new to guide their lives because they've lost sight of God's standard. They regard the Bible as a relic from the past. But God's laws are just as relevant and practical now as when He first gave them. His standards are more constant than the North Star and as unfailing as the law of gravity. To violate God's commands brings destruction to individuals and chaos to society. But to observe His Word brings peace. —H. W. R.

GOD'S WORD IS THE COMPASS THAT KEEPS YOU ON COURSE.

Oh, how I love Your law!
It is my meditation all the day.

PSALM 119:97

The jacaná is a unique tropical bird. It has spindly legs with long protruding toes, enabling it to skip along on floating weeds or stroll across lily pads. It has been given the nickname "lily-trotter." Even though it is capable of majestic flight, it seems content to move lazily from flower to flower or to drift slowly downstream.

Many Christians are like the jacaná bird in their Bible reading. They skip around on the surface, lighting on a few favorite verses that are beautiful and comforting. But they fail to learn the deeper truths of God's Word that can stabilize their lives. They seldom spend time studying their Bibles.

The psalmist meditated on God's Word throughout the day and gained great understanding and wisdom (Ps. 119:97–104). As believers, we would be wise to follow his example. Searching the Scriptures diligently (Acts 17:11) will cause us to grow in our knowledge of God's truth so that we understand how the Lord wants us to live and serve Him. —H. G. B.

WHEN YOU STUDY THE BIBLE "HIT OR MISS,"
YOU MISS MORE THAN YOU HIT.

The LORD . . . blesses the home of the just.

PROVERBS 3:33

The nearest thing to heaven on this earth is the home where husband and wife, parents and children live in love and peace together for the Lord and for each other. The nearest thing to hell on earth is an ungodly home, damaged by sin and iniquity, where parents quarrel and bicker, and children are abandoned to the devil and all the forces of wickedness.

In the wisdom of God, the family is the smallest complete unit of society on the earth. As goes the family, so goes the nation, and civilization, and the world.

No nation has ever risen higher morally, intellectually, or spiritually than the families of which that nation was constituted. All efforts, therefore, at improving moral and spiritual standards in the world, combating crime, infidelity, and violence, must begin with the home and with the family. —M. R. D.

THE HOME IS THE BUILDING BLOCK OF SOCIETY.

Let us lay aside every weight, . . . looking unto Jesus,
the author and finisher of our faith.

HEBREW 12:1–2

The Scottish preacher John McNeill liked to tell about an eagle that had been captured when it was young. The farmer who snared the bird put a restraint on it so it couldn't fly and turned it loose to roam in the barnyard. It wasn't long till the eagle began to act like the chickens, scratching and pecking at the ground. One day the farmer was visited by a shepherd who came down from the mountains where the eagles lived. Seeing the eagle, the shepherd said to the farmer, "What a shame to keep that bird hobbled here in your barnyard! Why don't you let it go?" The farmer agreed, so they cut off the restraint. But the eagle continued to wander around, scratching and pecking as before. The shepherd picked it up and set it on a high stone wall. For the first time in months, the eagle saw the grand expanse of blue sky and the glowing sun. Then it spread its wings and with a leap soared off into a tremendous spiral flight, up and up and up. At last it was acting like an eagle again.

Perhaps you have let yourself be comfortable in the barnyard of the world—refusing to claim your lofty position as God's child. He wants you to live in a higher realm. —P. R. V.

TO SOAR SPIRITUALLY, LOOK TO THE SON.

*No chastening seems to be joyful for the present, but painful;
nevertheless, afterward it yields the peaceable fruit of righteousness.*

HEBREWS 12:11

As the story goes, a little piece of wood once bitterly complained because its owner kept whittling away at it, gouging it and making holes in it. But the one who was cutting it paid no attention to the stick's protests. He was making a flute out of that piece of ebony, and he was too wise to stop when the wood complained.

The man said, "Little piece of wood, without these rifts and holes, and all this cutting, you'd be just a stick forever—a useless piece of ebony. What I am doing now may seem as if I am destroying you, but instead it will change you into a flute. Your sweet music will charm the souls of many and comfort sorrowing hearts."

The Lord is shaping us. Let's be patient and allow His chastening to do its work in our lives. —M. R. D.

PRESENT PAIN CAN LEAD TO PERMANENT GAIN.

Count it all joy when you fall into various trials.

JAMES 1:2

The human body is made up of ten trillion cells, which are home to some 100 trillion bacteria. A dime-sized patch of skin may hold up to two million bacteria. The presence of all those little critters might seem to be an overwhelming threat to our health. But scientists say that we would actually be sicker without the bugs than we are with them. The good bacteria apparently help fight off the bad bacteria that cause diseases.

God calls His children to show patience, love, and faith in a world polluted by sin and opposed to righteousness. Many of the troubles we encounter can help us avoid greater problems of independence, self-sufficiency, and pride that set in so quickly when all goes smoothly. The problems in our lives can drive us to depend on the Lord and to trust in His Word.

The difficulties we face can contribute to our spiritual health if we'll see them as tests of our faith and as opportunities to develop endurance. —M. R. D. II

**GOD WANTS TO USE OUR DIFFICULTIES
TO MAKE US BETTER—NOT BITTER.**

Every branch that bears fruit He prunes,
that it may bear more fruit.

JOHN 15:2

When Alexander Whyte (1837–1921), the great Scottish preacher, was a boy, he badly injured his arm in a threshing machine. Instead of going to a hospital for almost certain amputation, he was treated at home by a neighbor. When the boy complained of his suffering, she simply said to him, "I like the pain. I like the pain." She knew it was the first step to recovery.

Years later when people complained that Whyte's sermons were too critically soul-searching, he would reply, "I like the pain. I like the pain." He believed that conviction of sin was needed for their spiritual healing.

If you're going through a painful time, God's purpose may be to make you more spiritually fruitful. He sees the positive end-result and He "likes the pain." It's the first step to progress!—V. C. G.

PROBLEMS ARE OPPORTUNITIES FOR PROGRESS.

The entrance of Your words gives light;
it gives understanding to the simple.

PSALM 119:130

A minister flying to the West Coast struck up a conversation with the passenger next to him. "What's your occupation?" he asked. His seatmate replied, "I'm a professor of astronomy. And what about you?" "I'm a pastor," the minister answered.

The astronomer shifted a bit in his seat and then confessed, "I used to attend church when I was young, but my wife and I don't go very often now. But the way I look at it, the Bible is pretty simple. It all boils down to 'Get along with your neighbors and stay out of trouble.'"

"That's interesting," the pastor noted. "I feel the same way about what you do. For me, astronomy all boils down to 'Twinkle, twinkle, little star, how I wonder what you are.'"

The Bible is like the ocean. You can wade in it, feed from it, live on it—or swim in it. But those who take the time to learn its truths and practice them will be changed forever. —H. W. R.

THE BIBLE IS SIMPLE ENOUGH FOR A CHILD TO READ
YET TOO DEEP FOR A SCHOLAR TO MASTER.

He heals the brokenhearted. . . . He counts the number of the stars;
He calls them all by name.

PSALM 147:3–4

How many stars are there? Astronomers don't know. They simply assure us that the cosmos contains more stars than can be numbered. Billions for sure—probably trillions!

Figures like that are hard for us to grasp. Even a million is mind-boggling. If you were counting a million one-dollar bills at the rate of sixty a minute for eight hours a day five days a week, it would take you nearly seven weeks to complete the task. At the same rate it would take over 133 years to count a billion dollars.

So if we ever wonder whether God is able to carry us with all our burdens, let us remember that He is the sovereign of the stars. Surely He who is the guide of the galaxies can deal with our situations.—V. C. G.

THE ONE WHO UPHOLDS THE UNIVERSE
WILL NEVER LET YOU DOWN.

I saw heaven opened, and behold, a white horse.
And He who sat on him was called Faithful and True.

REVELATION 19:11

I was intrigued by a picture of a jubilant Hitler and a cheering crowd celebrating a German victory early in World War II. At that time, many people in Great Britain were completely discouraged. Ultimately, though, the Allies celebrated victory. How different the feelings of the British would have been early in the war if they could have witnessed the final scene!

When Jesus was arrested and led off to trial, His disciples were confused and afraid (Matt. 26:47–56). Their anguish increased as they saw Jesus on trial, scourged and seemingly helpless as He hung on a cross. They did not yet see the whole picture of their Messiah's role. Before fulfilling His role as Conqueror and King, He had to "give His life a ransom for many" (Matt. 20:28) and then break the power of death by resurrection (v.19).

Today we see much that discourages us. The forces of evil often seem to be in control. But if by faith we look beyond the present and focus on the final scene in God's plan, we can find reason to rejoice.
—H. V. L.

THE HOPE OF CHRIST'S COMING CAN KEEP US GOING.

Every good tree bears good fruit,
but a bad tree bears bad fruit.

MATTHEW 7:17

The renowned artist Paul Gustave Doré (1832–1883) lost his passport while traveling in Europe. When he came to a border crossing, he explained his predicament to one of the guards. Giving his name to the official, Doré hoped he would be recognized and allowed to pass. The guard, however, said that many people attempted to cross the border by claiming to be persons they were not.

Doré insisted that he was the man he claimed to be. "All right," said the official, "we'll give you a test, and if you pass it we'll allow you to go through." Handing him a pencil and a sheet of paper, he told the artist to sketch several peasants standing nearby. Doré did it so quickly and skillfully that the guard was convinced he was indeed who he claimed to be.

Someone has raised this heart-searching question: "If you were accused of being a Christian, would there be enough evidence to convict you?"—R. W. D.

ONE WHO WALKS WITH CHRIST IS A WALKING SERMON.

Blessed are you poor,
for yours is the kingdom of God.

LUKE 6:20

Many years ago I bought a used car that gave me nothing but trouble. I believed the owner when he told me it was in great shape and that the engine knock I heard was only a harmless "piston slap." The next day I found evidence that the car had been rolled. Two weeks later the engine self-destructed. I had a new motor installed, but I had problems with the car as long as I owned it.

Something C. S. Lewis wrote reminded me of that old car. He said that Christians journey through life with many strikes against them. Some people are poisoned by a bad upbringing, or saddled with unnatural urges, or nagged day in and day out by an inferiority complex. "If this describes you," said Lewis, "don't despair. You are one of the poor whom Jesus said are blessed. He knows what a wretched machine you are trying to drive. One day He will fling it on the scrap heap and give you a new one. And then you may astonish us all—not least yourself; for you have learned your driving in a hard school." —H. V. L.

HOPELESS SITUATIONS ARE REMINDERS
THAT WE ARE HELPLESS WITHOUT GOD.

*It is easier for heaven and earth to pass away
than for one tittle of the law to fail.*

LUKE 16:17

A cartoon in *Christianity Today* portrayed Moses atop Mount Sinai holding the Ten Commandments. Looking heavenward, he says to God, "They tend to lose interest rather quickly. Could I have a one-liner instead?"

In a sense, God did give "one-liners." His ten laws are clear and pointed.

1. Love the only true God.
2. Don't make an image of God.
3. Hallow His name.
4. Keep His day holy.
5. Honor your parents.
6. Don't murder.
7. Don't commit adultery.
8. Don't steal.
9. Don't lie.
10. Don't covet.

God's commandments work for our highest good. They are the law side of love. —D. J. D.

GOD GAVE TEN COMMANDMENTS, NOT TEN SUGGESTIONS.

If you forgive men their trespasses,
your heavenly Father will also forgive you.

MATTHEW 6:14

Leonardo da Vinci was a gifted artist. It is said that just before he began his painting of *The Last Supper*, he had a nasty quarrel with a fellow artist. Leonardo felt so bitter toward his rival that he determined to paint the face of his enemy as the face of Judas. In that way he would take revenge on the man. By picturing him as the betrayer of Jesus, he would make his face the object of scorn to all who viewed the painting.

The face of Judas was one of the first that da Vinci finished, and everyone could easily recognize it as the face of the painter with whom he had quarreled. But when Leonardo began to paint the face of Jesus, he could make no progress. Something seemed to be hindering his best efforts. According to the story, he finally came to the conclusion that the frustration he was experiencing was due to his continuing hatred of his enemy. Leonardo immediately painted out the face of Judas and began again on the face of Christ, this time with the success that the ages have come to acclaim. —H. W. R.

WE CAN STOP FORGIVING OTHERS
ONLY IF CHRIST STOPS FORGIVING US.

Present your bodies a living sacrifice . . . ,
which is your reasonable service.

ROMANS 12:1

Once when President Eisenhower was addressing the National Press Club, he opened his remarks by apologizing because he was not a great orator. Then he told his audience that the situation reminded him of a boyhood experience on a Kansas farm.

Eisenhower recalled, "An old farmer had a cow that we wanted to buy. We went over to visit him and asked about the cow's pedigree. The old farmer didn't know what pedigree meant, so we asked him about the cow's butterfat production. He told us that he hadn't any idea. Finally, we asked him if he knew how many pounds of milk the cow produced each year. The farmer shook his head and said, 'I don't know. But she's an honest old cow and she'll give you all the milk she has!'" Eisenhower then concluded his opening remarks, "Well, I'm like the cow: I'll give you everything I have."

The Lord doesn't expect from us any more than we have to offer, but He does want us to be faithful and to provide a quality of service that comes from doing our very best. May we say willingly and gladly, "Lord, I'll give you everything I have." —R. W. D.

A LITTLE IS A LOT WHEN YOU GIVE YOUR ALL.

There is forgiveness with You,
that You may be feared.

PSALM 130:4

*I*n a cemetery not far from New York City is a headstone engraved with a single word: FORGIVEN.

The message is simple, unembellished. There is no date of birth, no date of death, no epitaph. There is only a name and the solitary word *forgiven*. But that is the greatest word that can be applied to any man or woman, or written on any gravestone.

The psalmist said, "There is forgiveness with You, that You may be feared" (130:4). That refrain echoes in both the Old and New Testaments. God is honored and worshiped because He alone can clear our record. If God could not forgive us, we could only flee from Him in terror. Yet the God whose holiness threatens us is the God who through Christ redeems us. This dangerous God offers forgiveness for all our sins. We need only to ask for it. —H. W. R.

SIN INVITES JUDGMENT;
CONFESSION ENSURES FORGIVENESS.

Give me understanding according to Your word.

PSALM 119:169

Peter Deison tells about a friend who visited New York City and got lost among the maze of streets. So he took an elevator up to the observation deck of the Empire State Building and looked out over the city. He carefully noted prominent buildings, landmarks, and major streets. Having them firmly fixed in his mind, he said to a friend, "Now I understand where we are and where I want to go." Deison commented, "He went back down to the busy streets and never got lost again. He finally understood where to go because he got an overview of the city."

To get the most out of studying a portion of the Bible, we need the big picture. It's important to know the major divisions of the Bible, the Old and New Testaments, and how they are related. It helps to know the general themes of the Bible and the specific theme of each book, who wrote the books, to whom they were written, and their time period. It's also helpful to know that there are different types of literature in the Bible such as history, prophecy, and poetry. As you read God's Word the Author Himself will guide you. —R. W. D.

**To keep from getting lost in Bible verses,
be well-versed in the whole Bible.**

Do not worry about tomorrow . . . .
Sufficient for the day is its own trouble.

MATTHEW 6:34

"When I was a little boy," wrote H. P. Barker, "I used to help my mother store away apples. Putting my arms around ever so many, I tried to carry them all at once. I managed for a step or two, but then out fell one, and then another, and two or three more, till the apples were rolling all over the floor. Mother laughed. Putting my tiny hands around one apple, she then suggested that I take that one and then carry the others in the same way."

Mr. Barker made the following application: "Don't try to put your arms around a year or even a week. Rather say, 'Here is another day begun. Lord, help me to live it for You. Give me just now the help and strength that I need.'"

What good advice! How foolish it is to borrow trouble from tomorrow! We can trust God to meet our needs every day. So let's take just one "apple" at a time. —R. W. D.

WORRY IS CARRYING A BURDEN
GOD NEVER INTENDED US TO BEAR.

Let them . . . be rich in good works,
ready to give, willing to share.

1 TIMOTHY 6:18

John G. Wendel and his sisters were some of the most miserly people of all time. Although they had received a huge inheritance from their parents, they spent very little of it and did all they could to keep their wealth for themselves. John was able to influence five of his six sisters never to marry, and they lived in the same house in New York City for fifty years. When the last sister died in 1931, her estate was valued at more than $100 million. Her only dress was one that she had made herself, and she had worn it for twenty-five years.

The Wendels had such a compulsion to hold on to their possessions that they lived like paupers. Even worse, they were like the kind of person Jesus referred to "who lays up treasure for himself, and is not rich toward God" (Luke 12:21). Most of us will never come even close to being as rich as the Wendels. But if we are faithful stewards of the finances the Lord has entrusted to us, if we give unselfishly to His cause, and if we help people in need, we can be "rich in good works" and store up treasure in heaven (1 Tim. 6:18–19). —R. W. D.

**GOD CARES ABOUT THE SIZE OF YOUR HEART
MORE THAN THE SIZE OF YOUR BANK ACCOUNT.**

I am He who lives, and was dead,
and behold, I am alive forevermore.

REVELATION 1:18

On one occasion Michelangelo turned to his fellow artists and said with frustration in his voice, "Why do you keep filling gallery after gallery with endless pictures on the one theme of Christ in weakness, Christ on the cross, and most of all, Christ hanging dead?" he asked. "Why do you concentrate on that passing episode as if it were the last word, as if the curtain dropped down there on disaster and defeat? That dreadful scene lasted only a few hours. But to the unending eternity Christ is alive; Christ rules and reigns and triumphs!"

Michelangelo was right. Even though the cross is vitally important because of the redemption Jesus accomplished for us there, we must not emphasize His death to the exclusion of His resurrection victory. We should think of Him now in His glorified state in heaven. He is now our risen Lord, our Intercessor at the throne, and our soon-coming King.

Let's rejoice in His thrilling words, "I am alive forevermore!"

—H. G. B.

JESUS WHO DIED TO SAVE US NOW LIVES TO KEEP US.

God is my strength and power,
and He makes my way perfect.

2 SAMUEL 22:33

A man attending a major league baseball game caused a bit of commotion with the people around him. No matter which team made a hit or a run, the fan would cheer. Finally someone asked him, "Why are you rooting for both teams?" The man explained, "Well, I live way out in the country and I don't get to many games, so I pull for both sides. That way, no matter who wins, I go home happy."

You don't have to be a sports fan to know that if you have a strong loyalty for a team you won't root for both sides. Yet that's what we do if we talk and act like Christians when we are around fellow believers but act as if we don't know Jesus when we are with unbelievers. This kind of behavior may indicate that we really aren't sure which side is right, or that we lack the courage to be identified with Christ.

Let's not be wishy-washy. We know who the winner will be. So let's live like it. —JDB

STAND UP FOR CHRIST OR YOU'LL BE TRIPPED UP BY SATAN.

You have left your first love.
Remember therefore from where you have fallen.

REVELATION 2:4–5

Muynak was once a thriving fishing port on the Aral Sea. But today, according to James Rupert of the *Washington Post*, Muynak sits on the edge of a bitter, salty desert. Sand dunes are strewn with the rusted, hollow hulls of a fishing fleet that once sailed high above on the surface of Central Asia's fountain of life. Things began changing thirty years ago when Stalinist planners began diverting the Aral's water source to irrigate the world's largest cotton belt. No one, however, envisioned the environmental disaster that would result. Weather has become more extreme, the growing season has been shortened by two months, and 80 percent of the region's farmland has been ruined by salt storms that sweep in off the dry seabed.

What happened at Muynak parallels the history of the church of Ephesus. Once a thriving spiritual community, the Ephesian believers diverted their attention from Christ to works done in His name (Rev. 2:2–4). They had lost sight of what was most important in their relationship with Christ—their love for Him. May we recognize and repent of anything that diverts our attention from loving Him. —M. R. D. II

TO RENEW YOUR LOVE FOR CHRIST, REVIEW CHRIST'S LOVE FOR YOU.

Do not enter the path of the wicked . . . .
Avoid it, . . . turn away from it.

PROVERBS 4:14–15

Several artists were asked to illustrate their concepts of temptation. When their paintings were unveiled, some of them depicted man's attempt to achieve fame and fortune at any cost. Others pictured mankind's struggle against the alluring desires of the flesh. The prize-winning canvas, however, was quite different. It portrayed a quiet country lane with a man walking among inviting shade trees and lovely wild flowers. In the distance the way divided into two roads, the one leading to the right, the other to the left. The road that veered to the left seemed almost as inviting as the one that kept to the right. But if the traveler chose to take it, he would soon become mired in the mud. The artist was conveying the thought that sin's allurements are extremely subtle at first. They present themselves as an innocent-looking fork in the road.

The "path of the wicked" may seem harmless at first, and we tell ourselves that we would never fall into gross sin. But that's just the kind of thinking that can divert us from the path of righteousness. To avoid falling into sin, look beyond that seemingly harmless fork in the road.
—H. G. B.

**WHEN YOU MEET TEMPTATION ON THE ROAD OF LIFE,
KEEP TO THE RIGHT!**

I could wish that I myself
were accursed from Christ for my brethren.

ROMANS 9:3

George Sweeting, in his book *The No-Guilt Guide to Witnessing*, tells that during a serious shortage of currency in Great Britain, Oliver Cromwell (1599–1658) selected a group of men to search for silver to meet the need. Several months later they filed this report: "We have searched the empire in vain to find silver. To our dismay, we found none except in the great cathedrals, where the saints are constructed of choice silver."

When he heard that discouraging report, Cromwell issued this order: "Let's melt down the saints and put them into circulation." Sweeting concludes, "That's our need today!"

Yes, we all need a "meltdown" brought on by a burning compassion for lost sinners and a fiery zeal motivated by love to lead them to Christ. Let's ask the Lord to melt our hearts. —R. W. D.

THE CURE FOR COLD FEET IS A HEART ON FIRE FOR GOD.

You will keep him in perfect peace,
whose mind is stayed on You.

ISAIAH 26:3

*T*heard about a submarine that was on patrol during
wartime and had to remain submerged overnight. When it
resurfaced the next day, a friend on another ship radioed the captain,
"How did you fare in that terrible storm last night?" Surprised, the officer
exclaimed, "What storm? We didn't know there was one!" Although the
ocean's surface had been whipped into huge waves by high winds, the
vessel was not affected because the waters below remained calm and
tranquil.

Someone once outlined the words of Isaiah 26:3 this way:
"*You*—a precious God. *Perfect peace*—a priceless possession. *Whose mind
is stayed on You*—a present focus. *Because he trusts in You*—a powerful
faith." The believer who is confident of God's providence, who rests in
His grace, and who relies on His Holy Spirit will experience the miracle
of His quieting peace. —H. G. B.

WHEN WE KEEP OUR MIND ON GOD,
GOD KEEPS OUR MIND AT PEACE.

You cannot serve God and mammon.

LUKE 16:13

*G*odfrey Davis, who wrote a biography about the Duke of Wellington, said, "I found an old account ledger that showed how the Duke spent his money. It was a far better clue to what he thought was really important than the reading of his letters or speeches."

How we handle money reveals much about the depth of our commitment to Christ. That's why Jesus often talked about money. One-sixth of the gospels, including one out of every three parables, touches on stewardship. Jesus warned that we can become slaves to money. We may not think money means more to us than God, but Jesus didn't say we must serve God more than money. The issue isn't what occupies first place in our life, but whether we serve money *at all*.

Does your checkbook show that Christ is the Master in your life? —H. W. R.

TO BE RICH IN GOD IS FAR BETTER THAN TO BE RICH IN GOODS.

Well done, good and faithful servant.

MATTHEW 25:21

Rudolph was a young musician in Vienna with a burning desire to write a symphony. Finally the time came when he was able to do so. After writing and rewriting it many times, he showed the score to some friends and asked for their opinion. Without exception they agreed it was an excellent work. But Rudolph continued to labor over it, polishing and perfecting what he hoped would be a masterpiece. At last, he was ready to present it to the public.

The orchestra performed his symphony beautifully. After the last movement ended, there was a brief pause. Then the audience broke out in thunderous applause. Rudolph, however, seemed unmoved until an old white-haired man approached him. Placing his hands on the young man's shoulders, he exclaimed, "Well done, Rudolph! Well done!" Only then did the young musician smile with satisfaction. He had received approval from the one he wanted most to please—his respected mentor.

That's how we should view our work—as service for our Master. Recognition from people is encouraging, but it's the Master's approval that really counts! —R. W. D.

**WHEN YOU DO WHAT PLEASES GOD,
GOD IS PLEASED WITH YOU.**

*In this is love, not that we loved God, but that He loved us
and sent His Son to be the propitiation for our sins.*

1 JOHN 4:10

We hear it often: "TGIF" (Thank God it's Friday!).
Although many people use this phrase carelessly, without
reverence for their Creator, they're grateful because Friday marks the end
of the workweek.

On Good Friday, millions of Christians around the world are
especially thankful because it reminds them of what God accomplished
through His Son nearly 2,000 years ago.

But why do we call this day good? Was not this one of the
blackest days in history? God's sinless Son, who went about doing good,
healing the sick, and bringing hope to sin-ruined lives, was nailed to a
shameful cross by self-righteous religious leaders. That's evil at its worst.
Where is the good in that?

Paul gave us the answer. On this day centuries ago, God
demonstrated "His own love toward us, in that while we were still
sinners, Christ died for us" (Rom. 5:8). Such love is too profound for a
genius to fully grasp, yet so simple that a child can accept it.

TGIGF—thank God it's Good Friday! —D. J. D.

**CHRIST ENDURED THE DARKNESS
SO THAT WE CAN ENJOY THE LIGHT.**

"Not by might nor by power, but by My Spirit,"
*says the L*ORD *of hosts.*

ZECHARIAH 4:6

The builders of the Panama Canal faced enormous obstacles of geography, climate, and disease. Most of the construction was supervised by Colonel George Washington Goethals. He had to endure severe criticism from many back home who predicted that he would never complete the "impossible task." But the great engineer was resolute and pressed steadily forward in his work without responding to those who opposed him. "Aren't you going to answer your critics?" a subordinate inquired. "In time," Goethals replied. "How?" the man asked. The colonel smiled and said, "With the canal!" And his answer came on August 15, 1914, when the canal opened to traffic for the first time.

If we tried to respond to all who criticize us as we follow the Lord, nothing worthwhile would be accomplished. But if we are confident we are doing God's will, we can close our ears to ridicule and press on with the work. Completing the task is often the best way to silence the critics.
—R. W. D.

GOD JUDGES US BY WHAT WE DO,
NOT BY WHAT OTHERS SAY.

April

Grace to you and peace from . . . Jesus Christ,
who gave Himself for our sins.

GALATIANS 1:3-4

William D. Matheson, in *My Grandfather's War*, tells of a veteran who walked through the streets of his hometown with an empty sleeve. When a passerby commented on the loss of his arm, the veteran replied, "I didn't lose it. I gave it."

That describes what Jesus did for us. He didn't lose His life on the cross. He gave it. As today's verse says, He "gave Himself for our sins." He paid the penalty so that all who believe on Him would experience forgiveness of sin and have eternal life. In fulfillment of the Old Testament picture of the sacrifice of the lamb, He yielded His life for us.

Following Christ's example, we are to give ourselves unselfishly to His service and help others. That makes sense, though it may seem absurd to many. Our sacrifices will glorify the Lord and make an impact for Christ on our selfish world. —D. C. E.

CHRIST'S SACRIFICE OF HIMSELF FOR US
MOTIVATES US TO SACRIFICE OURSELVES FOR OTHERS.

While we were still sinners,
Christ died for us.

ROMANS 5:8

During the American Civil War, a farmer in New York was drafted for the Union army. His wife had died and he was the sole support of his young children. But then an unmarried man in the town who had no dependents came to his home and offered to go to war in his place. For the sake of his children, the farmer accepted the offer. The generous friend marched off to battle, and in the first engagement he was shot and killed. When the farmer heard what had happened, he went to the scene of the battle and brought back the body. He buried his friend in the village churchyard, and had these words engraved on the headstone: He Died for Me.

The truth of the gospel is that Jesus gave His life for us while we were His enemies (Rom. 5:8–10). The implications are staggering. If Christ died for us while we were enemies, how much more will the living Christ do for us now that He has made us His friends! We can be sure that not only will He preserve us from God's wrath against sin (v. 9), but He will give us everything we need (Rom. 8:32)—in this life and the next. —H. W. R.

JESUS TOOK OUR PLACE AND GAVE US HIS PEACE.

*These all wait for You, that You
may give them their food in due season.*

PSALM 104:27

The ant lion is a little insect whose larva (also called a doodle-bug) lives in regions of dry or sandy soil. It digs a pit about two inches deep and waits for ants to fall in. It is equipped with a highly sensitive alarm system that picks up the slightest vibration. A single grain of sand falling into its hole can activate it. Anchor-like appendages under its body enable it to grip the soil as it struggles with its victim. Even more remarkable is its complex mouth that forms a kind of "drinking straw," ideal for sucking fluids. When an ant is trapped, the ant lion injects it with a paralyzing drug and then with digestive juices that allows it to feed on its prey.

The eminent French zoologist Pierre-Paul Grassé says that Darwin's theory of natural selection can't explain the "avalanche of . . . chance occurrences" necessary for such a creature to evolve. The psalmist told us that God made all living things and feeds them, and we accept that by faith. Scientists marvel at nature's unique design, and they would not be at odds with the psalmist if they would merely believe what their findings point to—God, the great Designer. —D. J. D.

NATURE IS BUT A NAME FOR AN EFFECT WHOSE CAUSE IS GOD.

Let us lay aside every weight,
and the sin which so easily ensnares us.

HEBREWS 12:1

In her remarkable book *Teaching a Stone to Talk*, Annie Dillard tells about the ill-fated Franklin Expedition of 1845. The explorers sailed from England to find the Northwest Passage across the Arctic Ocean. They put aboard their two sailing ships many things they didn't need: a 1,200-volume library, fine china, crystal goblets, and sterling silverware. Amazingly, each ship took only a twelve-day supply of coal for their auxiliary steam engines.

The ships became trapped in vast frozen plains of Arctic ice. After several months, Lord Franklin died. The men decided to trek to safety in small groups but none survived. Two officers pulled a large sled more than sixty-five miles across the treacherous ice. When rescuers found their bodies, they discovered that the sled was filled with "a great deal of table silver." By carrying what they didn't need, these men were doomed to failure.

Do we do the same? Do we drag baggage through life that we don't need? Evil thoughts? Bad habits? Let's determine to "lay aside every weight, and the sin which so easily ensnares us" (Heb. 12:1). —D. C. E.

IF YOUR CHRISTIAN LIFE IS A DRAG,
WORLDLY WEIGHTS MAY BE TO BLAME.

I have finished the race,
I have kept the faith.

2 TIMOTHY 4:7

At 7 P.M. on October 20, 1968, a few thousand spectators remained in the Mexico City Olympic Stadium. The last of the marathon runners were stumbling across the finish line. Finally, the spectators heard the wail of sirens on police cars. As eyes turned to the gate, a lone runner wearing the colors of Tanzania staggered into the stadium. His name was John Stephen Akhwari. He was the last contestant to finish the 26-mile 385-yard contest. His leg had been injured in a fall and was bloodied and crudely bandaged. As he hobbled the final lap around the track the spectators rose and applauded him as though he were the winner. After he had crossed the finish line, someone asked him why he had not quit. He replied simply, "My country did not send me 7,000 miles to start the race. They sent me 7,000 miles to finish it."

Not all heroes receive medals. Yet those who faithfully live for Christ know that someday they will receive a crown of righteousness (2 Tim. 4:8). The Lord, the righteous Judge, will reward all those who long for Christ's return, are faithful in spite of difficulties, and who finish the race. —H. W. R.

WORK FOR GOD DONE WELL WILL RECEIVE GOD'S "WELL DONE!"

*Jesus our Lord . . . was raised
because of our justification.*

ROMANS 4:24–25

The resurrection of Jesus Christ is one of the most well-established events in history. Paul cited as irrefutable evidence the more than 500 eyewitnesses who saw Jesus after He arose, most of whom were still alive when the apostle wrote to the Corinthians.

Just as certain is the fact that Christ's sacrifice on the cross of Calvary fully paid the penalty for the sin of all mankind, so that everyone who trusts Him as Savior receives forgiveness. And it is Christ's resurrection that guarantees this. If just one sin had not been atoned for, Jesus would not have come out of the tomb.

In his book *The Resurrection of Jesus the Christ*, Fred John Meldau underscores the significance of Jesus' resurrection by describing Israel's annual Day of Atonement ritual. Meldau writes, "If [the High Priest] offered correctly, he came forth in due time; but . . . if he failed to offer correctly, he died there behind the veil. In like manner, the coming forth of Jesus the Christ, in His resurrection, after His atonement for our sins on the cross, shows that His offering was accepted. The empty tomb is God's 'Amen' to Christ's 'It is finished.'" —R. W. D.

CHRIST'S EMPTY TOMB GUARANTEES OUR FULL SALVATION.

Better to go to the house of mourning
than to go to the house of feasting.

ECCLESIASTES 7:2

If you visit some of the old New England churches, you'll notice that many of them have a cemetery in the churchyard. The windows in the sanctuary are filled with clear rather than stained glass so that the pastor would see the graveyard as he preached. Two hundred fifty years ago, Christians believed that the central mission of the church was to bring men and women into a right relationship with God. That's why they constructed their church buildings with see-through windows. They wanted their pastors to be continually reminded of the seriousness of their calling. Everyone who sat in the pews before them each Sunday would eventually fill a place in the cemetery and ultimately stand before God to be judged.

The preacher of Ecclesiastes also lived with the reality of death. He argued that it is better to go to a funeral than to a birthday party, because when we think about death we deal with the bedrock issues of our lives. Only those who've trusted in Christ for eternal life can live well—because they're prepared to die. —H. W. R.

YOU'RE NOT READY TO LIVE UNTIL YOU'RE READY TO DIE.

[Jesus] was moved with compassion for them,
and healed their sick.

MATTHEW 14:14

Many years ago, a back-country woman in Florida received news that her son had been killed in the war. Shortly thereafter, she was seen hoeing in her garden. "It just isn't fitting," chided a neighbor who thought it was inappropriate to be gardening instead of grieving. "Friend," said Effie Mae, "I know you mean well, but Jim rejoiced to see green things growing because it meant that his mother and the young ones would be eating. This is his hoe, and when I'm hoeing I can almost feel his big, strong hands under mine and hear his voice saying, 'That's good, Mom, that's good.' Working is the only headstone I can give him."

Is your heart broken today? Does life seem empty? Do you feel like giving up? There is hope in the Master's example. Take up whatever duties lie before you. Dedicate them to God. Refuse the luxury of self-pity. Do something to lift the burdens of others. —D. J. D.

TO EASE ANOTHER'S HEARTACHE
IS THE WAY TO FORGET YOUR OWN.

You have been . . . a refuge from the storm.

ISAIAH 25:4

The best correspondents for *Life* magazine were sent all over the world to ask the question, "What is the meaning of life?" They talked to philosophers and children, taxi drivers and Nile River boatmen. More than 100 premier photographers provided images. One dramatic photograph of a lighthouse off the Brittany Coast caught my eye. A huge Atlantic storm had sent gigantic waves around the mammoth brick structure, nearly swallowing it up. But on the sheltered side, literally surrounded by frothing, boiling waves, stood the lighthouse keeper. He was looking casually toward shore, his hands stuck nonchalantly in his pockets, as enormous waves crashed around him.

This powerful illustration reminded me of the many fierce storms of trial we face in life. Yet in God we are as safe as that lighthouse keeper. The words of Isaiah 25:4 are true for every believer: God is our refuge during the storms of physical affliction, emotional turmoil, and spiritual attack. With His protection we can endure any trial with the calm assurance that He who shields us cannot be moved. And that gives us peace no matter how turbulent our circumstances. —D. C. E.

**THE LORD MAY CALM THE STORM AROUND YOU,
BUT MORE OFTEN HE'LL CALM THE STORM WITHIN YOU.**

*It is God who arms me with strength,
and makes my way perfect.*

PSALM 18:32

Margaret Nikol was born into a pastor's family in Bulgaria. Her mother and father were murdered for their faith by the communists in the 1960s. Margaret was a brilliant violinist, and in spite of opposition she got an excellent education. She achieved fame throughout Europe and became concertmaster of the Dresden Symphony. But because of her faith in Christ, she was subjected to physical and emotional cruelty. Eventually, she was given a prison sentence—to begin as soon as the concert season was over. But God had other plans, and Margaret was invited to play in Vienna at an Easter concert in 1982. The communists repeatedly denied permission, but finally, because of outside pressure, they relented. "God was faster than they were," testifies Margaret. In Vienna she requested political asylum, and no less than five free nations offered it!

The same God who delivered Margaret from communist oppression, and who sent an angel to free the apostles from prison (Acts 5:19), can also rescue us from whatever is holding us captive—physically or spiritually. We must never give up hope! God is our great deliverer. —D. C. E.

THE GOD WHO HOLDS THE UNIVERSE IS THE GOD WHO IS HOLDING YOU.

Do not be overcome by evil,
but overcome evil with good.

ROMANS 12:21

Bruce Goodrich was being initiated into the cadet corps at Texas A&M University. One night, Bruce was forced to run until he dropped— but he never got up. Bruce Goodrich died before he even entered college. A short time after the tragedy, Bruce's father wrote this letter to the administration, faculty, student body, and the corps of cadets: "I would like to take this opportunity to express the appreciation of my family for the great outpouring of concern and sympathy from Texas A&M University and the college community over the loss of our son Bruce. We were deeply touched by the tribute paid to him in the battalion. We were particularly pleased to note that his Christian witness did not go unnoticed during his brief time on campus." Mr. Goodrich went on: "I hope it will be some comfort to know that we harbor no ill will in the matter. We know our God makes no mistakes. Bruce had an appointment with his Lord and is now secure in his celestial home."

Trusting in the sovereignty of God can turn outrage into understanding and hatred into compassion. —H. W. R.

NO TRAGEDY IS BEYOND GOD'S SOVEREIGNTY.

*When they had nothing with which to repay,
he freely forgave them both.*

LUKE 7:42

During the great depression of the 1930's, a shy elderly lady approached the front desk of an insurance office in Minneapolis. When asked what she wanted, she showed them a policy and explained that she was unable to make additional payments. She said that it was hard for her to get work, and what little she did get was scarcely enough to keep a roof over her head. After a quick investigation, the clerk saw that the policy was very valuable. He warned that it would not be wise to stop the payments. Besides, didn't her husband have anything to say? It was his policy, made out to her benefit. Her husband? She quickly explained that he had been dead for three years! Company officials soon discovered that she was telling the truth and gave her the full amount of the policy along with the overpaid premiums. The money kept her in comfort the rest of her days! She had not realized that she was entitled to the face value of the policy as soon as her husband died!

The greatest benefit of all time became due when Jesus died on the cross! But thousands of people keep trying to make payment on their soul's salvation while all they need to do is accept God's immeasurable gift! —M. R. D.

**THE WORLD IS DIVIDED INTO TWO GROUPS OF PEOPLE—
THE SAINTS AND THE AIN'TS!**

*When He has tested me,
I shall come forth as gold.*

JOB 23:10

It is said that a $5 bar of steel when made into horseshoes will be worth $10. If manufactured into needles, it is worth $350. But if it is made into delicate springs for expensive watches, its worth will rise to $250,000! It is made more valuable by passing through the heat again and again and by being hammered, manipulated, finished, and polished until it reaches its highest usefulness.

God, too, expends His efforts only on those lives that give promise of having greater potential after He has refined them. If you are suffering the heat of affliction, remember the Lord is seeking to rid your life of anything that might hinder your spiritual life or limit your usefulness to His kingdom. May we learn to say like Job, "When He has tested me, I shall come forth as gold."

GOD SENDS TRIALS NOT TO IMPAIR US, BUT TO IMPROVE US!

No one, having put his hand to the plow, and looking back,
is fit for the kingdom of God.

LUKE 9:62

In 1904 William Borden, heir to the Borden Dairy Estate, graduated from a Chicago high school a millionaire. His parents gave him a trip around the world. Traveling through Asia, the Middle East, and Europe gave Borden a burden for the world's hurting people. Writing home, he said, "I'm going to give my life to prepare for the mission field."

When he made this decision, he wrote in the back of his Bible two words: *No reserves.* Turning down high-paying job offers after graduating from Yale University, he entered two more words in his Bible: *No retreats.*

Completing studies at Princeton Seminary, Borden sailed for China to work with Muslims, stopping first at Egypt for some preparation. While there he was stricken with cerebral meningitis and died within a month. A waste, you say! Not in God's plan. In his Bible underneath the words *no reserves* and *no retreats,* he had written the words *no regrets.*

—D. J. D.

WHAT COUNTS IS NOT HOW LONG YOU LIVE
BUT HOW WELL YOU LIVE.

He was wounded for our transgressions,
He was bruised for our iniquities.

ISAIAH 53:5

The story is told of a man who was brought into court for trial and found guilty. The judge happened to be a close boyhood friend of the accused, although they had not seen each other for many years. Remaining impartial, the judge sentenced the man and levied a penalty appropriate to his crime. It was a fine so large that the accused could not pay it. A jail sentence, therefore, seemed to be the only alternative. The judge then did a very unusual thing. Leaving the bench, he approached the convicted man, shook his hand, and announced, "I'm paying the fine for you."

As we contemplate the great salvation God has provided, we must remember that He is both loving and just. Therefore, as much as He loves us, He could not simply overlook our sins. The penalty for violating His law had to be exacted. But by Jesus' death on the cross, God's love and justice were satisfied so that there is "no condemnation to those who are in Christ Jesus" (Rom. 8:1). Sin's penalty has been paid in full! —R. W. D.

SALVATION IS FREE, BUT IT COST OUR SAVIOR
AN ENORMOUS PRICE.

Be anxious for nothing, but . . .
let your requests be made known to God.

PHILIPPIANS 4:6

Several years ago the *Wall Street Journal* carried a story about Sally, an overly conscientious youngster who made herself miserable over the smallest failures and setbacks. Early one fall, when there was an exceptionally heavy snowstorm, Sally's grandfather took her for a drive. "Notice those elms," he said. "The branches are so badly broken that the trees may die. But just look at those pines and evergreens. They are completely undamaged by the storm. My child, there are two kinds of trees in the world: the foolish and the wise. An elm holds its branches rigid. As it becomes weighted down, eventually its limbs break. But when an evergreen is loaded, it simply relaxes, lowers its branches, and lets the burden slip away. And so it remains unharmed. Be a pine tree, granddaughter."

Christians who give up all their cares to the Lord can face life's burdens much better than those who try to bear the weight themselves. You can be like the elm tree that tries to bear all its troubles, only to break under the load. Or you can become like a pine because you are learning to roll all your burdens on the Lord. —H. G. B.

GOD INVITES US TO BURDEN HIM WITH WHAT BURDENS US.

Let us consider one another in order to stir up love and good works,
not forsaking the assembling of ourselves together.

HEBREWS 10:24–25

In 1660, John Bunyan was imprisoned in the Bedford jail for preaching the gospel. Except for his family and a few friends who visited him, he was cut off from the church for twelve years. Yet this forced confinement marked a deepening of his spiritual life. And during a later imprisonment he wrote *Pilgrim's Progress*.

If illness, imprisonment, the limitations of age, or any other legitimate reason keeps you away from church, don't feel guilty or forgotten. You are as much a part of the church as if you were present at all of its services. You can pray for its ministry, its needs, and its people.

And those of us who are not limited must take the church to those who can't attend. We must visit them regularly. When God's children can't attend, God still attends to them through His Spirit and through His people who show love and concern. —D. J. D.

BELIEVERS SEPARATED BY DISTANCE CAN STILL FEEL CLOSE
BECAUSE THEY ARE UNITED IN CHRIST.

Take My yoke upon you and learn from Me, . . .
and you will find rest for your souls.

MATTHEW 11:29

On one occasion F. B. Meyer visited D. L. Moody in Northfield, Massachusetts. Moody, showing Meyer a team of oxen, said that whenever one of those oxen was being yoked in, the other, which might be on the far side of the farmyard, would come trotting up and stand beside the other one until it was yoked in also.

Meyer then made this encouraging application to us in our relationship to Christ: "Jesus stands today with the yoke upon His shoulder. He calls to each one and says, 'Come and share My yoke, and let us plow together the long furrow of your life. I will be a true yokefellow to you. The burden shall be on Me.'"

When our burden seems heavy and our loads hard to bear, Christ has promised to lift our burdens and lighten our cares. That's how we find rest and peace in every area of life. —R. W. D.

IT'S NOT THE LOAD THAT BREAKS YOU DOWN,
IT'S THE FACT THAT YOU CARRY IT ALONE.

"Therefore I also have lent him to the LORD;
so long as he lives he shall be lent to the LORD."

1 SAMUEL 1:28

An elderly mother in Scotland had given up her son to the Lord. One day she went to a missionary society meeting where only contributing members were admitted. The doorkeeper asked, "Are you a contributor?" "I am afraid not," she answered. When he wouldn't let her in, she left disappointed. Pondering his words, she thought of her son who years before had gone as a missionary to Sierra Leone in West Africa. His body now lay buried in that distant land. She retraced her steps to the building and explained to the man, "I forgot. You asked me if I was a contributor. I gave my only boy, and he is buried out in Sierra Leone." The doorkeeper removed his cap, bowed graciously, and said, "Come in." He then led her to a front seat.

What more secure future could we want for our children than to give them to God! Only He can guide and keep them. —P. R. V.

TRAIN CHILDREN EARLY TO LOVE GOD'S WORD
SO THEY WILL FOLLOW ITS LIGHT ON THE PATH OF LIFE.

God has set the members, each one of them,
in the body just as He pleased.

1 CORINTHIANS 12:18

A sea captain and his chief engineer were at odds about whose job was the most vital on their ship. They decided that the best way to settle the question would be to exchange positions. The captain went below deck to run the engine room, and the chief engineer climbed to the bridge and grabbed the wheel.

Several hours later the captain appeared on deck, his clothes covered with oil and grease. "Chief," he yelled up to the bridge as he swung a wrench in hand, "come down here. I can't make 'er go!" "I know," yelled the chagrined chief engineer, "I've run 'er aground!"

The effectiveness of the Christian church is dependent on the cooperation of its members as each one does what God has equipped him or her to do best. Then, serving under the lordship of Christ, they will labor together in harmony. What task has God given you in His program? Stick to it. It's a job He intends just for you. —P. R. V.

THE CHRISTIAN WHO PULLS ON THE OARS
HAS NO TIME TO ROCK THE BOAT.

*The law of Your mouth is better to me
than thousands of coins of gold and silver.*

PSALM 119:72

The prospect of discovering millions of dollars in gold has driven men and women into high mountains, across hot deserts, and down to the ocean's floor. One such person was Mel Fisher. He spent twenty-three years of his life searching for sunken treasure. At last he discovered the wreck of the *Nuestra Senora de Atocha*, a Spanish vessel laden with gold. "Once you see the ocean bottom carpeted with gold coins," he said, "you'll never forget it." First his divers found a gold necklace, then silver and gold coins and bars worth millions of dollars.

That gold may be worth millions, bringing great personal satisfaction and wealth. But there are treasures of far greater value—the truths of the Bible—and they are available to all. The psalmist wrote of its value in today's text, "The law of Your mouth is better to me than thousands of [coins] of gold and silver." God's Word is far more valuable than sunken treasure. It is much more precious than gold. Have you discovered its riches? —D. C. E.

RICH TREASURES OF GOD'S TRUTH ARE WAITING TO BE DISCOVERED.

*I am the good shepherd; and I know My sheep,
and am known by My own.*

JOHN 10:14

Edward VII, the King of England from 1901 to 1910, was visiting a city to lay the cornerstone for a new hospital. Thousands of schoolchildren were present to sing for him. Following the ceremony, the King walked past the excited youngsters. After he was gone, a teacher saw one of her students crying. She asked her, "Why are you crying? Did you not see the King?" "Yes," the young girl sobbed, "but the King did not see me."

King Edward couldn't have taken notice of each child in that throng. Jesus, however, gives individual attention to each of us. He is the good shepherd who "calls his own sheep by name" (John 10:3). Think of it—Jesus knows who you are! You matter to Him. As you worship Him, tell Him you love Him. Then, as you fellowship with other believers, help them realize that they matter to Jesus. —P. R. V.

CHRIST KNOWS YOUR NAME AND YOUR NEED.

Offer the sacrifices of righteousness,
and put your trust in the LORD.

PSALM 4:5

British evangelist Billy Strachan told of sitting in his study, engaged in a serious discussion with a friend, when his daughter walked into the room. Her jump rope was hopelessly tangled. She handed it to her dad, said barely a word, and quietly left. Continuing his intense conversation with his friend, he untied the knots in her jump rope almost without thinking. A few moments later his daughter returned and said, "Thanks, Daddy," and skipped back out to play.

Billy commented, "Why can't we be like that with our heavenly Father? Why do we work so hard in our own efforts when we could turn our problems over to Him and let Him work them out? What we need is more trust in the Lord." We Christians seem determined at times to solve our problems ourselves rather than to trust God with childlike faith. We struggle and fuss and exert great effort, usually making matters worse, when we could be relaxed and confident by simply turning everything over to the Lord. —D. C. E.

TRUE FAITH IS NOT SIMPLY BELIEVING THAT GOD *CAN*
BUT THAT HE *WILL*.

Let each of you look out not only for his own interests,
but also for the interests of others.

PHILIPPIANS 2:4

A young artist submitted one of his works to be hung in a prestigious art exhibit, but the selection committee rejected it. One of its members, however, the renowned landscape painter Joseph Turner, insisted that they include the young man's work. The others denied his plea, saying that there was simply no room for it. Turner said no more but quietly removed one of his own pictures, replacing it with that of the budding young artist.

Life takes on new interest when we invest in the lives of others.

When it became necessary for Abram and Lot to go their separate ways, Abram graciously let his nephew choose whatever land he preferred. Abram said, "If you take the left, then I will go to the right; or, if you go to the right, then I will go to the left" (Gen. 13:9).

Let us live unselfishly today, so that as we close our eyes in sleep tonight we can do so with the satisfaction that comes from looking out for others. —R. W. D.

JESUS AND OTHERS AND YOU.
THAT'S THE WAY TO SPELL JOY!

Why do you look at the speck in your brother's eye,
but do not perceive the plank in your own eye?

LUKE 6:41

A woman named Ruth Knowlton lived in a tall apartment building in New York. Across the alley was another apartment building only a few feet away, and she could easily look into her neighbor's apartment. Ruth had never met the woman who lived there, but she could see her as she sewed and read each afternoon. After several months, she noticed that the figure by the window had become indistinct. She couldn't understand why the woman didn't wash her windows. One day Ruth decided to wash her windows. Later that day, as she sat down to rest by the window, to her amazement she could clearly and distinctly see her neighbor sitting by her window. Ruth said to herself, "Well, finally she washed her windows!" It never even occurred to Ruth that her windows were the ones that needed washing.

How often we overlook our own failures and sins while criticizing the faults in others! In fact, our judgment may reflect our own flaws, which usually are more serious than those we see in someone else. Are we looking through the smudges of our own lives and criticizing others?

—P. R. V.

OUR OWN FAULTS ARE THE ONES
WE CONDEMN MOST QUICKLY IN OTHERS.

When they had come to the place called Calvary,
there they crucified Him.

LUKE 23:33

*D*riving through West Virginia, Virginia, and North Carolina, my wife and I were captivated by the rolling foothills and sweeping mountains. But the most vivid memory of our drive down Interstate 77 was the repeated whisper of three crosses appearing on a knoll here, a sloping hillside there.

Those crosses call to mind a sermon I read some years ago by Myron J. Taylor titled "A Hill With Three Crosses." He said that one cross portrays a thief dying IN sin, and the other a thief dying TO sin. But the center cross speaks of the Redeemer dying FOR sin. It divides all humanity into one of two categories—those who reject Christ and die in sin, and those who receive Christ and can die to sin.

Those crosses confront us all along life's highway. Sin's penalty was paid and sin's power was broken on that center cross. By dying daily to our sins, we experience the fullness of eternal life. —D. J. D.

BECAUSE CHRIST DIED FOR SIN, WE CAN DIE TO SIN.

Let nothing be done through selfish ambition or conceit,
but . . . let each esteem others better than himself.

PHILIPPIANS 2:3

I read a story about a rich baker who sent for twenty of the poorest children in town and said to them, "In this basket is a loaf of bread for each of you. Take one and come back every day and I'll give you more." Immediately the youngsters began quarreling about who would get the largest loaf. Snatching from the basket, they left without even thanking the baker. Gretchen, a poorly dressed little girl, patiently waited until the others had left. She then took the smallest loaf, which remained in the basket, kissed the old man's hand, and went home. The next day the scene was repeated. But when Gretchen's mother sliced this loaf, she found many shiny silver pieces inside. When Gretchen took the money back to the baker, he said, "No, my child, it was not a mistake. I put them into the smallest loaf to reward you."

Self-interest is not wrong, but the Christ-like way is to look out also for the interests of others. To live for self and get ahead brings limited reward, but if we look on others' needs, we're honored by the Lord. —H. G. B.

FORGET YOURSELF FOR OTHERS,
AND OTHERS WILL NOT FORGET YOU.

You therefore must endure hardship
as a good soldier of Jesus Christ.

2 TIMOTHY 2:3

The knights in King Arthur's court had to be men of valor. Any soldier returning from battle without a wound heard this stern order: "Go get your scar!" The monarch expected his men to be so committed to him and his cause that they would willingly throw themselves into the thick of the conflict—risking injury or death. Only the brave met with his approval.

Jesus said, "If anyone desires to come after Me, let him deny himself, and take up his cross, and follow Me" (Matt. 16:24). This means we willingly obey Christ, disregarding our own desires and comforts. It means accepting ridicule, rejection, and even physical persecution. But Jesus takes note of it all. Peter said, "But rejoice to the extent that you partake of Christ's sufferings, that when His glory is revealed, you may also be glad with exceeding joy" (1 Pet. 4:13).

We will not have physical scars when we stand before Jesus someday. But everyone who has suffered in serving Him will be richly rewarded. —R. W. D.

NO SACRIFICE WE MAKE IS TOO GREAT
FOR THE ONE WHO SACRIFICED HIS ALL.

I will pray the Father, and He will give you another Helper.

JOHN 14:16

J. Allen Blair tells of a man who was struggling to get to Grand Central Station in New York City. The wind blew fiercely, and the rain beat down on him as he lugged his two heavy suitcases toward the terminal. Occasionally he would pause to rest and regain his strength before trudging on against the elements.

At one point he was almost ready to collapse, when a man suddenly appeared by his side, took the suitcases, and said in a strangely familiar voice, "We're going the same way. You look as if you could use some help." When they had reached the shelter of the station, the weary traveler, the renowned educator Booker T. Washington, asked the man,

"Please, sir, what is your name?" The man replied, "The name, my friend, is Roosevelt. Teddy Roosevelt."

We don't have to face life's storms alone. God sent the heavenly Helper to give us His strength and encouragement. Referring to Him, Jesus used the Greek word *parakletos*, which means "one called alongside to help" (John 14:16, 26). Are you depending on Him? —P. R. V.

**WITH THE HOLY SPIRIT ON THE INSIDE,
YOU CAN WIN ANY BATTLE ON THE OUTSIDE.**

I call to remembrance the genuine faith that is in you.

2 TIMOTHY 1:5

True Christians are characterized by a genuine faith. A good synonym for the word *genuine* in 2 Timothy 1:5 is the word *sincere*. If you look in a dictionary that lists word origins, you'll find that it comes from two Latin terms—*sine* and *cere*, meaning "without wax."

Years ago, a potter would often put his seal, or stamp, upon a completed vessel with the words *sine cere*. This meant that to his knowledge there was no flaw in that work. If a potter did crack a vessel, he would carefully patch that flawed vase or bowl by filling in the crack with wax. Then he would glaze it over. But it did not merit the stamp *sine cere*, "without wax," because it was not a flawless piece of pottery.

A phony faith will not stand the test of God's all seeing eye. He knows whether our profession of faith in Christ is real or whether it is merely a way of trying to satisfy a parent, a spouse, or a friend. Don't settle for a phony faith. Make sure it is genuine.—P. R. V.

**A FAITH THAT'S NOT ALL IT'S CRACKED UP TO BE
IS HEADED FOR A CRACKUP.**

May

*For to me, to live is Christ,
and to die is gain.*

PHILIPPIANS 1:21

George Atley was killed while serving with the Central African Mission. There were no witnesses, but the evidence indicates that Atley was confronted by a band of hostile tribesmen. He was carrying a fully loaded, ten-chamber Winchester rifle and had to choose either to shoot his attackers and run the risk of negating the work of the mission in that area, or not to defend himself and be killed. When his body was later found in a stream, it was evident that he had chosen the latter. Nearby lay his rifle—all ten chambers still loaded. He had made the supreme sacrifice, motivated by his burden for lost souls and his unswerving devotion to his Savior.

The apostle Paul said he wanted Christ to be magnified in his body, "whether by life or by death." Writing on Philippians 1:21 in *The Bible Knowledge Commentary*, Robert P. Lightner said, "Paul's concern was not what would happen to him but what testimony would be left for his Lord. Release would allow him to continue preaching Christ. But martyrdom would also advance the cause of Christ." —R. W. D.

**IT IS BETTER TO SUFFER FOR THE CAUSE OF CHRIST
THAN FOR THE CAUSE OF CHRIST TO SUFFER.**

Let your speech always be with grace,
seasoned with salt.

COLOSSIANS 4:6

If you were to evaporate a ton of water from the Pacific Ocean, you would get approximately 79 pounds of salt. A ton of Atlantic water would yield 81 pounds. And from the Dead Sea you would get almost 500 pounds of salt. As these statistics demonstrate, the earth's bodies of water vary greatly in their degree of saltiness. So do Christians. Jesus said that we are "the salt of the earth" (Matt. 5:13), but we all have different levels of "salt content." Let's look at a few Scripture references to see what it means to be "salty."

1. Salt enhances flavor (Job 6:6).
2. Salt indicates purity in speech (Col. 4:6).
3. Salt symbolizes keeping a promise (Num.18:19).
4. Salt speaks of goodness (Mark 9:50).

Now, check your salt content. Are you the kind of person others like to be around? Is your conversation pure? Do you keep promises? Are you characterized by goodness? An unbelieving world is watching and listening. —P. R. V.

AS THE "SALT OF THE EARTH," CHRISTIANS SHOULD MAKE OTHERS THIRSTY FOR THE WATER OF LIFE.

I am the way, the truth, and the life.
No one comes to the Father except through Me.

JOHN 14:6

One continuing concern about American tax structure is the problem of loopholes. Some people spend more time looking for loopholes than they do figuring how much tax they owe. Corporations hire experts to look for legal ways to avoid taxes—and they find them. The result for the U.S. government is the loss of millions of dollars.

Some people develop a "loophole mentality" in their relationship to God. I've heard that when W. C. Fields was on his deathbed, a visitor found him reading the Bible. Asked what he was doing, he replied, "Looking for loopholes, my friend. Looking for loopholes."

The Bible says that Jesus is the only way to heaven, and that we must repent of our sins and trust Him as our Savior. But many people secretly feel that when they die and stand before the judgment seat they will find some other way to get in. But they are wrong. Jesus is the only way to heaven. There are no loopholes. —D. C. E.

CHRIST IS THE ONLY WAY TO HEAVEN;
ALL OTHER PATHS ARE DETOURS TO DOOM.

Honor the LORD with your possessions,
and with the firstfruits of all your increase.

PROVERBS 3:9

An African convert who loved the Lord earned money by making and selling a special kind of bean cake. She had always been conscientious in her giving, but after suffering a severe foot injury in an accident her income ceased. It was many long months before she could resume her work. Eagerly she awaited the day she could sell her tasty cakes again. She promised the missionary that she would give one-third of her earnings to the Lord instead of just 10 percent. She said her goal for the first week of business was to make a profit of three shillings. The missionary was surprised, therefore, when the woman returned after only two days with one shilling as an offering for the Lord. "You surely haven't earned three shillings already!" he exclaimed. The woman was perplexed by his response. "Do you think I would give my Lord the last of the three?" she asked. "This is the first one and it belongs to Him—the other two I make will be for me."

One grace a child of God can show is giving from a generous heart, but if you wait until your riches grow you may never start. Practice "firstfruit" giving. —H. G. B.

WE SHOW WHO WE LOVE BY WHAT WE DO WITH WHAT WE HAVE.

If a man is overtaken in any trespass,
you who are spiritual restore such a one in a spirit of gentleness.

GALATIANS 6:1

I read about a group of residents in a Connecticut town who were terribly upset about the reckless driving on their suburban streets. So fifty-three of them signed a petition calling for tighter traffic control in their neighborhoods. The sheriff responded by setting up a watch a few nights later. He caught five violators in all—and each of them had signed the petition! They themselves were guilty of the very transgressions of which they were so critical.

Sometimes our fellow Christians need correcting, and we have a responsibility to help them. But before we undertake this delicate and challenging task, we must be honest about where we stand. When the apostle Paul wrote to the Galatian believers, he urged them to take steps to confront and restore a sinning brother (6:1). But he also called for it to be done in "a spirit of gentleness." Why? Because any one of us could fall to temptation and be found guilty of the same crime. —D. C. E.

IN SPEAKING OF A PERSON'S FAULTS, DON'T FORGET YOUR OWN!

*Daniel . . . knelt down on his knees three times that day,
and prayed and gave thanks before his God.*

DANIEL 6:10

In her book *A Practical Guide to Prayer*, Dorothy Haskins tells about a noted concert violinist who was asked the secret of her mastery of the instrument. The woman answered the question with two words: "Planned neglect." Then she explained, "There were many things that used to demand my time. When I went to my room after breakfast, I made my bed, straightened the room, dusted, and did whatever seemed necessary. When I finished my work, I turned to my violin practice. That system prevented me from accomplishing what I should on the violin. So I reversed things. I deliberately planned to neglect everything else until my practice period was complete. And that program of planned neglect is the secret of my success."

This same principle can be helpful as we plan a daily quiet time with the Lord. Unless we discipline ourselves and make a deliberate effort, trivial things will keep us from establishing a consistent devotional life. Let's give our time with the Lord top priority by "planned neglect" of things of lesser value. He deserves first place in our lives. —R.W.D.

**TO WALK WITH GOD, WE MUST MAKE IT
A PRACTICE TO TALK WITH GOD.**

*On this rock I will build My church,
and the gates of Hades shall not prevail against it.*

MATTHEW 16:18

Recently I came across some startling statistics in my reading, and they should produce a surge of optimism. Consider these facts: In Korea, the number of Christians has doubled every ten years since 1940 to more than 11 million believers today. That's 25 percent of the population! The number of Christians has doubled in Indonesia since 1965. In Africa there were 10 million Christians in 1900; today there are 203 million. From less than a million in 1900 in Latin America, the number of Christians has grown to 18 million. But the most growth has taken place in China. At the Communist takeover in 1949, there were about a million Chinese Protestants. But now there are an estimated 35 to 50 million Chinese believers.

I recognize that statistics don't tell the whole story. Not every "Christian statistic" is necessarily a true Christian. Even so, these figures give us reason to rejoice and know that God's Spirit is active in our world today, and that the church is growing. So don't be discouraged. God is building His church! —D. C. E.

**THE CHURCH CAN GO INTO THE WORLD
EVEN IF THE WORLD WON'T COME INTO THE CHURCH.**

Blessed be the LORD,
Who daily loads us with benefits.

PSALM 68:19

A Christian farmer went to the city on business and stopped at a small restaurant for lunch. When his food was served he bowed his head and gave God thanks, just as he always did at home. A young fellow at the next table noticed that the farmer was praying. Thinking that he was a little backward and not in touch with "city ways," he asked loudly to embarrass him, "Say, farmer, does everyone do that out in the country where you live?" The earnest Christian turned to him and replied kindly, "No, son, the pigs don't."

In Psalm 68, David reviewed the many ways God had cared for His people Israel. After surveying Jehovah's faithfulness, he exclaimed, "Blessed be the Lord, who daily loads us with benefits, the God of our salvation!" From a heart overflowing with love for the Lord, David gave thanks often. Should we not respond in like manner for every blessing God has so freely given? —P. R. V.

A THANKFUL HEART ENJOYS BLESSINGS TWICE—
WHEN THEY'RE RECEIVED AND WHEN THEY'RE REMEMBERED.

They sing the song of Moses, the servant of God,
and the song of the Lamb.

REVELATION 15:3

Emperor penguins love to sing. They are among the most musical creatures on earth. When courting, the male and female bow and sing to each other. Her voice is soft and gentle; he sings loud and long. When the mother penguin has laid her eggs, she goes off to the ocean for two weeks to feed. While she is gone, the father sits on the eggs and sings. After regaining her strength, the female comes back to the nest and sings as well. And shortly before a little one is hatched, if you lean your ear down close to the shell, you can hear the chick singing inside.

The people of God are also singers. When Moses led Israel out of Egypt, he paused to praise God in song (Exod. 15:1–18). Deborah sang in victory (Judges 5). David's songs were numerous. The disciples sang in the upper room (Mark 14:26).

If you have no song, something is wrong. Christians are a people who can't help but sing! —D. C. E.

REMEMBERING GOD'S GOODNESS PUTS A SONG IN THE HEART.

May the God of hope fill you with all joy and peace . . .
by the power of the Holy Spirit.

ROMANS 15:13

When the Norwegian explorer Fridtjof Nansen left for the North Pole in 1893, he took with him a strong, fast carrier pigeon. For many difficult months, Nansen explored the desolate Arctic regions. One day during that time, he penned a tiny message, attached it to the pigeon, and prepared to release the bird to travel the 2,000 miles back to Norway. Nansen took the trembling bird in his hand and flung her upward into the foreboding atmosphere. She circled three times and then headed south — a thousand miles over ice and another thousand over the ocean. When the bird finally arrived at the Nansen home, the explorer's wife knew her husband was safe.

Similarly, the heavenly Dove, the Holy Spirit, brought encouragement and hope to the early Christians on the Day of Pentecost. Before the Savior left this earth, He promised to send them a Helper, a Comforter.

Today the Holy Spirit bears witness with our spirit that we are God's children. He assures us that all is well. —P. R. V.

CHRIST DEPARTED SO THAT THE HOLY SPIRIT COULD BE IMPARTED.

Shall we indeed accept good from God,
and shall we not accept adversity?

JOB 2:10

The legendary Arabic author Lokman was originally a slave. He had always been treated well, but one time his master gave him an extremely bitter melon Lokman ate it without protesting. "How could you eat that nauseating fruit?" his owner inquired. "I've received many good things from you. Shouldn't I also be willing to take the bitter from your hand?" This response pleased the master, and he rewarded Lokman by giving him his freedom.

Job too endured some bitter experiences. The disease that plagued him may have been "black leprosy." It produces physical weakness, foul breath, difficulty in breathing, and tender, itchy skin. The body turns black, festering ulcers develop, and the legs swell to an enormous size. Even though the suffering was great, Job didn't rebel against the Lord. Instead, he said in faith, "Shall we indeed accept good from God and shall we not accept adversity?" All things are sent by God for our good, even the "bitter melon" of trial. Therefore, like Job, let's accept adversity with patient faith. —H. G. B.

THOSE WHO BLESS GOD *IN* THEIR TRIALS
ARE BLESSED *THROUGH* THEIR TRIALS.

*Grace, mercy, and peace from God our Father
and Jesus Christ our Lord.*

1 TIMOTHY 1:2

Among the safety rules a mountain climber must remember as he scales rocky cliffs is this: Keep three points on the rock. This means that if he moves one foot, his other foot and both hands must be solidly positioned. If he is going to move a hand to a new grip, his other hand and both feet must be secure.

This brings to mind a sermon I once heard called "Three Sisters of Salvation." These are grace, mercy, and peace. We are given our salvation as a gift of God's grace. His wrath is withheld from us because of His abundant mercy. And His peace helps us stand in quiet confidence when the howling gales of adversity swirl about our lives. They will give us security during our spiritual mountain climbing experience. Let's appropriate these gifts through prayer and obedience to God's Word. We will stand secure in the storms of temptation and evil if we keep advancing on these "three points on the Rock." —D. C. E.

**GOD'S GRACE IS IMMEASURABLE, HIS MERCY INEXHAUSTIBLE,
HIS PEACE INEXPRESSIBLE.**

*Unless you are converted and become as little children,
you will by no means enter the kingdom of heaven.*

M ATTHEW 18:3

Many years ago a doctor was comfortably seated in front of his fireplace, enjoying his shelter from the pouring rain. Suddenly he heard a knock at the door. Outside stood a distressed widow. "My boy, my Davy," she cried, he's very sick!" Oh no, he thought, not on a night like this! He knew this visit would be financially unprofitable. The woman obviously couldn't pay him. But the doctor loved children, and he had a strong sense of duty. So he went, and Davy's life was saved. That sick little boy recovered. His name was David Lloyd George. The doctor frequently looked back to that night when he took that five-mile walk in the drenching rain. He would say, "I never dreamed that in saving the life of that child, I was saving the life of the future Prime Minister of England!"

Nor do we know the eternal impact we can make when we seek opportunities to lead children to Christ.

Jesus is calling children to Himself. Ask God to give you opportunities to demonstrate His love for them. As we live for Christ, let's be careful not to offend children by our words and actions. Let's always look out for the little ones. —H. G. B.

EVERY CHILD IS A BUNDLE OF POTENTIALITY.

Casting all your care upon Him,
for He cares for you.

1 PETER 5:7

As Sarah Smiley was preparing to descend a 5,000 foot Rigi Mountain peak in central Switzerland, her guide told her that she should let him carry her load. She agreed to give some of it to him, but she kept a few items. As they made their way down the mountainside, Sarah felt hindered by her load. Soon she had to stop and rest. When she did, her guide demanded that she give him everything except her Alpine walking stick. This time she agreed and transferred the load to his strong shoulders. Without the extra weight, she made the rest of the trip with ease. It was as if her Lord was trying to say to her, "O foolish, willful heart, have you indeed given up your last burden? You have no need to carry them, or even the right."

How often we are just like Sarah Smiley! When we face a difficulty, we carry the burden by ourselves. God invites us to cast all of our cares on Him, and He is strong enough to shoulder the burden. Let's take Him up on the offer. Our pathway will be easier and our steps lighter. —P. R. V.

OUR WORK IS TO CAST CARE;
GOD'S WORK IS TO TAKE CARE.

I have not come to call the righteous,
but sinners, to repentance.

LUKE 5:32

When F. B. Meyer became pastor of Christ Church in England, only middle-class and wealthy people attended services. He decided to change this by making friends with the poor people in the slums nearby. One morning a garbage collecter shouted from his wagon, "Good morning, Brother Meyer." The preacher replied, "Good morning, dear Brother." When the man jumped down, Meyer extended his hand. The garbage collector drew back, saying, "Excuse me, sir, my hand is not fit for the likes of you." "There's lots of soap and water at Christ Church," Meyer responded. "Please give me your hand." So they shook hands, and the two walked together down the street. Soon they met four other men, and the garbage collector held up his hand. "Look here, mates," he said, "the new parson has shaken that filthy hand." One replied, "Well, if he'll do that, he'll do to listen to." And they all came to hear the gospel.

Jesus was not afraid to dirty His hands (or His reputation, in the eyes of some) in order to call sinners to repentance. Are we willing to do the same? —D. J. D.

WHILE WE ARE PRAYING FOR SINNERS TO COME TO CHRIST,
HE IS PLEADING FOR US TO GO TO SINNERS.

*When he was still a great way off, his father saw him
and had compassion, and ran and fell on his neck and kissed him.*

LUKE 15:20

A Chinese artist was commissioned to portray the parable of the prodigal son. So he chose that part of the story where the wayward boy returns home after having wasted his resources in reckless living. He depicted the father standing by the gate waiting for his son, who could be seen approaching in the distance.

When the artist showed the painting to a Christian friend, the man exclaimed, "Oh no, you don't have it right at all! The father shouldn't be standing still, he should be eagerly running to meet his son!" "But no Chinese father would ever consider doing that to one who had been so wayward," answered the other in surprise. "Ah," said the Christian, "but this parable depicts the heart of God. He is far more loving than even the best of human parents."

How marvelous is God's love for penitent sinners! Be assured that He eagerly waits to welcome any repentant sinner and forgive all his sins.
— H. G. B.

GOD DOES NOT FORGET THE SINNER. HE FORGETS THE SIN.

*Put on the whole armor of God, that you may be able
to stand against the wiles of the devil.*

EPHESIANS 6:11

One of the most unusual creatures of the sea is the lobster. It runs backwards. It hears with its legs and tastes with its feet. It chews its food with teeth in its stomach. And because the lobster is delicious food for other sea creatures, the Lord gave it a full suit of armor. A thick plate covers its claws and its body. Overlapping sheets of armor encase its lower body and its tail. Although many old lobsters have numerous scrapes and gouges on their shells, they survive attacks from most predators because of the armor God gave them to protect them.

The Lord supplies us with a suit of armor too—a helmet, a breastplate, a shield, a belt, and shoes—to keep us safe from the attacks of our powerful spiritual foes. But we must be sure to use our armor. Take the helmet of salvation to assure you of your position in Christ, the breastplate to live righteously, and the shield of faith to protect you at all times. Finally, be sure to walk in truth and peace. Omitting any part of God's provision invites spiritual injury. Like the lobster, let's take full advantage of our armor! —D. C. E.

GOD'S ARMOR IS TAILOR-MADE, BUT WE MUST PUT IT ON.

Then a voice came from heaven,
"You are My beloved Son, in whom I am well pleased."

MARK 1:11

An old shoemaker was once visited by a preacher who expressed pity for him because he filled such a "menial" position. The man gently rebuked the pastor by pointing to a motto over his workbench that read, "A shoemaker by the grace of God." The motto reminded him of the dignity of his work as a Christian.

For three years Jesus engaged in a dramatic public ministry of healing and teaching. He died on the cross for the sins of the world; then He arose from the dead. But we often forget those silent years of routine labor as a carpenter (Mark 6:3). Even there, He never faltered but remained diligent and faithful to the Father's will. The years when Jesus worked as a craftsman in wood were certainly included in the Father's loving affirmation, "I am well pleased."

God allots to each of His children some work in which He expects them to be faithful. It may be on an assembly line, part of a construction crew, in an office, or in the home. Let's follow Jesus' example by performing our work well for our heavenly Father. —H. G. B.

GOD DOESN'T ASK YOU TO BE THE BEST, ONLY TO DO YOUR BEST.

*Those who wait on the LORD . . . shall run and not be weary,
they shall walk and not faint.*

ISAIAH 40:31

read a cute little story of a first grader who wondered why her father brought home a briefcase full of work every evening. Her mother explained, "Daddy has so much to do that he can't finish it all at the office." "Well, then," asked the child innocently, "why don't they put him in a slower group?"

We are not all made to go at the same speed. Some people run on high-powered motors while others must crank their engines to get going, and they never run very fast. Even so, there's a pace uniquely suited to our own temperament, talents, and energies. When we let ourselves be driven by worry, greed, worldly ambition, and unsatisfied egos, we easily sacrifice priorities, fall into sin, or become emotionally drained.

Life's race isn't always won by those who are constantly on the go. It's won by believers who wait on the Lord to renew their strength. They run and are not weary; they walk and don't faint. They've learned Christ's secret by the Father's timing. —D. J. D.

WHEN WE LEARN TO WAIT UPON THE LORD,
HIS STRENGTH WILL BE OUR SURE REWARD.

He [chastened us] for our profit,
that we may be partakers of His holiness.

HEBREWS 12:10

Amy Carmichael (1867–1951) labored in India as a missionary for fifty-five years. Of a childhood experience she wrote, "When I was small, I used to thrust my hands into the flour bin whenever I had the chance. Not sealskin, kitten's fur, velvet, or even water seemed to me so wonderful in deliciousness of gentleness as that fine flour.

"Later when I read Leviticus and Numbers, and found that fine flour was used as a type of our Lord Jesus Christ, I understood at least one reason He was like fine flour in the texture of His being. Fine flour . . . has been milled to the uttermost. Our Holy Savior was fine flour from the beginning, and yet in an awful sense, He 'went through the mill' of hard human experience; He suffered, being tempted."

The ways of God with His children, even in chastening, are to conform us to the image of His Son, to make us "fine" like Jesus. If the grinding of some pressure seems never to end, if your trial or chastening is severe, remember that your loving Father is using that experience to refine you. —P. R. V.

IF GOD SHOULD SPARE US FROM ALL PAIN,
WE WOULD LIVE OUR LIVES IN VAIN.

A man's heart plans his way,
but the LORD directs his steps.

PROVERBS 16:9

In his book *The Person Reborn*, Paul Tournier tells of a visit from a dear friend who was having great inner turmoil. He had made a life-changing decision, which at the time he believed was God's will. Subsequent events, however, gave him serious second thoughts about whether he had made a mistake.

Each morning Dr. Tournier and his friend read the Bible and prayed together. One day they came to the story of Lot's wife, who was turned into a pillar of salt because she looked back (Gen. 19:26). Suddenly the distressed man said with a burst of insight, "I am like Lot's wife! My life is petrified because I keep looking back. I turn that problem over and over uselessly, without ever discovering whether I did right or not."

If we have prayerfully sought God's will, we must not keep second-guessing our decision. We are assured that God "works out everything for His own ends" (Prov. 15:4). And that includes all the "what ifs" we can think of. —D. J. D.

WHERE GOD'S FINGER POINTS HIS HAND WILL MAKE THE WAY.

Train up a child in the way he should go,
and when he is old he will not depart from it.

PROVERBS 22:6

A friend called on Michelangelo as he was putting what appeared to be the finishing touches on a sculpture. Later when the visitor stopped in to see the artist again, he was surprised to find him busy on the same statue. Seeing no evident changes, he exclaimed "You haven't been working on that statue all this time, have you!" "Yes, I have," the sculptor replied. "I've been busy retouching this part, and polishing that part; I have softened this feature, and brought out that muscle; I've given more expression to the lips, and more energy to that arm." "But all those things are so insignificant," said his visitor. "They are mere trifles." "That may be so," replied Michelangelo, "but trifles make perfection, and perfection is no trifle."

The training of a child demands that same kind of diligence. By reading the Bible, telling its stories, praying, and teaching "line upon line," parents must day after day shape and mold the character of their children so that they will choose to be like Christ. Yes, the proper training of a child is the making of a masterpiece. —R. W. D.

THE CHARACTER OF OUR CHILDREN TOMORROW
IS SHAPED BY WHAT THEY LEARN FROM US TODAY.

Blessed is he whose transgression is forgiven,
whose sin is covered.

PSALM 32:1

A little boy named Bobby had just been tucked into bed by his mother, who was waiting to hear his prayers. But he had been naughty that day and now it was bothering him. So he said, "Mama, I wish you'd go now and leave me alone. I want to pray by myself."

Sensing that something was wrong, she asked, "Bobby, is there anything you ought to tell me?" "No Mommy," he replied. "You would just scold me, but God will forgive me and forget about it." That little boy understood one of the greatest salvation benefits of all—the reality of sins forgiven. The Bible indicates that in Christ "we have redemption through His blood, the forgiveness of sins" (Col. 1:14). We who have received the Lord Jesus as Savior enjoy freedom from sin's eternal condemnation (Rom. 8:1), and we can also have daily forgiveness and cleansing (1 John 1:9).

When we acknowledge our guilt with true repentance, God stands ready to forgive because of what Jesus did on the cross. It's up to us to accept it. —R.W.D.

WHEN GOD FORGIVES, HE ALSO FORGETS.

Even though our outward man is perishing,
yet the inward man is being renewed day by day.

2 CORINTHIANS 4:16

A traveler visiting Amsterdam was intrigued by a chiming tower in the middle of the city. Every hour when the melody was played on the chimes, he would watch and listen. He became so interested that he asked permission to climb to the tower room to watch the musician. Once he got there, however, he didn't hear any music. All he heard was the thump and bang of the keys. In the chime room there was nothing but a terrible clatter, yet beautiful music floated across the city.

In a small way this illustrates the difference between what we see happening in our lives and the beautiful work God is accomplishing in us as He works through us. Often in the clatter and thump of life, we wonder what is happening. But if we are faithful to God and obedient to His Spirit, others will see and hear the beauty and harmony of Christ's life in us. Let's hope in God. No matter how discordant things seem, He keeps the melody playing. —P. R. V.

WE GO FROM STRENGTH TO STRENGTH
AS WE GO FROM STRUGGLE TO STRUGGLE.

How I love Your law!
It is my meditation all the day.

PSALM 119:97

Some Christian women had gathered in a home for Bible study. When the teacher discovered that she had forgotten to bring her Bible, the hostess offered her the use of her own Bible and went to get it.

Looking where she usually kept it, she was surprised that it wasn't there.

She searched for it everywhere but still no Bible. What will those women think of me, she thought, if I can't even find my own Bible! Running upstairs, she found the cleaning woman, who had just started working there. "Betty," she asked, "have you seen my Bible anyplace?" The maid responded with a "Praise the Lord! Praise the Lord!" "Why in the world do you say that?" the distressed woman asked. "Because," Betty replied with a big smile on her face, "the first thing I do when I begin at a new place is hide the Bible. I do it just to find out how long it takes people to miss it. I put yours in the linen closet under the sheets!"

If someone were to hide your Bible, how long would it take before you missed it? Let's not neglect the Word—not even for a day. —R. W. D.

**TOO MANY PEOPLE PUT THE BIBLE ON THE SHELF
INSTEAD OF IN THEIR HEARTS.**

What the law could not do in that it was weak through the flesh,
God did by sending His own Son.

ROMANS 8:3

Experiments with uranium were part of Louis Slotin's job as a research scientist in 1946. In one of his experiments, Slotin conducted a test in which he would bring two pieces of uranium close together. Just as an atomic reaction would begin, he would separate the two segments with a screwdriver and stop it. One day, while performing the experiment, the screwdriver slipped and the pieces of uranium got too close together. The reaction instantly filled the room with a dazzling bluish light. Slotin did not run to protect himself from the dangerous radiation. Rather, he tore the pieces of uranium apart with his hands, stopping the chain reaction. His quick action saved the lives of the other scientists in the room, but nine days later he died in agony.

What this unselfish scientist did is a picture of what Christ did for us nearly 2,000 years ago. The Lord Jesus took to Himself sin's most deadly radiation. He willingly accepted its curse on our behalf. He let it bring Him to a horrible death. In so doing, He broke the chain reaction that entrapped us. —D. C. E.

**JESUS IS THE ONLY PHYSICIAN WHO CAN
CURE HIS PATIENTS BY TAKING THEIR DISEASE.**

We also glory in tribulations,
knowing that tribulation produces perseverance.

ROMANS 5:3

After William Carey was well established in his pioneer missionary work in India, his supporters in England sent a printer to assist him. Soon the two men were turning out portions of the Bible for distribution. Carey had spent many years learning the language so that he could produce the Scriptures in the local dialect. He had also prepared dictionaries and grammars for the use of his successors.

One day while Carey was away, a fire broke out and completely destroyed the building, the presses, many Bibles, and the precious manuscripts, dictionaries and grammars. When he returned and was told of the tragic loss, he showed no sign of despair or impatience. Instead, he knelt and thanked God that he still had the strength to do the work over again. He started immediately, not wasting a moment in self-pity. Before his death, he had duplicated and even improved on his earlier achievements.

The next time you face a trying situation, ask the Lord for perseverance. Then pick up the pieces and start over again. —H. G. B.

GREAT ENDURANCE IS ESSENTIAL TO GREAT ACHIEVEMENT.

*He who glories, let him glory in the L*ORD.

1 CORINTHIANS 1:31

François Fenelón was the court preacher for King Louis XIV of France in the seventeenth century. One Sunday when the king and his attendants arrived at the chapel for the regular service, no one else was there but the preacher. King Louis demanded, "What does this mean?" Fenelón replied, "I had published that you would not come to church today, in order that Your Majesty might see who serves God in truth and who flatters the king."

Why do you go to church? To meet your friends, to hear the preacher, to fulfill an obligation? These reasons are not wrong, but they do not represent our highest motivation. Our primary reason must be to worship Christ.

When we gather with God's people, let's not do so to be seen, nor to flatter the preacher. Let's be united in heart and keep Christ preeminent. Make worshiping Him your primary reason for going to church. —P. R. V.

TRUE WORSHIP ACKNOWLEDGES THE TRUE WORTH-SHIP OF **C**HRIST.

That which we have seen and heard we declare to you,
that you also may have fellowship with us.

1 JOHN 1:3

We are hearing a lot these days about networking. This term refers to the people in our lives—relatives, friends, and associates—who are part of our emotional and physical support base. They are the people we can count on for help. When we're out of a job looking for an emergency loan, or grieving, they are the ones who stand by us.

The idea of networking is closely akin to the Christian concept of fellowship. It transcends racial, social, economic, and sexual differences and unites a wide variety of people in the worship and service of Christ.

The true nature of Christian fellowship may be clarified by contrasting the use of two German words. The first, gesellschaft, refers to people thrown together without deep ties, such as all the people riding the same bus. The second, gemeinschaft, refers to those with intimate ties of family or community.

We need the fellowship of a community of believers who love, encourage, and pray for one another. —D. C. E.

WE NEED ENCOURAGEMENT TO BUILD US UP
AND SUPPORT TO HOLD US UP.

What is man that You are mindful of him,
and the son of man that You visit him?

P SALM 8:4

A highly acclaimed astronomer was giving an address on recent discoveries about the vast workings of our universe. The information was amazing!

When the astronomer fielded questions, someone asked, "Professor, after all you have told us about the complexity of our universe, do you think a God great enough to make such a world could be concerned about us mortals?" After careful thought, the professor answered, "It depends on how great your God is!"

Planet earth is a mere speck of dust traveling through space. And we, its passengers, might well be viewed as less noticeable than the tiny, almost invisible insects that we unwittingly trample underfoot. But God is not like man. His power is so great that He sees us. He knows us. He cares for us. He seeks us. He meets our need. Yes, this all-powerful God loves us. —R. W. D.

GOD LOVES US NOT BECAUSE OF WHO WE ARE
BUT BECAUSE OF WHO HE IS.

*The eyes of the LORD are on the righteous,
and His ears are open to their cry.*

PSALM 34:15

The story is told of an eastern monarch who recognized how difficult it was for the common people in his realm to come to him with their requests. Sometimes it was nearly impossible for them to make their way through the guards and attendants surrounding him. So the king decided to become more accessible to his subjects. He had a bell installed next to his throne with a long, thin chain attached to it. He then ordered that the chain be let down through a window into the street below so that anyone could get his attention at any time just by ringing the bell.

This is a beautiful and striking picture of God's availability to His children through prayer. Although He is surrounded by indescribable splendor and glory, His ear is open to the faintest cry of the most needy of His followers on earth. We can always "pull the chain" of intercession and have an immediate audience with the King of heaven and earth.

Christian, don't despair. Keep the prayer bell ringing! —H. G. B.

GOD'S HELP IS ONLY A PRAYER AWAY!

June

Through love serve one another.

GALATIANS 5:13

At the annual homecoming of William and Mary College, many of the returning alumni wear white jackets. This is true even of graduates who have gained high positions—including a college president, a state governor, and many business and professional leaders. Why the white jackets? To show that they were among the many students who helped earn their way through college by waiting on tables. Their job and their white jackets symbolized a willingness to serve in a not-so-glamorous job.

Our tendency is to serve only in places of high visibility, or because we feel guilty. But we should humble ourselves and sacrifice time and energy for the sake of others because that's Christ's way. He was the holy Son, yet He washed the dirt from the disciples' feet. Let's learn how to serve as He did, so that we may glorify God. —D. C. E.

IF YOU SERVE FOR THE APPLAUSE OF MEN,
YOU SACRIFICE THE APPROVAL OF GOD.

You will show me the path of life;
in Your presence is fullness of joy.

PSALM 16:11

One dark, rainy night a salesman had a flat tire on a lonely road. To his dismay he had no lug wrench. So he began walking to a farmhouse nearby. Surely the farmer would have a lug wrench. But would he come to the door? And if he did, he'd probably be furious for being awakened. By now the salesman was angry just thinking about the farmer. Why he's just a selfish old clod for refusing to help me, he thought. Reaching the house, the salesman banged on the door. Who's there!" shouted a voice from a window overhead. "You know good and well," yelled the salesman. "It's me. And you can keep your old lug wrench! I wouldn't use it if it were the last one in the county."

Are you like that? Do you tend to look on the dark side of things? Do you always expect the worst? Instead, think positively about doing God's will, and stay close to Jesus. That will keep you from always looking for trouble. —D. J. D.

MANY OF OUR TROUBLES ARE OF OUR OWN MAKING.

*It is good to give thanks to the L*ORD.

PSALM 92:1

Finding it difficult to be thankful? Fulton Oursler learned thankfulness from a woman who helped care for him when he was a little boy. She told him, "Looking for good things is a kind of game an old preacher taught me to play. Take this morning. I woke up and thought, what's there to praise God for today? You know what? I couldn't think of a thing! Then from the kitchen came the most delicious odor that ever tickled my nose. Coffee! 'Much obliged, Lord, for the coffee,' I said, 'and much obliged too for the smell of it.'"

Many years later, Oursler stood at the bedside of that woman as she lay dying. Seeing her in much pain, he wondered if she could still find something to be grateful for. Just then she opened her eyes, looked at the others gathered around her bedside, and quietly said with a smile, "Much obliged, Lord, for such fine friends."

I can't think of a better time than today to begin looking for things to be grateful for. It won't matter what words you use whether you say, "Thank You, Father," or "Much obliged, Lord." The important thing is to say it! —H. V. L.

IF YOU CAN'T THINK OF ANYTHING TO BE THANKFUL FOR, YOU HAVE A POOR MEMORY.

Cleanse me from secret faults.
Keep back Your servant also from presumptuous sins.

PSALM 19:12–13

We don't like to think that sins lying beneath the surface need to be cleansed. We're like the four-year-old who didn't like soap and water, especially when his mother used it to clean those hard-to-get-at places on his face. One day she tried to reason with him and said, "But you want to be clean, don't you?" "Yes," he whimpered, "but can't you just dust me off?"

In the spiritual realm, a once-a-week dusting by going to church and confessing our outward sins is much easier than a daily discipline of letting God's Spirit show us from the Word what needs to be confessed. The inner filth remains undisturbed in our lives. In contrast, the psalmist prayed, "Cleanse me from secret faults." This should be the yearning desire of every child of God. He who is not concerned about his secret faults will sooner or later reveal serious character flaws. —H. G. B.

IT'S THE SIN WE COVER UP THAT EVENTUALLY BRINGS US DOWN.

With great power the apostles gave witness
to the resurrection of the Lord Jesus.

ACTS 4:33

The renowned conductor Reichel was leading a great orchestra and choir in the final rehearsal of Messiah. They had come to that point where the soprano soloist takes up the refrain, "I know that my Redeemer liveth." With the chorus quiet, her elegant voice rang out. It was marked by perfect technique in breathing and enunciation. She sang with near perfection.

As the final note faded into silence, the entire orchestra expected to see Reichel's nod of approval. But instead, he stepped down from the podium and made his way to the singer. With a look of sorrow, he said, "My daughter, you do not really know that your Redeemer lives, do you?" "Why, yes," she blushingly replied. "Then sing it!" cried Reichel. "Tell it to me so that I will know, and all who hear you will know that you know the joy and power of it!" Turning to the orchestra, he motioned to begin again. This time the soloist sang the truth as she knew it in her own soul. Those listening wept under the powerful witness. —P. R. V.

THEY WITNESS BEST WHO WITNESS WITH THEIR LIVES.

His eyes are on the ways of man,
and He sees all his steps.

JOB 34:21

New techniques to detect and identify fingerprints are making it easier to apprehend and convict criminals. One of these methods uses a laser, which causes latent prints to glow when scanned by a laser. Body oils and perspiration, even on porous materials, leave traces that respond to laser light to such an extent that they can be photographed. Variation in color helps to determine the age of the prints, revealing the time sequence of a crime. Even very old prints that cannot be detected by powders and chemicals can be seen clearly by this new technique. For example, a forty-year-old fingerprint was detected on a postcard written during World War II.

If finite man can invent such methods of detection, what must be the infinite capacities of our God? He sees and knows everything! It is a frightening discovery to the sinner to realize that every thought and deed is known to God. But how reassuring to the child of God who is under the loving eye and gracious hand of his heavenly Father! —P. R. V.

KNOWING THAT GOD SEES EVERYTHING
WILL EITHER GIVE CONVICTION OR CONFIDENCE.

*I am the living bread
which came down from heaven.*

JOHN 6:51

After renowned missionary Jonathan Goforth (1859–1936) had spoken in a chapel in southern China, a man asked to talk to him. He said, "I have heard you speak three times, and you always have the same theme. You always speak of Jesus Christ. Why?"

The missionary replied, "Sir, before answering your question, let me ask, 'What did you have for dinner today?'" "Rice," replied the man. "What did you have yesterday?" "The same thing." "And what do you expect to eat tomorrow?" "Rice of course. It gives me strength. I could not do without it. Sir, it is—" the man hesitated as if looking for a strong word. Then he added, "Sir, it is my very life!" The missionary responded quickly, "What you have said of rice, Jesus is to our soul! He is the 'rice' or 'bread of life.'"

Are you nourishing your soul with the Bread of Life? Through prayer and meditation on God's Word, you will find that Christ is your very life. —H. G. B.

ONLY THE BREAD OF LIFE CAN SATISFY SPIRITUAL HUNGER.

God has not given us a spirit of fear,
but of power and of love and of a sound mind.

2 TIMOTHY 1:7

As the city fathers of New York contemplated the future growth of the city, they laid out the streets and numbered them from the center outward. When they began, there were only six or seven streets. In their planning maps, they projected how large they thought the city might grow. Reaching beyond their wildest imagination, they drew streets on the map all the way out to Nineteenth Street. They called it "Boundary Street" because they were sure that's all the larger New York City would become. But history has proven them to be shortsighted. At last count, the city had reached 284th Street—far exceeding their expectations!

We, like those city fathers, sometimes set the boundaries too close in our spiritual expectations. We shrink back from taking a step of faith. We are shortsighted in our concept of God and His power to change our lives.

Let's stop dreaming only little dreams and start expanding our horizons. We'll never reach new heights if we set limits on God.
—D. C. E.

IF WE'RE NOT AS SPIRITUAL AS WE COULD BE,
WE'RE NOT AS SPIRITUAL AS WE SHOULD BE.

Well done, good servant; because you were faithful in a very little,
have authority over ten cities.

LUKE 19:17

One stormy night an elderly couple entered the lobby of a small hotel and asked for a room. The clerk said they were filled, as were all the hotels in town. "But I can't send a fine couple like you out in the rain," he said. "Would you be willing to sleep in my room?" The couple hesitated, but the clerk insisted. The next morning when the man paid his bill, he said, "You're the kind of man who should be managing the best hotel in the United States. Someday I'll build you one." The clerk smiled politely.

A few years later the clerk received a letter from the elderly man, recalling that stormy night and asking him to come to New York. A round-trip ticket was enclosed. When the clerk arrived, his host took him to the corner of Fifth Avenue and Thirty-Fourth Street, where stood a magnificent new building. "That," explained the man, "is the hotel I have built for you to manage." The man was William Waldorf Astor, and that hotel was the original Waldorf-Astoria. The young clerk, George C. Boldt, became its first manager.

Never downplay the importance of what you are doing for Jesus. He sees it all. He rewards it all. —D. J. D.

GOD REQUIRES FAITHFULNESS; GOD REWARDS WITH FRUITFULNESS.

*I will make you an eternal excellence,
a joy of many generations.*

Isaiah 60:15

Scientific measurements indicate that we are moving even when we are standing still. Continental land masses sit on enormous slabs of rock that slide very slowly at the rate of one to eight inches per year. America is gradually moving westward, away from Europe, at the rate of three inches per year.

If that doesn't impress you, consider this. Our Milky Way galaxy is hurtling through space at 375 miles per second or 1.3 million miles per hour. But that's not all. Within our own galaxy the sun and its solar system are zooming along at 12.4 miles per second (43,000 mph) in the direction of the star Vega in the constellation Lyra.

Just as we are hurtling through the heavens at unimaginable speeds, so too we are moving from here to eternity. Our days and opportunities to live for the Lord pass so rapidly that we cannot afford to waste time.

May our measured days be spent as a gift from God. —M. R. D. II

HOW YOU SPEND TIME DETERMINES HOW YOU SPEND ETERNITY.

My God shall supply all your need
according to His riches in glory by Christ Jesus.

PHILIPPIANS 4:19

During the pioneer era in America, a poverty-stricken old man found his way into a settlement on the western frontier. He had run out of supplies, so he was looking for food. As he walked through the camp, someone stopped to talk with him and noticed that he wore a small pouch on a ribbon around his neck. The old man explained that it was a charm given to him many years before. He opened it, removed a crumpled paper, and handed it to his inquirer. Upon examining it, the villager discovered that it was a regular discharge from the federal army. It was signed by General George Washington himself, and it entitled the man to a pension for life. How surprised the old soldier was to find out that all these years he had been carrying a bona fide promise that his needs would be met! Because he had not claimed it, though, he had been a wandering, hungry, penniless man.

We too sometimes wander around in the wilderness of spiritual poverty while God's ample provision goes unused. We forget that God has opened to us "His riches in glory" through the work and merits of Jesus Christ. —P. R. V.

INSTEAD OF SITTING ON THE PREMISES
TRY STANDING ON THE PROMISES.

"With everlasting kindness I will have mercy on you,"
says the LORD, your Redeemer.

ISAIAH 54:8

A large sum of money was given to Rowland Hill to dispense to a poor pastor. Thinking that the amount was too much to send all at once, Hill forwarded just a portion along with a note that said simply, "More to follow." In a few days the man received another envelope containing the same amount and with the same message, "More to follow." At regular intervals, there came a third, and a fourth. In fact, they continued, along with those cheering words, until the entire sum had been received.

C. H. Spurgeon used this story to illustrate that the good things we receive from God always come with the same prospect of more to follow:

When God forgives our sins, there's more forgiveness to follow.

He justifies us in the righteousness of Christ, but there's more to follow.

He adopts us into His family, but there's more to follow.

He prepares us for heaven, but there's more to follow.

He gives us grace, but there's more to follow. —R. W. D.

MAN'S LOVE HAS LIMITS; GOD'S LOVE IS LIMITLESS.

*[Do] the will of God from the heart, with goodwill doing service,
as to the Lord, and not to men.*

EPHESIANS 6:6–7

I stood in the cold pre-dawn darkness outside a New York City hotel waiting for the airport bus. The street was deserted. My attention was drawn to one lone man who was cleaning the glass on the doors at the entrance of the hotel. With great care he removed every smudge. He even dusted overhead so that no dirt or cobwebs would collect. What made his work so noteworthy was that no one was inspecting it, and throughout the day many people would go through those doors, smearing the windows with their handprints. Nevertheless, he worked diligently and faithfully with special care to make sure those glass panels were spotless.

What a lesson, I thought, for Christians! All of our work should be characterized by such diligence and thoroughness. Even when no human eye looks on and no tongue commends our efforts, we must strive to do our best as to the Lord. Our willingness to work hard should not result from a desire to win the approval of others but from a deep awareness that we are "servants of Christ." —P. R. V.

THE WORLD CROWNS SUCCESS; GOD CROWNS FAITHFULNESS.

The LORD will give strength to His people;
the LORD will bless His people with peace.

PSALM 29:11

*D*uring the depression a man lost his job, his fortune, his wife, and his home, but tenaciously held to his faith—the only thing he had left. One day he stopped to watch some men building a stone church. One of them was chiseling a triangular piece of rock. "What are you going to do with that?" asked the man. The workman said, "Do you see that little opening way up there near the spire? Well, I'm shaping this down here so that it will fit in up there." Tears filled the eyes of the heartbroken man as he walked away. It seemed that God had spoken through the workman to explain the ordeal through which he was passing.

Perhaps you have recently suffered a great loss. Or maybe you are experiencing physical or emotional pain. The outward man seems to be "perishing." Yet, if you know the Lord as your Savior, you need not despair. All these things are under the loving hand of your heavenly Father. The pressure of His hand may hurt, but remember, He is getting you in shape down here so you will fit in up there! —H. G. B.

WHAT WE CALL ADVERSITY, GOD CALLS OPPORTUNITY.

*Whoever drinks of the water
that I shall give him will never thirst.*

JOHN 4:14

*I*n the middle ages, people built castles where they could flee for safety and defend themselves from the enemy. But one of the problems was the water supply. If the enemy surrounded them, they would not have access to life-giving springs and fresh-flowing streams to quench their thirst. Their defeat would be just a matter of time. The problem was solved in the castle of Edinburgh, however. It was constructed above an underground spring that gushed forth with all the fresh water the besieged defenders would ever need. Nourished from within, they were practically invulnerable.

When Jesus spoke about living water to a woman of Samaria He was referring to an inner source of spiritual refreshment—a living water that would quench forever the God-thirst of a human soul in search of forgiveness and life. Only in Him can our arid and parched lives be refreshed. —D. C. E.

ONLY JESUS, THE LIVING WATER
CAN QUENCH THE DRIVING THIRST OF THE SOUL.

The fruit of righteousness is sown
in peace by those who make peace.

JAMES 3:18

Some of mankind's greatest contributions have come from people who decided that no sacrifice was too large and no effort too great to accomplish what they set out to do. Edward Gibbon spent twenty-six years writing *The History of the Decline and Fall of the Roman Empire.* Noah Webster worked diligently for thirty-six years to bring into print the first edition of his dictionary. It is said that the Roman orator Cicero practiced before friends every day for thirty years in order to perfect his public speaking. What stamina! What persistence!

Now let's think about how much energy we put into the Lord's work. The comparison can be rather embarrassing. The apostle Paul gave us a clear definition of our duty when he said, "And whatever you do, do it heartily, as to the Lord" (Col. 3:23). Our service for Christ must be marked by persistent, prayerful, energetic effort. That's how to serve heartily. —P. R. V.

SOME CHRISTIANS MAY DO NOTHING,
BUT NO CHRISTIAN HAS NOTHING TO DO.

He who believes in Him is not condemned;
but he who does not believe is condemned already.

JOHN 3:18

The story is told of a professor of psychology who had no children of his own, but whenever he saw a neighbor scolding a child for some wrongdoing he would say, "You should love your boy, not punish him." One hot summer day the professor was repairing his concrete driveway. Tired after several hours of work, he laid down the trowel, wiped the perspiration from his forehead, and started toward the house. Just then, out of the corner of his eye, he saw a mischievous little boy putting his foot in the fresh cement. He rushed over, grabbed him, and was about to spank him when a neighbor leaned out his window and said, "Watch it, Professor! Don't you remember? You must love the child!" At this, he yelled back furiously, "I do love him in the abstract but not in the concrete!"

How easy it is to talk sentimentally about love as an intangible thing! But it's much more difficult to put it into practice in the trying situations of real life. In the Sermon on the Mount Jesus commands us to display kindness and grace, and even to pray for those who mistreat or show ill will toward us. That's the test of real love. —H. G. B.

RETURNING GOOD FOR GOOD IS COMMENDABLE;
RETURNING GOOD FOR EVIL IS CHRISTLIKE.

Blessed is that man who makes the LORD his trust.

PSALM 40:4

*P*erhaps no animal provides a more striking example of obedience than the Australian sheep dog. When it comes time to move the sheep from one pasture to another, these skillful herders work in perfect harmony with the shepherd to get the reluctant animals moving. The shepherd rides out into the field on horseback, the dogs trotting happily alongside. Then he gives a command, and the dogs begin to move the sheep. A steady stream of whistles and calls gives the dogs their orders, and they respond in perfect obedience. The shepherd, surveying the entire flock, sees the sheep that are lagging behind or straying. His clear, short commands convey his desires to the dogs, and they bring them into line through their unquestioning obedience.

Christ is our Master, the One who leads, who gives commands. And we don't have to wonder what He wants us to do, for God has revealed His will to us in the Bible. As we learn its principles and specific commands, made known to us by the Holy Spirit, we are to obey them exactly and without question. And when we do, His work among His people is accomplished. —D. C. E.

**THE BEST RESPONSE TO UNDESERVED BLESSING
IS UNRESERVED OBEDIENCE.**

You enlarged my path under me;
so my feet did not slip.

2 SAMUEL 22:37

A wide area of Kentucky receives electricity that is generated by turbines on the Kentucky River. One night the power failed and lights were darkened all over that section of the state. Engineers first inspected the turbines, but found nothing wrong. After several hours of fruitless searching, the engineers sent a man to examine the wires that carried the current from the generating station. There he found the trouble. A snake had crawled up to those wires and had started across them. As it touched both at once, it was instantly electrocuted. Its body had short-circuited the current and caused the power to fail.

Something similar can take place in the Christian life. When the spiritual power that should be produced in our lives by the Holy Spirit stops flowing we need to investigate what has cut off the power. The apostle Paul said that lying, sinful anger, stealing, corrupt talk, bitterness, wrath, fighting, slander, hatred, unkindness, and an unforgiving attitude can block the power of the Holy Spirit in our lives. We need to be constantly alert so that none of these sins wriggles into our lives and causes a short-circuit. —P. R. V.

A LITTLE SIN WILL ADD TO YOUR TROUBLE
AND MULTIPLY YOUR DIFFICULTIES.

He who heeds the word wisely will find good,
and whoever trusts in the LORD, happy is he.

PROVERBS 16:20

In the early days when people were crossing America on horseback, a party of explorers came to the Susquehanna River. It was the spring of the year and the waters were turbulent and deep. Surveying the situation they decided they would have to ford the river in spite of the flood. As their horses waded out toward midstream, one of the riders was almost overcome with dizziness. Seeing the swirling waters on all sides, he began to sway in the saddle. His companion, noting his plight—and fearful lest he should fall from his mount—shouted, "Look up, man! Look up!" The dizzy traveler heeded the command and regained his balance.

How much we are like that rider! Instead of resting on the promises of God, we start viewing the boisterous billows of life, the treacherous winds of adversity, and our own inadequacy to cope with our problems. The result? We become panic-stricken. As soon as we look at anything else but the Lord and His Word, we are bound to sink beneath the waves of circumstances. The essential thing is to keep looking up—to keep our eyes on Jesus. —H. G. B.

IF YOU CAN'T FIND A WAY OUT, TRY LOOKING UP!

His delight is in the law of the LORD,
and in His law he meditates day and night.

PSALM 1:2

When I began to paint duck decoys, I learned that there are two kinds of ducks: puddle ducks and divers. Puddle ducks, such as mallards and redheads, simply paddle around the edge of marshes and ponds and feed in the shallow water. They eat only what they can reach from the surface. Diver ducks, however, are able to dive to surprising depths in a lake to feed from the plants at its bottom. Mergansers and canvasbacks are typical of this group, some of which can dive to depths of 150 feet for their food!

When it comes to studying Scriptures, Christians can be a bit like those ducks. Some, like puddle ducks, stay near the surface, satisfied with the nourishment they find in the shallows. Others, however, are like divers. Following the example of the psalmist, they plunge deeply into the Word through study, reflection, and meditation "day and night."

What about it? Have you established a satisfying, deepening study of God's Word? Or are you content to stay near the surface? —D. C. E.

TREASURES OF TRUTH FROM GOD'S WORD
LIE DEEP BENEATH THE SURFACE.

I have laid the foundation, and another builds on it.
But let each one take heed how he builds on it.

1 CORINTHIANS 3:10

Outside a Minneapolis church several years ago, as the chairman of the board was about to enter the building, he saw an elderly man standing at the corner of the building. He seemed to be caressing the bricks. The chairman was fascinated by the action of the man, so he approached him and said, "Pardon me, sir, but you seem to have some special interest in this corner of our building. I'm curious to know what's so interesting about those bricks?" The old man answered, "Yes, I have a special interest. You see, when this building was erected many years ago, I was a workman on the project." Patting the bricks, he said, "These bricks—I set them here." With a smile of satisfaction, he added, "And I think I did a pretty good job." He had used good materials and had built well. The building was solid, and "his corner" was plumb to the line. His work stood approved.

How about the corner where God has placed you? Whether it's your work in the church or your daily occupation, a task done well can be a clear testimony of God's work in your life. —P. R. V.

WORK DONE WELL FOR CHRIST
WILL RECEIVE A "WELL DONE" FROM CHRIST.

In this you greatly rejoice, though now for a little while,
if need be, you have been grieved by various trials.

1 PETER 1:6

A. B. Cooper said that one autumn day when he went to a chrysanthemum show, he asked of a gardener, "How do you manage to produce such marvelous flowers?" "Well, sir, we concentrate all the strength of the plant in one bloom. If we would allow it to bear all the flowers it could, none would be worth showing. If you want a prize specimen, you must be content with a single chrysanthemum instead of many." So too, God prunes from our lives certain habits and practices, which in themselves may not be wrong, so that He may perfect in us the one exquisite white blossom of holiness.

Those who accept trouble graciously grow rich by their losses, rise by their falls, and find new life in Christ by dying to self. This is one blessed answer to the "why" of suffering! —H. G. B.

ANYTHING SUFFERED IN THE BODY CAN PROFIT THE SOUL.

He first found his own brother Simon, and said to him,
"We have found the Messiah."

JOHN 1:41

In his book *The Twelve*, Leslie B. Flynn wrote about a businessman who walked by a restaurant and noticed a poor boy peering in, his nose pressed flat against the glass pane. "Are you hungry?" asked the man. The boy timidly replied, "Sure am, Mister." The man took the boy inside and ordered a hearty meal for him. But the boy kept looking outside, showing little interest in the delicious food. The man tapped him on the shoulder, "Why don't you eat? You said you were hungry." He answered, "See that boy looking in through the window? That's my little brother. How can I eat with him standing there looking at me like that?"

When we find what satisfies us, we will want others to have it too. We who have experienced salvation through faith in Christ have an "inside" connection with Jesus. But there are many still on the "outside" who have never trusted him as their personal Savior. May we respond to their need by introducing them to Jesus. —D. C. E.

WE MUST GO TO SINNERS
IF WE EXPECT SINNERS TO COME TO THE SAVIOR.

*He said to them, "Come aside by yourselves
to a deserted place and rest a while."*

MARK 6:31

Greek legend tells us that in ancient Athens a man noticed the great storyteller Aesop playing childish games with some little boys. The observer laughed and jeered at Aesop for this undignified behavior. Instead of replying, Aesop picked up a bow that he sometimes used for playing a stringed instrument. He unstrung it and laid it on the ground. Then he said to the critical Athenian, "Now, answer the riddle, if you can, and tell us what the unstrained bow implies." The man could not tell him. He had no idea what it meant. Aesop explained, "If you keep a bow always bent, it will break eventually; but if you let it go slack, it will be more fit for use when you want it."

It's like that with people too. That's why we need to take time to rest—when the bow of life can be relaxed. God "rested from all His work" (Gen. 2:3). Shouldn't we follow His example? You can't do your best for the Lord if you don't rest a while. —P. R. V.

TIME IN CHRIST'S SERVICE REQUIRES TIME OUT FOR RENEWAL.

Show me Your ways, O LORD;
teach me Your paths.

PSALM 25:4

Evangelist Sam Jones frequently referred to his father's horse named "Old Charlie." When the animal was hitched to a plow, he would balk and become a problem. But when he was hitched to a red-wheeled buggy with a fancy harness, he held his head high, and was full of excitement and vigor. It was never necessary to coax him or use the whip. It was as if the horse was eager to be seen in fancy trappings—especially when he had a light load to pull. Sam Jones said, "Human nature is like that too. Some people simply won't work for the Lord in a humble capacity. They must have a prominent office with a high-sounding title before they'll do their best."

How contrary this is to the spirit of Christianity! Any opportunity to glorify God should never be considered too small or too insignificant to command our best efforts. No matter how menial the task, if it's in the line of duty we can view it as service to God and do it gladly without complaining or self-seeking. —H. G. B.

THOUGH THE DEED BE SMALL, GIVE IT YOUR ALL.

Until now you have asked nothing in My name.
Ask, and you will receive, that your joy may be full.

JOHN 16:24

Among those who served in the court of Alexander the Great was a famous philosopher who had outstanding ability but little money. He asked Alexander for financial help and was told he could draw whatever cash he needed from the imperial treasury. When he submitted to the treasurer a request for an amount equal to $50,000, he was promptly refused. The treasurer had to verify that such a large sum was indeed authorized. But when he asked Alexander, the ruler replied, "Pay the money at once. The philosopher has done me a singular honor. By the largeness of his request he shows that he has understood both my wealth and generosity."

People who exercise great faith by asking God to provide for their needs demonstrate a similar understanding of His vast wealth and goodness. When we request help from God, asking according to His will, we are saying to Him that we trust Him and that we believe He will supply what's best from His boundless goodness. That kind of asking honors Him. —P. R. V.

LARGE ASKING RESULTS IN LARGE RECEIVING.

*Flee also youthful lusts; but pursue righteousness, faith, love,
peace with those who call on the Lord out of a pure heart.*

2 TIMOTHY 2:22

A boy named Bobby asked his mother if he could go play ball with his friends. She consented, but she knew that the boys had to pass their favorite "swimming hole," so she told him not to go swimming. When Bobby left the house, however, he took his bathing suit with him—just in case! Well, you know what he did when he saw his friends enjoying themselves in the pond. Bobby had invited temptation by taking his swimsuit with him.

How different the attitude displayed by the youngster who said, "When I go past a watermelon patch, I can't keep my mouth from watering, but I can run!" His action exemplifies what Paul was saying to young Timothy in today's Scripture reading. According to 1 Corinthians 10:13, God is faithful and will not allow us to be tempted beyond what we are able, but will with the temptation also make the way of escape, that we may be able to bear it. When temptation comes, God will do His part—He will provide "the way of escape." But it's up to us to run!
—R. W. D.

EVERY TEMPTATION IS AN OPPORTUNITY TO FLEE TO GOD.

Be strong and of good courage . . .
for the LORD your God is with you wherever you go.

JOSHUA 1:9

The seventeenth-century German pastor and songwriter Paul Gerhardt faced many trials during his life. During the Thirty Years' War, he and his family were forced to flee their home. One night as they stayed in a small village inn, homeless and afraid, his wife wept openly in despair. To comfort her, Gerhardt reminded her of Scripture promises about God's provision and keeping. Then he went out to a garden where he too burst into tears. Not long afterward, he sensed anew the presence of the Lord. He took a pen and began to write a hymn, the last lines of which are, "Give to the winds thy fears, and be thou undismayed; God hears thy sighs and counts thy tears—God shall lift up thy head." Gerhardt had been given a song in the night! A short time later, God delivered the family from danger and gave the young pastor a new church.

Often it is in the darkest times of life that God makes His presence known most clearly to us. Are you facing struggles right now? Take heart. In the midst of suffering, put your life in God's hands. He still gives songs in the night. —P. R. V.

WHEN TROUBLES CALL, CALL ON GOD.

Praying always with all prayer and supplication in the Spirit,
being watchful to this end with all perseverance.

EPHESIANS 6:18

It is said that the early Christians never met without invoking God's blessing and never parted without a word of thanksgiving. We are told also that during the Middle Ages many occurrences would summon the faithful to immediate prayer. When night erased the shadows on a sundial, when a tolling bell announced a death, or when a flight of birds signaled a change of seasons, they bowed to offer an appropriate petition.

It was the custom of John Fletcher of Madeley, England, never to meet a Christian without saying, "Friend, do I meet you praying?" This unusual salutation reminded the person that his life should be an unbroken expression of prayer and fellowship with God.

If someone today were to give you John Fletcher's unusual greeting, how would you respond? Is your life characterized by joyous contact with Jesus and an unwavering perseverance in prayer? —H. G. B.

A PRAYERLESS CHRISTIAN IS A POWERLESS CHRISTIAN.

July

For this is God, our God forever and ever;
He will be our guide even to death.

PSALM 48:14

t the dedication of a great cathedral in Milan, Italy, a little girl in the crowd cried out, "I helped build it. I helped build it!" "What!" exclaimed one of the guards who was standing nearby. "Tell me what you did." The child replied, "I brought my daddy's lunch to him when he worked here." She was right. Although she didn't actually take part in the construction, her efforts did contribute to the completion of that beautiful edifice.

Heaven is going to be filled with many surprises. Among them, I think, will be the recognition given to those believers who serve the Lord unknown and unappreciated. We sometimes get the idea that the ones engaged at the "front" in spiritual conflict with the evil one are going to be more fully rewarded by the Lord than others. But all believers who faithfully fill God's place for them will hear the Savior say, "Well done." —R. W. D.

A SMALL DEED DONE IN JESUS' NAME IS NO SMALL DEED.

*If we confess our sins, He is faithful and just to forgive us our sins
and to cleanse us from all unrighteousness.*

1 JOHN 1:9

*D*id you read about the man whose guilty conscience
prompted him to send a letter to the Internal Revenue
Service? The note read, "I haven't been able to sleep because last year
when I filled out my income tax report I deliberately misrepresented my
income. I am enclosing a check for $150, and if I still can't sleep, I'll send
you the rest."

Now, it's commendable that the man confessed his wrongdoing,
but his halfhearted restitution showed the shallowness of his regret. His
confession was prompted by his desire for personal peace, not by
remorse for a moral transgression.

When we believe on Jesus Christ, we are declared righteous. The
sins of our past, present, and future are forgiven. But because we are
defiled by sin in our day-by-day walk, we need the daily cleansing of
confession. This restores fellowship between us and our heavenly Father.
But we must be genuine. We must come to Him with a sincere sorrow
for our sins and an honest desire to forsake them. —R. W. D.

GOD HAS PROMISED PARDON TO THOSE WHO REPENT.

Pure and undefiled religion before God and the Father is this:
to visit orphans and widows in their trouble.

JAMES 1:27

Christian businessman heard his pastor tell about a widow who had been evicted from her home because she had no money to pay her rent. Her furniture was piled up on the lawn. She didn't know where she would go or what she would do. The pastor said that if someone would help her, he would have a "foretaste of heaven." The businessman went to the home to see what he could do. He returned to church that evening and said, "I have just been in heaven. I went to see that widow, paid her back rent, helped her move her belongings into the house again, and stocked her cupboards with food. It is the most joy I have experienced in many years."

Do you want to be in heaven without leaving this earth? Do something kind and unselfish for someone in need. The joy and gratitude you see on the faces of people you help will make you feel so good that you will wonder how heaven could be any better. —H. V. L.

WHEN YOU LOOK UPON YOUR BROTHER'S NEED,
LOVE DEMANDS THE LOVING DEED.

Cause me to know the way in which I should walk,
for I lift up my soul to You.

PSALM 143:8

When Raphael's picture "The Sistine Madonna" was brought to Dresden, Germany, it was displayed in the castle before the king. However, the spot where the light was best was already occupied by the throne. Observing the situation, the king immediately stepped down from his royal chair, saying, "Make room for the immortal Raphael!"

So too, there is but one throne in the human heart, and the most important question for any of us to answer is this: Who is to occupy that place of authority? Will it be Christ or self? If we are to emulate His example and learn of Him, our selfish desire must be set aside.

This day let us ask the question, "Who is on the throne of my life—self or the Savior?" If it is self, let's learn of Him who is gentle and lowly in heart. Let's make room for Jesus. —H. G. B.

GIVE GOD THE SAME PLACE IN YOUR HEART
THAT HE HOLDS IN THE UNIVERSE.

Therefore I say to you,
do not worry about your life.

MATTHEW 6:25

I heard about a woman who kept a box in her kitchen that she called her "Worry Box." Every time something arose that troubled her, she would write it down on a piece of paper and place it in that box. She resolved that she would give these problems no thought as long as they were in the box. Every so often she would open it, take out the slips of paper, and review the concerns written on them. Following this procedure enabled the woman to put troubles out of her mind completely. She knew that they could be dealt with later. Then, because she had not been drained by anxiety over her difficulties she was in a relaxed frame of mind and better able to find solutions to her problems. Many times, however, she discovered to her delight that most of the troubles she had been worried about no longer existed.

Writing your worries on paper and putting them in a box may be helpful, but how much better to place them in the hands of God and forget about them! Worry robs us of joy, drains us of our energy, stunts our spiritual growth, stifles our testimony, and worst of all, dishonors God. —R. W. D.

PUT YOUR CARES IN GOD'S HANDS;
HE'LL PUT PEACE IN YOUR HEART.

He gives wisdom to the wise and
knowledge to those who have understanding.

DANIEL 2:21

God does not change. Haddon Robinson illustrated this truth by calling attention to a famous clock. He wrote, "In the town hall in Copenhagen stands the world's most complicated clock. It took forty years to build, at a cost of more than a million dollars. That clock has ten faces, 15,000 parts, and is accurate to two-fifths of a second every 300 years. The clock computes the time of day, the days of the week, the months and years, and the movements of the planets for 2,500 years. Some parts of the clock will not move until twenty-five centuries have passed."

"What is intriguing," Robinson added, "is that the clock is not accurate. It loses two-fifths of a second every 300 years. Like all clocks, that timepiece in Copenhagen must be regulated by a more precise clock, the universe itself. This mighty astronomical clock with its billions of moving parts, from atoms to stars, rolls on century after century with movements so reliable that all time on earth can be measured against it."

Clocks stop. Cars break down. Financial institutions go bankrupt. People disappoint us. But God and His universe remain the same. He is the reliable God! —D. C. E.

GOD CANNOT FAIL FOR HE IS GOD.

I know whom I have believed and am persuaded that He
is able to keep what I have committed to Him until that Day.

2 TIMOTHY 1:12

Stonewall Jackson and his sister were crossing a treacherous torrent just below the mighty Niagara Falls. The current so rocked and tossed the boat that the woman became terrified. Jackson took her firmly by the arm and turning to one of the two boatmen said, "How often have you crossed here before?" "Continually, sir, for the past twelve years." "Did you ever meet with an accident?" "Never, sir." "Never capsized and never lost a life?" "Nothing of the kind, sir." Turning to his sister, Jackson reassuringly replied, "You heard what the boatman said. Unless you think you can row better than he does, just sit still and trust him as I do."

Similar words of reassurance are what spiritually troubled Christians need to hear when tossed by the billows of doubt and uncertainty. Jesus has never lost a soul entrusted to His care. We are safe in the refuge of God's love, secure for time and eternity because of His grace! —H. G. B.

GOD PERFORMS WHAT HE PROMISES
AND COMPLETES WHAT HE COMMENCES.

Make me understand the way of Your precepts;
so shall I meditate on Your wonderful works.

PSALM 119:27

While visiting a space exhibit at the Smithsonian Institution in Washington, D. C., Princess Anne was introduced to Neil Armstrong. Later during her tour, she noticed a display of astronauts' spacesuits. Turning to Armstrong, she asked, "Is there any danger of a rip?" The one who had taken great risks in being the first to walk on the moon replied, "Yes, the difference between life and death up there is only about one-hundredth of an inch of rubber!"

Our lives are a fragile gift from God. Realizing the brevity of life, David wrote in the Psalms, "Lord, make me to know my end, and what is the measure of my days, that I may know how frail I am" (Ps. 39:4).

Having that awareness will motivate us to live each day totally for the Lord. And it will enable us to take that final step without fear!

—H. G. B.

YOU'RE NOT READY TO LIVE UNTIL YOU'RE READY TO DIE.

I love those who love me,
and those who seek me diligently will find me.

PROVERBS 8:17

When an ocean liner sank along the Irish coast many years ago, the maritime world was bewildered. Because the ship's captain was an excellent seaman, no one could figure out what caused the accident. Divers were sent down, and one of the items they brought up to examine was the ship's compass. As they opened the compass box, they found the point of a knife blade inside. Apparently, while cleaning the compass, an unwary sailor had broken off the tip of his knife, which had become lodged inside the device. It was just a tiny piece of metal, but it was enough to cause the compass to give a bad reading. As a result, the ship took the wrong course and crashed into the rocky coast.

As Christians, we too can be shipwrecked if we begin to think that little things—little sins—are not harmful. That's why our words, our deeds, and our attitudes must always be kept free of any sin that can disrupt our testimony and damage our relationship with God. —P. R. V.

NO SIN IS LITTLE, FOR IT IS AN OFFENSE TO AN INFINITE GOD.

*Narrow is the gate and difficult is the way which leads to life,
and there are few who find it.*

MATTHEW 7:14

I have always been amazed to watch the freighters go through the Soo Locks that join Lake Superior and Lake Huron in Michigan's Upper Peninsula. To me, it's a wonder of piloting as I see the captain inch his 1,000-foot-long ore boat safely through the Poe or the Davis Lock. There it can be lowered to the level of Lake Huron or raised so that it can enter Lake Superior.

The captain eases the boat through the gates of the lock at a barely discernible pace because it is only a couple feet wider than the ship itself. The process may take a while, but it gets the ship safely through. It would be much easier for the captain to approach the wide mouth of the St. Mary's River that flows alongside the locks and joins the two lakes. But it is shallow, fast-moving, and filled with huge rocks and white-water rapids. A freighter trying that route would be doomed to destruction. If you were the ship's captain, which way would you choose? The narrow way, of course. It's the only safe way.

There is a narrow way in the spiritual life; the way of faith in Christ. It leads to heaven. Trust Jesus today. Take the narrow way!

—D. C. E.

A WELL-BEATEN PATH IS NOT NECESSARILY THE RIGHT PATH.

*Lift up your eyes on high,
and see who has created these things.*

ISAIAH 40:26

*M*y friend Mark was on a golf course he had played many times before. Suddenly he exclaimed to his golfing partners, "Look at that beautiful sight!" There, stretching away over the golden sand dunes, was a marvelous view of Lake Michigan, its sparkling blue waters shimmering in summer splendor. Always before on that particular hole, Mark had been concerned with a golfing problem—the chip he had to make or the putt he had to sink. His eyes had always been focused downward. "I never looked up from here before!" he exclaimed.

Sometimes we become so involved in a difficulty or so overwhelmed with a situation that we lose our perspective on God. We get in problem places that absorb our interest and limit our vision. It could be at our desk at work or in the presence of a difficult person. It might be in a hospital bed or sickroom. We're discouraged and weakened. If so, we need to look up and see again the grandeur and power of our all-sufficient God. —D. C. E.

**BELIEVE THE WONDERS GOD CAN DO,
AND HE WILL SEE YOU THROUGH.**

Blessed be the God and Father of our Lord Jesus Christ,
who has blessed us with every spiritual blessing.

EPHESIANS 1:3

A little boy had an accident and was taken to a hospital. After he was made comfortable, a nurse brought him a large glass of milk. He looked longingly at it, but did not pick it up. He had come from a poor home where his hunger was seldom satisfied. If he ever received a glass of milk, it was only partly filled, and even that had to be shared with another child. Finally he looked up at the nurse and asked, "How deep may I drink?" The nurse tenderly replied, "Drink it all! There's more."

So too, there is no limit to the grace of God of which we may freely partake. The springs of spiritual refreshing are continuously flowing to provide for the believer's every need. We are blessed with "every spiritual blessing in the heavenly places in Christ." He invites us to draw freely by faith on His infinite resources until we are fully satisfied. —H. G. B.

OUR GREATEST NEEDS CANNOT EXCEED GOD'S GREAT RESOURCES.

I have learned in whatever state I am, to be content.

PHILIPPIANS 4:11

Leaning on his fence one day, a devout Quaker was watching a new neighbor move in next door. After all kinds of modern appliances, electronic gadgets, and plush furnishings had been carried in, the onlooker called over, "If you find you're lacking anything, neighbor, let me know, and I'll show you how to live without it."

If chronic dissatisfaction plagues your life, ask yourself these simple questions: Is Jesus Christ at the center of all my endeavors? Am I confusing my needs with my wants? Can I be happy with less? Economic pressures may be an opportunity for some of us to restructure our lives. Practicing self-discipline in our spending could allow us to give more to the Lord's work. We may actually develop a simpler lifestyle that proves more satisfying than when we had more and worried more. —D. J. D.

CONTENTMENT IS NOT FOUND IN HAVING EVERYTHING,
BUT IN BEING SATISFIED WITH EVERYTHING YOU HAVE.

I will both lie down in peace, and sleep;
for You alone, O LORD, make me dwell in safety.

PSALM 4:8

Two young brothers had wandered away from their home, which stood next to a dense forest. As the evening shadows darkened their pathway the little fellows became confused and were soon lost. When they did not return, their family began looking for them—searching all night and the next day until they finally found the boys. Relieved, the parents asked the boys what they had done when they realized that they were lost in the woods. The older boy replied, "When it got dark, I kneeled down and asked God to take care of Jimmy and me. Then we went to sleep."

When our faith is like that—when it is so strong that we can simply ask God for help and then leave the results to Him—we can make it through life's times of stress. Are you experiencing the panic of being lost amid life's forest of problems, fears, and perplexities? Don't despair. There's hope. Put your faith in the heavenly Father. —P. R. V.

HE WHO ABANDONS HIMSELF TO GOD
WILL NEVER BE ABANDONED BY GOD.

*All things work together for good to those who love God,
to those who are the called according to His purpose.*

ROMANS 8:28

It has been said that when George Frederick Handel's health and finances were at a low point, he rose to the greatest heights of his creative experience. His creditors were threatening him with imprisonment, and he was suffering from partial paralysis. He then went into seclusion and prayed to God as never before. During that time, God enabled him to write the grandest of all his oratorios, *Messiah*. The notes seemed to fly from his pen.

It may seem that difficulties would prevent us from being productive in the Lord's service, but actually the opposite can be true. Through God's intervention, our losses can be turned into great gain, and the outcome of our trials will become a blessing to others. In all things, even our afflictions, God is working everything together for our benefit. Overruling the bad to produce good is no problem to an all-powerful, good God! —H. G. B.

TRIALS CAN PREPARE ORDINARY CHRISTIANS
FOR EXTRAORDINARY SERVICE.

We walk by faith, not by sight.

2 CORINTHIANS 5:7

A colony of small water-bugs living in a pond noticed that every once in a while one of their fellow bugs would climb up a lily stem and never be seen again. They agreed that if this should ever happen to one of them, they would return to tell the others about their journey. Sure enough, the day came when one of the bugs found himself going up the stalk and crawling onto the lily pad at the top. He fell asleep in the warm sunshine, and when he awakened he stretched himself, only to hear a crackling sound as his old outer coat fell off. He sensed that somehow he was larger, cleaner, and freer than ever before. Spreading his wings, he flew into the air as a beautiful green dragonfly. Suddenly he remembered his promise. But then he realized why none of the others had ever returned. He couldn't go back and tell his friends what to expect because he was no longer a part of their world. Besides, one day they too would experience the wonderful freedom he now enjoyed.

We naturally shrink from the mysterious thought of dying. But we need not fear. Nor do we need a message from a departed loved one. God has told us all we need to know. So let's "walk by faith" and wait in hope. —H. V. L.

FAITH LOOKS BEYOND THE DARKNESS OF EARTH TO THE BRIGHTNESS OF HEAVEN.

*Your Father knows the things
you have need of before you ask Him.*

MATTHEW 6:8

A story is told of a Roman emperor who was parading through the streets of the imperial city in a victory celebration. Tall legionnaires lined the route to keep back the cheering masses. At one place along the way was a platform on which the royal family was sitting. As the emperor approached, his youngest son, who was just a little boy, jumped down, burrowed through the crowd, and tried to run out to meet him. "You can't do that," said one of the guards as he scooped up the lad. "Don't you know who's in that chariot? That's the emperor!" Quickly the youngster replied, "He may be your emperor, but he's my father!"

All believers can approach God with that same confidence and intimacy. In fact, Christians are the only people who have the right to address God as their Father. The next time you pray, quiet your heart with the wonderful thought that you are coming into the presence of Almighty God and can say, "You are my Father." —D. J. D.

**YOU CAN'T CLAIM GOD AS YOUR FATHER
UNTIL YOU CLAIM CHRIST AS YOUR SAVIOR.**

The love of money is a root of all kinds of evil.

1 TIMOTHY 6:10

Coming downstairs one morning, a wealthy man heard his cook exclaim, "Oh, if I only had five dollars, wouldn't I be content!" Thinking the matter over and wanting to see the woman satisfied, he handed her a five dollar bill. She thanked him profusely. He paused outside the kitchen door to hear if she would express the same satisfaction and thanks to God. As soon as she thought he was out of earshot, he heard her mutter in disgust, "Oh, why didn't I say ten dollars!" That's the typical cry of the covetous heart.

A Christian magazine reported that a songbook had a misprint in one line of the hymn, "Guide Me, O Thou Great Jehovah." It should have read, "Land me safe on Canaan's shore," but it was printed, "Land my safe on Canaan's shore." The editor observed, "The revised version might be acceptable to many who have fallen into the trap of the love of money."

To find the joy and satisfaction that comes from God—that's contentment. —H. G. B.

**THE REAL MEASURE OF OUR WEALTH
IS WHAT WILL BE OURS IN ETERNITY.**

He who has My commandments and keeps them,
it is he who loves Me.

JOHN 14:21

As Pastor A. J. Gordon walked to his Boston church one day, he saw a young boy carrying some birds in a cage. "Where did you get those birds?" asked Gordon. "Trapped them in the field," the boy replied. "What are you going to do with them?" Gordon asked. "Oh, I'm going to play with them for a while and then I'll feed them to the old cat at home," the boy answered. "They're just field birds and can't sing very well." The preacher responded, "I'll give you two dollars for the cage and the birds." "It's a deal," the boy answered, "but you're making a bad bargain." Gordon carried the cage behind his church and released the birds, which flew away—free and singing. The next Sunday, Gordon had the cage on the pulpit as he told the story. "When I released them," he told his congregation, "they went singing away into the blue and it seems they were singing, 'Redeemed, redeemed.'"

People who don't know Jesus as their Savior are like those birds before they were released. They "can't sing very well" because they are trapped in the cage of sin. But Jesus can give freedom that puts a song in the heart. —P. R. V.

TO HAVE A SAVED SOUL IS TO HAVE A SONG IN YOUR HEART.

You shall love the LORD your God with all your heart,
with all your soul, and with all your mind.

MATTHEW 22:37

King Alfonso XIX of Spain learned that the boys who served in his court were forgetting to pray before their meals. So he decided to teach them a lesson. He gave a banquet and invited them to attend. Midway through the dinner a ragged beggar came in, sat down, and began eating ravenously. When he was finished, he went out without saying a word. "That ungrateful wretch ought to be whipped," shouted the boys. "He ate the king's food and never showed gratitude." Quietly the king rose to his feet, and silence fell over the group. "Daily you have taken the rich blessings of life from the hand of your heavenly Father," said the king. "You've enjoyed His sunshine, breathed His air, eaten food He has provided and you have not bothered to say 'thank you' for any of them. You are more ungrateful than that beggar."

Let us never settle for a full stomach and a soul famished by ingratitude. —D. J. D.

HE WHO FORGETS THE LANGUAGE OF GRATITUDE
IS NOT LIKELY TO BE ON SPEAKING TERMS WITH GOD.

God is our refuge and strength,
a very present help in trouble.

PSALM 46:1

An ocean liner encountered a severe storm while crossing the Atlantic. One of the sailors was tending his duties on deck when he was washed into the sea. Instantly the cry went up, "Man overboard!" A crewman quickly grabbed a life preserver and threw it over the stern. In a few moments he felt a tug on the lifeline. Peering into the darkness, he shouted to the man in the water, "Have you got the line?" A faint reply came back, "No, but the line has me!" The exhausted sailor had slipped the lifesaver over his shoulders and under his arms, realizing he didn't have enough strength to hold on to it.

As Christians, we experience storms and trials in life that sometimes overwhelm us. We come to the end of our own strength. Even though our faith may be weak, or we feel we have no faith left, God supports us and lifts us out of despair. It's His strength, not ours, that is sufficient. —H. G. B.

WHEN YOU HAVE NOTHING LEFT BUT GOD,
YOU FIND THAT GOD IS ENOUGH.

*These things I have written to you who believe in the name
of the Son of God, that you may know that you have eternal life.*

1 JOHN 5:13

When George B. McClellan was commissioned Major General of the Army, he wrote his wife, "I don't feel any different than I did yesterday. Indeed, I have not yet put on my new uniform. I am sure, however, that I am in command of the Union Army because President Lincoln's order to that effect now lies before me."

Accepting the authoritative word of his Commander in Chief, McClellan was confident of his position. Similarly, all who receive Jesus Christ as Savior can completely trust God's Word, the Bible, which says that we are "justified by faith" (Rom. 5:1) and have "passed from death to life" (1 John 3:14). Our assurance of salvation is based on facts, not feelings.—H. G. B.

**WHEN A MAN IS IN CHRIST, HE IS SAFE;
ALL THE DEVIL CAN DO IS WORRY HIM.**

Comfort each other and edify one another,
just as you also are doing.

1 THESSALONIANS 5:11

Bruce Larson illustrated the power of encouragement in his book *Wind and Fire*. Writing about sand-hill cranes, he said, "These large birds, who fly great distances across continents, have three remarkable qualities. First, they rotate leadership. No one bird stays out in front all the time. Second, they choose leaders who can handle turbulence. And then, all during the time one bird is leading, the rest are honking their affirmation." Larson commented, "That's not a bad model for the church. Certainly we need leaders who can handle turbulence and who are aware that leadership ought to be shared. But most of all, we need a church where we are all honking encouragement."

There's a lesson for each of us in the unique habits of the sand-hill crane. Let's begin to offer encouragement, to support our leaders, to build one another up. Who can tell what might happen in our church if we started "honking encouragement." —D. C. E.

LIVE TO BUILD PEOPLE UP, NOT TO TEAR THEM DOWN.

Call upon Me in the day of trouble;
I will deliver you, and you shall glorify Me.

PSALM 50:15

An ancient legend tells of a monarch who hired some people to make tapestries for him. Among them was a young child who was especially skilled at weaving. The king gave the silk and the patterns to the workers with instructions to ask for his help if any difficulties arose.

The boy made quiet and steady progress while the others were distressed by their many failures. One day they gathered around the youngster and asked, "Why are you so happy and successful while we are always having trouble? Either our silk becomes tangled or our weaving varies from the pattern." The lad answered, "Don't you remember the words of the king when he told us to send for him whenever it was necessary? Didn't you notice how often I called for him?" he inquired. "Yes, but he's very busy, and we thought you were wrong in disturbing him so frequently." "Well," replied the boy, "I just took him at his word, and he was always happy to help me!"

Jesus encourages us to call on Him. If we cast our care on Him, He will assist us before the threads of our lives become tangled. —H. G. B.

PRAYER IS THE PLACE WHERE BURDENS CHANGE SHOULDERS.

Let him who thinks he stands take heed lest he fall.

1 CORINTHIANS 10:12

Several years ago a severe ice storm hit southern lower Michigan, causing great damage to trees. As I surveyed the destruction, I checked the two large white birches in my backyard. One had lost some of its limbs, but its partner had suffered a worse fate. The entire tree had toppled over and was completely uprooted. Why the one and not the other? The answer was simple. Instead of standing straight up, this thirty-five-foot tree had grown at a pronounced angle. So when the heavy ice accumulated on its branches, it fell in the direction it was leaning.

If we don't live in fellowship with the Lord each day, our lives will lean toward some weakness or besetting sin. Then if a crisis comes or if we are caught off guard, we will be unable to resist the pressure of our circumstances. Let's stand tall in the strength of the Lord so it won't happen to us. —D. J. D.

WE NEED GOD'S STRENGTH TO KEEP US TRUE AND STRAIGHT IN EVERYTHING WE DO.

Blessed are those servants whom the master,
when he comes, will find watching.

LUKE 12:37

*D*ean Frederic Farrar was a personal friend of Queen Victoria of England. On one occasion he told of a conversation he had with Her Majesty after she had heard one of her chaplains preach a message on Christ's return. She said, "Oh, Dean Farrar, how I wish the Lord would come during my lifetime!" When he asked why she desired this, her countenance brightened, and with deep emotion she replied, "Because I would love to lay my crown at His blessed feet in reverent adoration!"

This way of thinking touches the heart and motivates a person to godly living and a hopeful expectation of seeing Jesus face to face. The apostle John said that everyone who has the hope of Christ's return burning brightly in his heart "purifies himself, just as He is pure" (1 John 3:3). These folks are living for His glory and want to give Him praise and adoration for all He has done for them. —H. G. B.

WILL CHRIST'S RETURN FIND US ANXIOUS OR ANTICIPATING?

Great is our LORD, and mighty in power;
His understanding is infinite.

PSALM 147:5

Bible teacher Warren Wiersbe tells the story of a little boy who was leading his younger sister up a steep mountain path. The climbing was difficult, for there were many rocks in the way. Finally, the little girl, exasperated by the hard climb, said to her brother, "This isn't a path at all. It's all rocky and bumpy." "Sure," her brother replied, "but the bumps are what you climb on."

Are there obstacles in your way? Rocks in the path? Do you feel like quitting? Turn to the Lord for the strength, the grace, and the direction that come only from Him. Take your eyes off the difficulties and keep them steadfast on the goal of being prepared for greater usefulness. God did not promise to remove all the stones from your path, but He has promised to help you every step of the way.

Remember, "bumps are what you climb on." —D. C. E.

GOD CAN TURN OBSTACLES INTO OPPORTUNITIES.

If any of you lacks wisdom, let him ask of God, . . .
and it will be given to him.

JAMES 1:5

The weakest among us can participate in athletics, but only the strongest can survive as spectators. According to a heart specialist, when you become a sports spectator rather than a participant, the wrong things go up and the wrong things come down. Body weight, blood pressure, heart rate, cholesterol, and triglycerides go up. Vital capacity, oxygen consumption, flexibility, stamina, and strength go down.

Being an onlooker in the arena of Christian living is also risky. The wrong things go up, and the wrong things come down. Criticism, discouragement, disillusionment, and boredom go up. Sensitivity to sin and human need, and receptivity to Divine resources and the Word of God go down. Sure, there's a certain amount of thrill and excitement in hearing someone's testimony about how God has worked. But it's nothing like knowing that joy yourself. There's no substitute for cutting out your own path of peace, piling up your own experiences of faith, and using your own God-given abilities in behalf of others. —M. R. D. II

**GOD CALLED US TO GET INTO THE GAME,
NOT TO KEEP THE SCORE.**

Be steadfast, immovable,
always abounding in the work of the Lord.

1 CORINTHIANS 15:58

Newspaper copy editor Robert Manry piloted the smallest ship ever to sail the Atlantic Ocean. The trip aboard the *Tinkerbelle* was long and difficult. He dared not sleep in the shipping lanes. The rudder broke several times. He was washed overboard often, saved only by the rope he had tied to himself and to his 13-foot vessel. Finally, after 78 days, Manry approached Falmouth, England. He thought only of tying up to some dock, finding a hotel room, and getting some sleep. But an enthusiastic crowd had other ideas. A fleet of about 300 small boats came out to greet him, all blowing their horns in salute. Forty thousand well-wishers lined the docks, cheering him on. What a welcome he received!

Something like that awaits faithful Christians who have weathered life's storms and remained true to the Savior. When these believers finally reach heaven's shore, they will be given an abundant entrance into the everlasting kingdom where they will come into the presence of Christ Himself. —D. C. E.

GAINING HEAVEN MORE THAN COMPENSATES FOR THE LOSSES OF EARTH.

That great Shepherd of the sheep, . . .
[is] working in you what is well pleasing in His sight.

HEBREWS 13:20-21

A brilliant young concert pianist was performing for the first time in public. The audience sat enthralled as beautiful music flowed from his disciplined fingers. The people could hardly take their eyes off this young virtuoso. As the final note faded, the audience burst into applause. Everyone was standing—except one old man up front. The pianist walked off the stage crestfallen. The stage manager praised the performance, but the young man said, "I was no good, it was a failure." The manager replied, "Look out there, everyone is on his feet except one old man!" "Yes," said the youth dejectedly, "but that one old man is my teacher."

Whether we work in the limelight or labor unnoticed behind the scenes, when we do our task with faith, diligence, thankfulness, and caring, God is pleased. But more wonderful still, He helps us by "working in [us] what is well pleasing in His sight through Jesus Christ" (Heb. 13:21). —D. J. D.

WHEN YOU DO WHAT YOU PLEASE,
DOES WHAT YOU DO PLEASE GOD?

Do not forget to do good and to share,
for with such sacrifices God is well pleased.

HEBREWS 13:16

A vital part of worship is giving. Leslie B. Flynn illustrated this kind of personal giving in his book *Worship*. He wrote, "A man was packing a shipment of food contributed by a school for the poor people of Appalachia. He was separating beans from powdered milk, and canned vegetables from canned meats. Reaching into a box filled with various cans, he pulled out a little brown paper sack. Apparently one of the pupils had brought something different from the items on the suggested list. Out of the paper bag fell a peanut butter sandwich, an apple, and a cookie. Crayoned in large letters was a little girl's name, 'Christy—Room 104.' She had given up her lunch for some hungry person."

Whenever we give out of a heart of concern for people in need, we are making a sacrifice that pleases the Lord. "But do not forget to do good and to share, for with such sacrifices God is well pleased" (Heb. 13:16). God considers such gifts as given to Him. —D. C. E.

GOD LOOKS AT THE HEART, NOT THE HAND;
THE GIVER, NOT THE GIFT.

August

Seek first the kingdom of God and His righteousness,
and all these things shall be added to you.

MATTHEW 6:33

During the reign of Queen Elizabeth I, a busy merchant was chosen by Her Majesty to fulfill an important ambassadorial mission. Informed of this honor, he asked to be excused, saying that it would cause him monetary loss and severely interrupt the supervision of his industrial activities. To this the Queen replied, "You look after my business abroad, and I will look after yours at home." The gentleman accepted the appointment and was gone for several years. When he returned, he found that the Queen, true to her word, had more than adequately taken care of his affairs.

To be faithful disciples of Jesus requires that we give the Savior top priority in all things, trusting Him fully to take care of our needs.

God gives His best blessings to those who put Christ first. Does He have top priority in your life? —H. G. B.

HE WHO OFFERS GOD SECOND PLACE OFFERS HIM NO PLACE.

All our righteousnesses are like filthy rags.

ISAIAH 64:6

A dirty, poorly clothed boy walked into a London orphanage. The superintendent saw him and asked, "What are you doing here, young man?" "Why, I'd like to live here," he answered. The man replied, "But I don't know you. What do you have as a recommendation?" The youngster held up his torn coat—nothing more than rags—and said, "If you please, sir, I thought this would be all I would need." Immediately the superintendent swept him into his arms and into the orphanage, where he was fed and clothed and warmly accepted. For his old rags the boy received new garments.

What a picture of a sinner coming to Christ! All we have to offer Him is our sinfulness—our lost condition. But that in itself is good news because a sinner is the only kind of person He saves. Our "rags" become our claim to the robe of His righteousness. —P. R. V.

**NO ONE IS TOO GOOD—NOR TOO BAD—
TO BE A CANDIDATE FOR SALVATION.**

You are my hope, O Lord God;
You are my trust from my youth.

PSALM 71:5

My friend Ralph Abuhl had the thrilling experience of going on a short cruise on the aircraft carrier *U.S.S. Kennedy*. He saw jet fighters take off, land, and demonstrate bombing maneuvers. He was told about a practice that is followed on all U.S. aircraft carriers. Whenever the planes are taking off or landing—a dangerous operation on a carrier-the captain watches from the bridge. Even if the planes are flying around the clock, he stays on the bridge, catnapping between runs if necessary. Therefore, each time a pilot takes off in his high-speed aircraft or lands on the deck of that "floating airfield," he knows that his captain is watching.

As Christians we know God is watching over us. Wherever we are, whatever bold endeavor we are involved in for Him, or whatever battle we may be fighting with our spiritual enemy, we have the confidence that the Lord of hosts is with us. And what's more, He guides, protects, and leads us. He's always on the bridge! —D. C. E.

WE FIND SAFETY NOT IN THE ABSENCE OF DANGER BUT IN THE PRESENCE OF GOD.

*He will teach us His ways,
and we shall walk in His paths.*

MICAH 4:2

read a story about an aged lighthouse keeper who had been on the job more than twenty years. At his lighthouse, a gun was set to go off every hour to warn the ships. Year after year the keeper had heard the blast of the shotgun on the hour throughout the day and night. Then the inevitable happened. Something went wrong with the mechanism in the middle of the night, and the gun didn't go off. Within minutes the keeper was startled awake and said, "What was that?" The absence of the sound had alarmed him.

Likewise, the habits of the Christian life should be so instilled in us that missing one of them will sound a silent "alarm" inside us. When we neglect prayer, disobey the Lord, fail to fellowship with God's people, or fall short in one of the other Christian virtues, something inside alerts us. Like the old lighthouse keeper, we will respond, "What was that?" —D. C. E.

THE WAY OF OBEDIENCE IS THE WAY OF BLESSING.

If anyone sins, we have an Advocate with the Father,
Jesus Christ the righteous.

1 JOHN 2:1

When Abraham Lincoln was President, his son Robert had a close friend who entered the army as a private. Robert sent word to his friend, saying, "Write to me, and I will intercede with Father and get you something better." A few years went by before Robert heard from the soldier again. When they got together, Lincoln's friend said, "I never took advantage of your offer, but you do not know what a comfort it was to me. Often after a weary march I would throw myself on the ground and say, 'If it becomes beyond human endurance, I can write to Bob Lincoln and get relief; and I would rather have his intercession than that of the President's cabinet, because he is the President's son.' "

We too know a Son to whom we can go for help—Jesus Christ, our Advocate. An advocate is one who can assist us, either by pleading on our behalf or by giving evidence that supports our case. Jesus can do this for us because of His position at God's right hand. Praise God! We have a Friend in the court of heaven. —P. R. V.

THE ONE WHO DIED AS OUR SUBSTITUTE
NOW LIVES AS OUR ADVOCATE.

God was in Christ reconciling the world to Himself,
not imputing their trespasses to them.

2 CORINTHIANS 5:19

There's a story about a bell that hung in the belfry of an old church. When some visitors tried to ring it, nothing happened. So they investigated and discovered something most unusual. The bottom of the bell was plugged with wood. Stranger yet, a door had been cut in the side of the bell and a padlock had been used to secure the door. The church was using the old bell as a strongbox in which to store money. This was a clever idea, but it certainly wasn't what the bell was designed for.

Just as a bell is made for ringing, Christians are meant to sound out the good news of salvation. But many remain silent and keep the precious message all to themselves. Think carefully about your own life. Do you keep your knowledge of Scripture and your joy of knowing God locked up inside? Sound out the gospel story! —P. R. V.

IF CHRISTIANITY IS WORTH HAVING, IT'S WORTH SHARING.

We have this treasure in earthen vessels,
that the excellence of the power may be of God and not of us.

2 CORINTHIANS 4:7

Advice columnist Abigail Van Buren illustrated the human ability to overcome obstacles when she wrote:

- Cripple him, and you have a Sir Walter Scott.
- Lock him in a prison cell, and you have a John Bunyan.
- Bury him in the snows of Valley Forge, and you have a George Washington.
- Afflict him with asthma as a child, and you have a Theodore Roosevelt.
- Make him play second fiddle in an obscure South American orchestra, and you have a Toscanini.
- Deny her the ability to see, hear, and speak, and you have a Helen Keller.

I'm sure you get the point. If you are using some limitation or hardship as an excuse for falling short of God's best, it's time to change your attitude. In the power of God, and following the example of others, you can be a winner! —D. C. E.

GOD DOES NOT DEMAND SUCCESS, BUT OBEDIENCE.

*Inasmuch as you did it to one of the least of these My brethren,
you did it to Me.*

MATTHEW 25:40

In the late 1700s, the manager of Baltimore's largest hotel refused lodging to a man dressed like a farmer because he thought the fellow's appearance would discredit his inn. So the man left. Later that evening, the innkeeper discovered that he had turned away none other than Thomas Jefferson! Immediately he sent a note to the famed patriot, asking him to come back and be his guest. Jefferson replied by instructing his messenger as follows: "Tell him I have already engaged a room. I value his good intentions highly, but if he has no place for a dirty American farmer, he has none for the Vice President of the United States."

It makes me wonder. Do we push the Lord aside in our lives because we disregard folks who are needy? Christ may be in the small child who needs attention, the exhausted wife who needs encouragement, or the frustrated laborer who needs recognition. When we show kindness to the "least of these," we do so as unto Christ. —M. R. D. II

LIVING TO HELP OTHERS IS LIVING FOR GOD.

By the grace of God I am what I am,
and His grace toward me was not in vain.

1 CORINTHIANS 15:10

A shepherd who had been given a position of great honor by one of Scotland's kings would often go alone to a certain room in the palace. The king became suspicious and thought he was plotting a conspiracy. So he asked to look inside this secret room. There, to his surprise, he found only a chair, a shepherd's crook, and an old plaid scarf. "What does this mean?" asked the king. The nobleman answered, "I was a humble shepherd when your Majesty promoted me. I come to this room to look at the crook and the plaid. They remind me of what I was—and that I am nothing but what the grace of the king has made me."

All of us who trust Jesus should take the backward look often. It will fill us with praise that God should send His Son to die for us. Like that shepherd, we can say, "I am nothing but what the grace of the King has made me." —D. J. D.

GOD'S GRACE MAKES NEW CREATURES
OUT OF THE BEST AND THE WORST OF SINNERS.

Let your conduct be without covetousness;
be content with such things as you have.

HEBREWS 13:5

An ancient Persian legend tells of a wealthy man by the name of Al Haffed who owned a large farm. One evening a visitor related to him tales of fabulous amounts of diamonds that could be found in other parts of the world, and of the great riches they could bring him. The vision of all this wealth made him feel poor by comparison. So instead of caring for his own prosperous farm he sold it and set out to find these treasures. But the search proved to be fruitless. Finally, penniless and in despair, he committed suicide by jumping into the sea.

Meanwhile, the man who had purchased his farm noticed one day the glint of an unusual stone in a shallow stream on the property. He reached into the water, and to his amazement he pulled out a huge diamond. Later when working in his garden, he uncovered many more valuable gems. Poor Al Haffed had spent his life traveling to distant lands seeking jewels when on the farm he had left behind were all the precious stones his heart could have ever desired.

Beware of covetousness! —H. G. B.

EARTHLY THINGS DON'T SATISFY;
CONTENTMENT COMES FROM THE LORD'S SUPPLY.

I will look to the LORD;
I will wait for the God of my salvation.

MICAH 7:7

The slave-making ants of the Amazon are intriguing insects that can teach us a lesson. Hundreds of these ants periodically swarm out of their nest to capture neighboring colonies of weaker ants. After destroying resisting defenders, they carry off cocoons containing the larvae of worker ants. When these "captured children" hatch, they assume that they are part of the family and launch into the tasks they were born to do. They never realize that they are forced-labor victims of the enemy.

Just as these little creatures are bound from the time of their birth, so we enter the world enslaved to sin and Satan. But there is a solution. By receiving Christ we are released from the condemnation of sin. Then by the Holy Spirit's power we can begin serving Christ where we are.

We are all servants of one master or the other. Our decision is not whether we will serve, but whom we will serve. —M. R. D. II

TRUE FREEDOM IS FOUND IN BONDAGE TO CHRIST.

We speak, not as pleasing men,
but God who tests our hearts.

1 THESSALONIANS 2:4

An old fable tells about an elderly man who was traveling with a boy and a donkey. As they walked through a village the man was leading the donkey and the boy was walking behind. The townspeople said the old man was a fool for not riding, so to please them he climbed up on the animal's back. When they came to the next village, the people said the old man was cruel to let the child walk while he enjoyed the ride. So, to please them, he got off and set the boy on the animal's back and continued on his way. In the third village, people accused the child of being lazy for making the old man walk, and the suggestion was made that they both ride. So the man climbed on and they set off again. In the fourth village, the townspeople were indignant at the cruelty to the donkey because he was made to carry two people. The frustrated man was last seen carrying the donkey down the road.

We smile, but this story makes a good point! We can't please everybody, and if we try we end up carrying a heavy burden. The One we must please above all others is Christ. —D. C. E.

WHAT WE NEED IS THE APPROVAL OF GOD,
NOT THE OPINIONS OF OTHERS.

He said to them, "My soul is exceedingly sorrowful, even to death. Stay here and watch with Me."

MATTHEW 26:38

The Sequoia trees of California tower as much as 300 feet above the ground. Strangely, these giants have unusually shallow root systems that reach out in all directions to capture the greatest amount of surface moisture. Seldom will you see a redwood standing alone, because high winds would quickly uproot it. That's why they grow in clusters. Their intertwining roots provide support for one another against the storms.

Support is what Jesus wanted from Peter, James, and John in Gethsemane as He faced Calvary. In that dark hour, He looked to His disciples for prayer and compassion. If Jesus looked to human support in His crisis hour, how much more do Christians need one another when they suffer! Let's be willing to ask someone to pray for us and with us. And let's be alert for opportunities to lend our support to others who are suffering. —D. J. D.

THOSE WHO SUFFER NEED MORE THAN SYMPATHY,
THEY NEED COMPANIONSHIP.

Thanks be to God who always leads us in triumph in Christ.

2 CORINTHIANS 2:14

British writer Guy King told of standing on a railroad station platform, waiting for a train from London. Another train pulled into the station from the opposite direction, and the members of a soccer team got out. The players were returning from a game in another city. News had not reached home as to the outcome of the game, so those awaiting the team didn't know if they had won or lost. A small boy wiggled his way through the crowd and asked one of the players the score. As soon as he heard it, he ran excitedly up and down the platform shouting, "We won! We won!" That youngster was brimming with joy because he identified himself with the players. In one sense, their victory was his victory.

You and I can live triumphantly because almost 2,000 years ago Jesus paid sin's penalty by dying on the cross and broke its power by rising from the dead. We share in His victory through faith. Friend, we won! We won! —P. R. V.

**WE ARE MORE THAN CONQUERORS THROUGH
THE ALL-CONQUERING CHRIST.**

Blessed are those who keep His testimonies,
who seek Him with the whole heart.

PSALM 119:2

Today we have the complete written revelation of God—the Bible. An unknown writer said, "This Book is the mind of God, the state of man, the way of salvation, the doom of sinners, and the happiness of believers. Its doctrines are holy, its precepts are binding; its histories are true, and its decisions are immutable. Read it to be wise, believe it to be safe, practice it to be holy. It contains light to direct you, food to support you, and comfort to cheer you. It is the traveler's map, the pilgrim's staff, the pilot's compass, the soldier's sword, and the Christian's character. Here paradise is restored, heaven opened, and the gates of hell disclosed. Christ is its grand subject, our good its design, and the glory of God its end. It should fill the memory, rule the heart, and guide the feet. Read it slowly, frequently, prayerfully. It is a mine of wealth, a paradise of glory, and a river of pleasure. Follow its precepts and it will lead you to Calvary, to the empty tomb, to a resurrected life in Christ; yes, to glory itself, for eternity."

Yes, the Bible is all of that—and more. An entire lifetime of study and obedience could not exhaust its riches. —D. C. E

OUR LOVE FOR GOD LEADS US TO LOVE GOD'S WORD.

*Walk in the Spirit,
and you shall not fulfill the lust of the flesh.*

GALATIANS 5:16

Douglas Corrigan was called "wrong-way Corrigan." He acquired this title in 1938 when he took off in his plane from Brooklyn, New York, on an announced flight to Long Beach, California. A little over twenty-three hours later, however, he touched down in Dublin, Ireland, and asked officials, "Is this Los Angeles?" For years people laughed at his "miscalculations," but finally in 1963 he admitted that his trip across the Atlantic had really been planned. Unable to get clearance to cross the ocean, he went ahead and made the flight "by mistake" on purpose.

There's a striking parallel between Corrigan's action and much of our own experience as Christians. Although we are new creatures in Christ, the strong, willful tendency remains in us. The Bible clearly indicates that every believer experiences a struggle between the flesh and the indwelling Spirit (Gal. 5:16–17). That's why we must determine to submit to Him, for He gives us a desire to follow righteousness.
—M. R. D. II

**THOSE WHO FULLY SURRENDER TO THE LORD
WILL NEVER DELIBERATELY SURRENDER TO THE ENEMY.**

Do not let the sun go down on your wrath.

EPHESIANS 4:26

The story is told about a little boy who got into a fight with his older brother one morning. Somewhat outmatched, he took quite a beating. It was his pride, however, that suffered the most. The whole experience left him feeling bitter. In fact, he refused to talk to his brother all day. Bedtime came, and their mother, very much wanting to see the two make up, said to the younger, "Don't you think you should forgive your brother before you go to sleep? Remember, the Bible says, 'Do not let the sun go down on your wrath.'" The youngster looked perplexed. He thought for a few moments and then blurted out, "Well, how can I keep the sun from going down?" He had no intention of getting rid of his grudge.

What can we do if we are holding a grudge against someone? There's only one thing we can do. We cannot change that person's heart, but we can change our attitude. The Bible says, "And be kind to one another, tenderhearted, forgiving one another, just as God in Christ also forgave you" (Eph. 4:32). We can't keep the sun from going down. But we can keep it from setting—on our anger. —R. W. D.

EVERY MINUTE YOU ARE ANGRY,

YOU LOSE SIXTY SECONDS OF HAPPINESS.

The LORD is far from the wicked,
but He hears the prayer of the righteous.

PROVERBS 15:29

Dr. Helen Roseveare, missionary to Zaire, told the following story. "A mother at our mission station died after giving birth to a premature baby. We tried to improvise an incubator to keep the infant alive, but the only hot water bottle we had was beyond repair. So we asked the children to pray for the baby and for her sister. One of the girls responded, 'Dear God, please send a hot water bottle today. Tomorrow will be too late because by then the baby will be dead. And dear Lord, send a doll for the sister so she won't feel so lonely.' That afternoon a large package arrived from England. The children watched eagerly as we opened it. Much to their surprise, under some clothing was a hot water bottle! Immediately the girl who had prayed so earnestly started to dig deeper exclaiming, 'If God sent that, I'm sure He also sent a doll!' And she was right! The heavenly Father knew in advance of that child's sincere requests, and five months earlier He had led a ladies' group to include both of those specific articles."

Not all of our prayers are answered so dramatically, but we know that God always sends what is best. —H. G. B.

GOD NOT ONLY PROMPTS THE ASKING,
HE ALSO PROVIDES THE ANSWER.

On that day the LORD exalted Joshua
in the sight of all Israel.

JOSHUA 4:14

One of the most demanding track events is the 400-meter relay. In this race, each team has four sprinters, each of whom runs 100 meters. Winning the race depends on passing a baton successfully from runner to runner. If this transfer is not handled smoothly, the team has no chance of winning the race. In fact, a few years ago in the Olympics, the fastest relay team ever assembled lost a race they should have won in world record time because one runner fumbled the baton.

Perhaps you are at one of those times in your life when you are being called on to "pass the baton." Maybe you have been asked to relinquish your position to someone else. Perhaps it's time to realign some of your family duties. Or you could be leaving one job behind as you prepare to begin another. If so, think again about the honor and privilege of passing on the baton. Anticipate with gladness the next step in your journey. —D. C. E.

WE CANNOT ALTER THE PAST,
BUT WE CAN BE ALERT FOR THE FUTURE.

Godliness with contentment is great gain.

1 TIMOTHY 6:6

Leslie Flynn tells the story of a prestigious alumni association that was trying to discover the levels of wealth and success of its graduates. One of the questionnaires was sent to a former student, now a missionary in Colombia, South America. Here are some of the questions they asked and the answers they received: (1) Do you own your own home? Yes. (He had paid the tribes people $125 for his palm-thatched dwelling in the Amazon basin.) (2) Do you rent quarters elsewhere? Yes. (He and his family occasionally stayed in a house where missionaries were crowded together for conferences.) (3) Do you own a boat? Yes. (He had a dugout canoe tied up at the riverbank below his house.) (4) Do you plan to travel abroad during the next 2 years? Yes. (He and his family were going home on furlough.) (5) What is your income? Under $10,000 per year.

Flynn suggests that the computer probably spit out an analysis with the notation, "Data incompatible." But this man is both rich and successful! He possesses great spiritual wealth as a child of God and as a citizen of heaven. He is successful because he is doing the work to which God called him—a work of eternal value. —H. V. L.

TO BE RICH IN GOD IS BETTER THAN TO BE RICH IN GOODS.

Let each of you look out not only for his own interests,
but also for the interests of others.

PHILIPPIANS 2:4

In his book *Open the Door Wide to Happy Living*, T. Huffman Harris told of a young man named Eddie who became tired of life and decided to leap from a bridge into a turbulent river. Jim, a total stranger, saw Eddie being swept downstream and plunged into the water in an effort to save him. Eddie, a good swimmer, noticed the man floundering desperately in the strong current and knew that without his help he would drown. Something stirred within him. With all of his strength, Eddie swam over to the man and rescued him. Saving that stranger, who had attempted to save him, brought new hope and meaning to Eddie's life.

We as Christians can become so immersed in our own troubles that we think only of ourselves, and all sorts of negative thoughts flood our soul. At a time like that we need to look upward to Christ and outward to a needy world. Then as we reach out to help others, the Holy Spirit works a change in us. Hope is born when we help others in Jesus' name. —D. J. D.

WHEN WE EASE THE BURDEN OF ANOTHER, WE FORGET OUR OWN.

Restore to me the joy of Your salvation,
and uphold me by Your generous Spirit.

PSALM 51:12

It isn't easy to make a forty-foot, forty-five-ton, untrained whale do what you want it to do, even if it's for its own good. That's what well-wishing friends found out when a humpback whale, affectionately named Humphrey made a wrong turn during his migration along the California coast. The wayward mammal became a national celebrity when he turned in to San Francisco Bay, swam under the Golden Gate Bridge, and managed to navigate seventy miles upriver. For more than three weeks, Humphrey defied all efforts to get him back to salt water. Finally, marine biologists tried to lure him with the recorded sounds of feeding humpbacks. It worked. Humphrey responded to the "happy humpbacks" and followed "them" back to the Pacific.

The lure of happy sounds works not only with lost whales but also with lost people. God makes the lives of His saints appealing to those who don't know Him. Love, joy, and peace are the appealing qualities of those who are feeding on the goodness of God. And they are the "sounds" that can lead the lost to the freedom found in the ocean of God's infinite grace. —M. R. D. II

YOU CAN ATTRACT SINNERS TO CHRIST
WHEN YOU HAVE HIS SONG IN YOUR HEART.

Where do wars and fights come from among you?
Do they not come from your desires for pleasure . . . ?

JAMES 4:1

The world is in turmoil. Terrorists hijack airplanes. Gunmen take hostages. Internal strife plagues nations. Government officials are being criticized. What is the underlying cause of all this unrest? A student in Wales offers an answer to this question. In replying to a statement that the laboring man was responsible for the economic crisis in Great Britain, she said, "No, it's not just the workers. They get the blame day after day, but others are at fault as well. Everyone is out for himself—the employee, the manager, the politician. The whole world is one big selfish mess!"

Isn't this exactly what the Bible teaches? The reason for family quarrels, neighborhood feuds, strife between labor and management, and war among nations is the inherent self-centeredness of human beings. Since everybody is seeking his own interests, sooner or later he comes into conflict with the selfish desires of others. Society will show little improvement until individuals experience a change of heart by letting Christ begin to rule in their heart. —H. V. L.

GOD'S GRACE CREATES AN OPEN HAND AND A GIVING HEART.

Do not be deceived, God is not mocked;
for whatever a man sows, that he will also reap.

GALATIANS 6:7

once read a fable about a farmhand who was given instructions to plant a field of barley. He acted immediately, but he sowed oats instead of barley. After several weeks, the owner of the farm went out to inspect the crop and was astonished to see oats growing instead of barley. The workman was told to report to the owner's office at once. "I told you to plant barley," he said. "Why did you sow oats?" "Oh," the man responded, "I didn't think it would make any difference. I figured that even if I planted oats, I could expect barley to come up." Enraged, the owner shouted, "Are you crazy, man? What ever made you think that?" The farmhand replied, "I got that idea from you, sir. I've been watching the way you live. And I've noticed that even though you're constantly sowing 'seeds of evil,' you expect to be reaping 'fruits of virtue'!"

No one can avoid the natural laws of sowing and reaping. Whatever we sow, we will reap. What are you sowing? —R. W. D.

THE COST OF LIVING GOES UP AND DOWN,
BUT THE COST OF SOWING WILD OATS REMAINS THE SAME.

"Take, eat; this is My body which is broken for you;
do this in remembrance of Me."

1 CORINTHIANS 11:24

I once heard my friend Roger Rose tell this story. He said that when he was a boy, his family lived on a farm alongside a dirt road. Only on rare occasions would an automobile pass by. But one day as Roger's young brother was crossing the road on his bicycle, a car came roaring down a nearby hill, struck the boy, and killed him. Roger said, "Later, when my father picked up the mangled, twisted bike, I heard him sob out loud for the first time in my life. He carried it to the barn and placed it in a spot we seldom used. Father's terrible sorrow eased with the passing of time, but for many years whenever he saw that bike, tears began streaming down his face." Roger continued, "Since then I have often prayed, 'Lord, keep the memory of Your death as fresh as that to me! Every time I partake of Your memorial supper, let my heart be stirred as though You died only yesterday. Never let the communion service become a mere formality, but always a tender and touching experience.'"

As we partake of the Lord's Supper, meditating on His suffering and death should always fill us with a deep sense of gratitude to God for providing our redemption. —H. G. B.

REMEMBERING CHRIST'S WOUNDS
SHOULD ENCOURAGE US TO DO HIS WILL.

Whatever you do,
do all to the glory of God.

1 CORINTHIANS 10:31

Drifting snow and bitter cold threatened the lives of Indian evangelist Sadhu Sundar Singh and his Tibetan companion as they crossed a Himalayan mountain pass. Fighting the "sleep of death," they stumbled over a mound in the trail. It was a man, half-dead. The Tibetan refused to stop but continued on alone. The compassionate Sadhu, however, shouldered the burden the best he could. Through his struggling, he began to warm up, as did the unconscious man. But before reaching the village they found the Tibetan—frozen to death.

Jesus taught that if we put our selfish desires first, we become losers. But if we use our lives for His sake, we receive life in abundance. Only when life's energies are put into the cause of Christ do we know the joy of being finders instead of losers. —D. J. D.

YOU DENY CHRIST WHEN YOU
FAIL TO DENY YOURSELF FOR CHRIST.

That your charitable deed may be in secret;
and your Father who sees in secret will Himself reward you openly.

MATTHEW 6:4

As Christians, we should not display a "cash and carry" attitude of expecting immediate appreciation for the good we do. God wants us to remember that someday He Himself will richly reward us.

A newspaper article reminded me of the kind of "delayed returns" we should be living for. It told of a car dealer who went out of his way to give a foreign student an honest deal on a new automobile. Fifteen years later, the young man had become the sole purchasing agent for the Iranian Contractors Association. He showed his gratitude for the kindness he had received by placing a multimillion-dollar order with that dealer for 750 heavy dump trucks and 350 pickups. "It's unbelievable!" exclaimed the businessman. The good he had done was rewarded years later beyond his wildest imagination.

If we do good to others for the immediate thanks we receive, we already have our reward. But if we do it for God, the future return will be as sure and generous as He is. —M. R. D. II

**THERE IS NO REWARD FROM GOD
TO THOSE WHO SEEK IT FROM MEN.**

Keep your heart with all diligence,
for out of it spring the issues of life.

PROVERBS 4:23

When I was a boy our family water supply came from a spring just a few feet from the house. The water, which was pure, cold, and sweet, bubbled up through a large pipe about the size of a barrel that had been sunken upright into the ground. As I was about to dip out some water one morning, I saw two huge frogs at the bottom looking up at me with doleful eyes. No one in the family wanted any of that water until we had removed the frogs and had allowed it to run over the sides for several hours. We all wanted to make sure it was perfectly clean and pure again.

Those frogs remind me of the bad thoughts that can spring from our hearts. How important it is to guard what comes into the mind! We become what we think! If we permit hateful thoughts to remain, we will become cruel and heartless. If we let in lustful thoughts, we will become immoral. But when we dwell on lovely, pure, and unselfish thoughts, what flows from our mouths and comes forth in our conduct will be pleasing to God and a blessing to others. —H. V. L.

**NOTHING SO THREATENS CHRISTIAN CHARACTER
AS IMPURE THOUGHTS.**

The Son of Man has power on earth to forgive sins.

MATTHEW 9:6

An anonymous author made this striking comparison: "Socrates taught for forty years, Plato for fifty, Aristotle for forty, and Jesus for only three. Yet the influence of Christ's three-year ministry infinitely transcends the impact left by the combined 130 years of teaching from these men who were among the greatest philosophers of all antiquity. Jesus painted no pictures; yet some of the finest paintings of Raphael, Michelangelo, and Leonardo da Vinci received their inspiration from Him. Jesus wrote no poetry; but Dante, Milton, and scores of the world's greatest poets were inspired by Him. Jesus composed no music; still Haydn, Handel, Beethoven, Bach, and Mendelssohn reached their highest perfection of melody in the hymns, symphonies, and oratorios they composed in His praise. Every sphere of human greatness has been enriched by this humble Carpenter of Nazareth.

"His unique contribution to the race of men is the salvation of the soul! Philosophy could not accomplish that. Nor art. Nor literature. Nor music. Only Jesus Christ can break the enslaving chains of sin and Satan." — H. G. B.

BELIEVING CHRIST DIED, THAT'S HISTORY.
BELIEVING CHRIST DIED FOR ME, THAT'S SALVATION.

This is the victory that has overcome the world—our faith.

1 JOHN 5:4

In his book *Forever Triumphant*, F. J. Huegel told a story that came out of World War II. After General Jonathan Wainwright was captured by the Japanese, he was held prisoner in a Manchurian concentration camp. Cruelly treated, he became "a broken, crushed, hopeless, starving man." Finally the Japanese surrendered and the war ended. A United States army colonel was sent to the camp to announce personally to the general that Japan had been defeated and that he was free and in command. After Wainwright heard the news, he returned to his quarters and was confronted by some guards who began to mistreat him as they had done in the past. Wainwright, however, with the news of the allied victory still fresh in his mind, declared with authority, "No, I am in command here! These are my orders." Huegel observed that from that moment on, General Wainwright was in control.

Huegel made this application: "Have you been informed of the victory of your Savior in the greatest conflict of the ages? . . . Then rise up to assert your rights. . . . Never again go under when the enemy comes to oppress. Claim the victory in Jesus' Name." —R. W. D.

GOD WANTS YOU TO BE A VICTOR, NOT A VICTIM.

Blessed are those who hunger and thirst for righteousness,
for they shall be filled.

MATTHEW 5:6

Everything was set for our first bass fishing expedition of the year. We had some exotic new lures that would be irresistible to those big six-pounders lurking beneath the surface of our favorite lake. We would tempt them with Sassy Shads, with brightly colored new Hula Poppers, and buzz baits. And, if all else failed, we had some fresh Canadian crawlers. We were out at dawn, hitting all the best spots with our assortment of delectable temptations. But nothing happened. We worked the shore. We cast along the weeds. We tried every lure in the tackle box—even the crawlers. Finally we gave up. As we motored back to the cabin, we concluded, "The fish just aren't hungry."

That experience reminds me of temptation. Satan has a whole "tacklebox" of alluring devices he uses to tempt us. Some of them are gaudy and exotic, easy to spot, while others whet our appetites in quiet and subtle ways. But with mental discipline and the help of the Holy Spirit, we can keep our hearts full of goodness. Then, in frustration, Satan will have to say, "They just aren't hungry!" —D. C. E.

EVERY STEP AWAY FROM THE DEVIL LEADS ONE STEP CLOSER TO GOD.

September

SEPTEMBER 1

The testing of your faith produces patience.

JAMES 1:3

Almost everyone would rather have sunshine than showers. Franklin Elmer, Jr., described a region in Chile between the great Andes mountain range and the Pacific Ocean where that is actually true, where rain never falls. He wrote, "Morning after morning the sun rises brilliantly over the tall mountains to the east; each noon it shines brightly down from overhead; evening brings a picturesque sunset. Although storms are often seen raging high in the mountains, and heavy fog banks are observed far out over the sea, the sun continues to shine on this favored and protected strip of land. One would imagine this area to be an earthly paradise; but it is not. Instead, it is a sterile and desolate desert! There are no streams of water, and nothing grows there."

Elmer then made this application: "Too often we long for total sunshine and joy in life. We have wished to be rid of burdensome responsibilities. But, like this sunny, unfertile part of Chile, life without its burdens and trials would not be creative, productive, or challenging. We need sunshine *and* showers." —R. W. D.

ALL SUNSHINE AND NO RAIN MAKES A DESERT.

*And let us consider one another
in order to stir up love and good works.*

HEBREWS 10:24

Loneliness is a growing problem in our society. A study by the American Council of Life Insurance reported that the loneliest people in America are college students. That's surprising! Next on the list are divorced people, welfare recipients, single mothers, rural students, housewives, and the elderly. To point out how lonely people can be, Charles Swindoll mentioned an ad in a Kansas newspaper. It read, "I will listen to you talk for thirty minutes without comment for $5.00." Swindoll said, "Sounds like a hoax, doesn't it? But the person was serious. Did anybody call? You bet. It wasn't long before this individual was receiving ten to twenty calls a day. The pain of loneliness was so sharp that some were willing to try anything for a half hour of companionship."

If you are lonely, realize that Christ understands your loneliness. Claim His promise never to leave you. If you know someone who is lonely, reach out to that person. Share your life and Christ's love.

—D. C. E.

WE'RE NEVER ALONE WHEN WE'RE ALONE WITH JESUS.

Christ will be magnified in my body,
whether by life or by death.

PHILIPPIANS 1:20

The eighteenth-century English pastor Rowland Hill lived to a ripe old age. In fact, he outlived most of his friends. Missing them very much and anxious to join them on the other side, he grew more homesick for heaven with each passing day. It seemed so long since some of them had gone to glory that he would often jokingly say with a wink, "Do you think they'll remember me?" It was not unusual for him to go to some other believer well along in years with this request: "If you should go before I do, give my love to everyone. Be sure to tell them that old Rowley, although staying behind a little while, is coming on as fast as he can."

For the Christian, death holds some wonderful blessings. It's a release from the pains, the heartaches, and the testings of this present life. It's the doorway to incomprehensible glory. And at the moment a Christian takes his last breath, faith is turned to sight as he enters the presence of the Savior Himself, for to be absent from the body is to be present with the Lord (2 Cor. 5:8). That's the greatest death benefit of all!
—R. W. D.

FOR THE CHRISTIAN, DEATH IS NOT GLOOM BUT GLORY.

By grace you have been saved through faith,
and that not of yourselves; it is the gift of God.

EPHESIANS 2:8

Bible teacher G. Campbell Morgan told of a coalminer who came to him and said, "I would give anything to believe that God would forgive my sins, but I cannot believe that He will forgive them if I just ask Him. It is too cheap." Morgan said, "My dear friend, have you been working today?" "Yes, I was down in the mine." "How did you get out of the pit? Did you pay?" "Of course not. I just got into the cage and was pulled to the top." "Were you not afraid to entrust yourself to that cage? Was it not too cheap?" Morgan asked. "Oh, no," said the miner, "it was cheap for me, but it cost the company a lot of money to sink the shaft." Suddenly, the truth struck him. What had not cost him anything—salvation—had not come cheap to God. This miner had never thought of the great price God paid to send His Son so He could rescue fallen humanity. Now he realized that all anyone had to do was to "get into the cage" by faith.

Because of God's grace, salvation is a free gift. But to receive it, we must stop trying to pay for it and start trusting what Christ has done on the cross. It's free, but it's not cheap. —P. R. V.

SALVATION IS FREE, BUT IT COST SOMEONE AN ENORMOUS PRICE.

[He] comforts us in all our tribulation,
that we may be able to comfort those who are in any trouble.

2 CORINTHIANS 1:4

The English artist Joseph Turner once invited the clergyman and novelist Charles Kingsley to his studio to see a picture he had just completed of a storm at sea. Filled with admiration, Kingsley inquired, "How did you make it so realistic?" The artist replied, "When I decided to paint this scene, I thought it would be best to go to the coast of Holland and hire a fisherman to take me out in his boat during an actual storm. I knew this was the only way I could get a feel for my subject. The boatman bound me to the mast so I could watch the squall in safety. I not only observed it and sensed its power, but the tempest blew itself into me until I seemed to become a part of it. When it was over, I was able to depict on canvas all the fury I had felt at sea."

So too, in the Christian life we may acquire some wisdom in times of prosperity, but oh, the deeper lessons we can learn in the school of tribulation and sorrow! Experience is a great teacher. We learn the most from what affects us personally. If you have received consolation from the Lord in time of tribulation, God wants you to share with others the lessons you've learned. —H. G. B.

GOD COMFORTS US NOT TO MAKE US COMFORTABLE,
BUT TO MAKE US COMFORTERS.

Why do you judge your brother? . . .
We shall all stand before the judgment seat of Christ.

ROMANS 14:10

I like the story of the young man whose habit of criticizing backfired on him. One evening, while waiting for a bus, he was standing with a crowd of people looking in the window of a taxidermist shop. In the center of the window was a large owl that attracted the attention of all who passed by. The self-appointed expert began to criticize the job done on it. "If I couldn't do better than that," he said pompously, "I'd find another business. Just look at it. The head is out of proportion, the pose of the body is unnatural, and the feet are pointed in the wrong direction." Just then the owl turned his head and gave the fellow a broad wink. The crowd laughed as the critic slinked away.

One of the more destructive practices is to be unnecessarily critical. Too often we are like the person in the anonymous poem who said of himself: "Faults in others I can see; but praise the Lord, there's none in me." When we want to cast stones at others let's ask the Lord to remind us of our own faults. —D. C. E.

BE PATIENT WITH THE FAULTS OF OTHERS;
THEY HAVE TO BE PATIENT WITH YOURS.

If anyone thinks himself to be something,
when he is nothing, he deceives himself.

GALATIANS 6:3

Disaster always results when we try to build ourselves up by minimizing the worth of others. That's the message of an old fable about a little frog who was startled when he looked up and saw an ox drinking out of the pond. He had never seen such a huge creature. Immediately he hopped away to tell his grandfather about the enormous ox. Determined that no one should seem larger in the eyes of his grandson than he, the old bullfrog began to puff himself up as he asked, "Was he bigger than this?" "Oh, yes, Grandfather," answered the little frog, "much larger." He inflated himself more. "Bigger than this?" he queried. "Lots bigger!" replied the grandson. The old frog continued to puff until he exploded.

Now, it's healthy to have a good self-image, but there's a big difference between a sense of our God-given worth as His handiwork and an ego that is inflated by pride. That's why we must be quick to acknowledge that what we accomplish is done solely by God's grace. Only then can we see how foolish it is to promote our selfish interests.
—P. R. V.

GOD WANTS PEOPLE GREAT ENOUGH
TO BE SMALL ENOUGH TO BE USED.

Ask, and it will be given to you; seek, and you will find;
knock, and it will be opened to you.

MATTHEW 7:7

In an interview with Samuel F. B. Morse, the inventor of telegraph, George Hervey inquired, "Professor Morse, when you were making your experiments at the university, did you ever come to a standstill, not knowing what to do next?" "Oh, yes, more than once." "Then what did you do?" "I've never discussed this with anyone, so the public knows nothing about it. But now that you ask me, I'll tell you frankly—I prayed for more light." "And did God give you the wisdom and knowledge you needed?" "Yes, He did," said Morse. "That's why I never felt I deserved the honors that came to me from America and Europe because of the invention associated with my name. I had made a valuable application of the use of electrical power, but it was all through God's help. It wasn't because I was superior to other scientists. When the Lord wanted to bestow this gift on mankind, He had to use someone. I'm just grateful He chose to reveal it to me."

In view of these facts, it's not surprising that the inventor's first message over the telegraph was: "What hath God wrought!" —H. G. B.

TRUE WISDOM STARTS WITH A HEART FULL OF FAITH,
NOT A HEAD FULL OF FACTS.

Indeed these are the mere edges of His ways,
and how small a whisper we hear of Him!

JOB 26:14

Writing in his syndicated column, George Will described a space telescope designed to study light that travels toward earth from near the edge of the universe. Such a telescope is designed to be operated from outer space. It weighs twelve tons, is the size of a bus, and is more precise than the finest watch. Because it will be stationed above the earth's atmosphere, it will be a "clean window" on the universe. This is important to astronomers, because looking through the atmosphere with a conventional telescope has been compared to "bird-watching from the bottom of a lake."

We have a similar problem with our spiritual vision. Although God has come to us in Christ and has given us His Word and His Spirit, we still "see in a mirror, dimly" (1 Cor. 13:12). As we look through the dim atmosphere of physical trouble from our limited perspective, we see only faintly the glory and splendor of God. Things may not always go our way, but we have the hope and assurance that one day we will see Jesus face-to-face, and our perspective will be totally clear. —M. R. D. II

IN HEAVEN, GOD WILL REVEAL WHAT ON EARTH
HE CHOSE TO CONCEAL.

The grass withers, the flower fades,
but the word of our God stands forever.

ISAIAH 40:8

Before the discovery of the Dead Sea Scrolls in 1947, the oldest Hebrew manuscripts dated about A. D. 900. The Dead Sea Scrolls, in startling agreement with the Masoretic text, dated to about 150 B.C. But now archeologists have discovered a pair of tiny silver scrolls that date back to about 600 B.C.! While digging at the site of a fifth-century church in Jerusalem, researchers found a Roman legionnaires' cemetery. Exploring still deeper, they found a small burial cave containing the scrolls. Very carefully, less than a hundredth of an inch at a time, the scrolls were unrolled. On each of them appeared an excerpt from the book of Numbers that included the word *Jehovah*. And these scrolls date back to the days before the exile to Babylon, earlier than liberal scholars supposed that the Pentateuch had even been written!

The Bible has been wonderfully and accurately preserved. Copies of portions of the New Testament, dating to within fifty years of the original manuscripts, have been found, and they coincide with what we have today. The Bible can be trusted as the inspired, inerrant Word of God.—D. C. E.

THE BIBLE DOMINATES THE WORLD AND CHALLENGES THE CENTURIES.

*It is God who works in you both to will
and to do for His good pleasure.*

Every day we make many decisions with no more effort than it takes to breathe. But those big ones—such as the choice of a mate or our life's work—give us trouble. Two extremes must be avoided: acting on desire alone, and letting time and circumstances decide for us. Fear of making a wrong choice can so paralyze us that the decision is made for us. We are like the supposedly experienced paratrooper who was asked how many jumps he had to his credit. "Twenty-five," was his reply, but then he added sheepishly, "Really only one. The other twenty-four I had to be pushed."

Here are some guidelines to keep us from being "pushed" by people, events, or the passing of time. First, start with prayer. Second, list the options and write out the pros and cons of each one. Third, base your decision on biblical principles. If you don't have peace and you cannot delay the decision, ask God to block it if it is wrong. Then go forward in confidence. Difficult decisions are never too difficult for Him! —D. J. D.

DECISIONS THAT DON'T BEGIN WITH GOD END IN FAILURE.

My covenant I will not break,
nor alter the word that has gone out of My lips.

PSALM 89:34

When a couple left for vacation, their newly married son and daughter-in-law promised to watch the house, take in the mail, and keep the lawn mowed. The couple hadn't been gone very long before they began to worry. What if the young people were careless about locking the doors, and all their possessions were stolen? What if they didn't pick up the mail, and some checks were stolen? And what if the lawn weren't mowed? What would the neighbors think? The couple nearly ruined their vacation with worry, and they even cut it short a couple days. When they returned, however, they found the lawn mowed, the mail taken care of, and the house in perfect order. They realized how foolish they had been, because their children had kept their word.

So it is with God. He keeps His word. This brings us great comfort and can free us from worry. Why? Because it means that every promise of God will be kept. Are you fretting or doubting unnecessarily? If so, it's time you laid hold of a promise and reminded yourself that God always keeps His word. —D. C. E.

**WORRY MEANS WE BELIEVE MORE IN OUR PROBLEMS
THAN IN GOD'S PROMISES.**

Whom He called, these He also justified;
and whom He justified, these He also glorified.

ROMANS 8:30

A theology student was writing a term paper about confession of sin. At one point he started to type, "When we confess our sins, He takes away our guilt." The young man couldn't type too well, and when he came to the word *guilt*, he hit the letter "q" by mistake. This made his sentence read, "When we confess our sins, He takes away our quilt." When the paper was returned, the student grinned as he read the marginal note from the professor: "Never fear, my friend, you'll never freeze, because God has given us a Comforter."

Using his keen wit, the professor had conveyed a marvelous truth. Ever since the day of Pentecost, the Holy Spirit has been faithfully carrying on His ministry in the lives of believers. He guides us into truth (John 16:13); He assures us we are God's children (Rom. 8:16); He helps us pray (Rom. 8:26); He transforms us into Christ's image (2 Cor. 3:18); He strengthens us (Eph. 3:16). We can face each day with confidence because of His blessed ministry in our lives. —D. J. D.

THE CHRISTIAN'S HEART IS THE HOLY SPIRIT'S HOME.

Do not enter the path of the wicked,
and do not walk in the way of evil.

PROVERBS 4:14

The story is told of a young girl who accepted Christ as her Savior and applied for membership in a local church. "Were you a sinner before you received the Lord Jesus into your life?" inquired an old deacon. "Yes, sir," she replied. "Well, are you still a sinner?" "To tell you the truth, I feel I'm a greater sinner than ever." "Then what real change have you experienced?" "I don't quite know how to explain it," she said, "except I used to be a sinner running after sin, but now that I am saved I'm a sinner running from sin!" She was received into the fellowship of the church.

Our attitude toward sin is a pretty good indicator of our spiritual vitality. If we take sin lightly, we might well question the genuineness of our relationship to Christ. As believers, we must determine with His help to shun anything that might make us stumble or could lead us into a state of spiritual defeat. —H. G. B.

BELIEVERS ARE NOT SINLESS, BUT THEY SHOULD SIN LESS.

This hope we have as an anchor of the soul,
both sure and steadfast.

HEBREWS 6:19

A newsboy, thinly clad and drenched by the soaking rain, stood shivering in a doorway one cold day in November. First one bare foot and then the other was lifted for a moment and pressed against his leg to get a little warmth. Every few minutes his shrill cry could be heard, "Morning paper! Morning paper!" A man who was well protected by his coat and umbrella stopped to buy the early edition. Noting the boy's discomfort, he said, "This kind of weather is pretty hard on you, isn't it?" Looking up with a smile, the youngster replied, "I don't mind too much, Mister. The sun will shine again."

What a picture of the Christian life! Chilling winds of adversity and grey skies of a sinful environment can easily discourage us. But we can always count on better days because we know God is working in our lives. How fitting that this hope is called an "anchor of the soul"! —D. J. D.

IT IS ALWAYS DARKEST JUST BEFORE DAWN.

Do not despise the chastening of the LORD,
nor be discouraged when you are rebuked by Him.

HEBREWS 12:5

Here is how one writer has described the balance between mercy and discipline. "The Christian life is like the dial of a clock. The hands are God's hands, passing over and over again—the short hand of discipline and the long hand of mercy. Slowly and surely the hand of discipline must pass, and God speaks at each stroke. But over and over passes the hand of mercy, showering down a twelve-fold blessing for each stroke of discipline and trial. Both hands are fastened to one secure pivot: the great unchanging heart of our God of love."

Since "no chastening seems to be joyful for the present, but grievous" (Heb. 12:11), why can't God leave out the chastening? The answer is simple. If He were to do that, our spiritual growth would be stunted. We need every trial because each is designed by God to help us mature and to conform us to the image of His Son. —P. R. V.

GOD CAN EITHER CHANGE THE CIRCUMSTANCES
OR HE CAN CHANGE US.

The discretion of a man makes him slow to anger.

PROVERBS 19:11

A man from Michigan had an idea for removing a tree stump from the yard of a friend. He decided to use a few sticks of dynamite he had stored away in his house. First he tried six sticks of the explosive, but that didn't do the job. Next he tried nine sticks. That did the trick. It turned the stump into an airborne missile that traveled 163 feet downrange before crashing through a neighbor's roof. The stump opened a three-foot hole in his roof, split the rafters, and pushed through the ceiling of his dining room.

We, too, have sometimes used explosive power to try to solve problems. We do this when we resort to anger, which can cause worse problems than the situation that upset us in the first place. It may get some action, but it leaves much damage in its wake. Anger, like dynamite, is explosive. Take care to handle it with wisdom and self-control. —M. R. D. II

**WHEN A MAN'S TEMPER GETS THE BEST OF HIM,
IT REVEALS THE WORST OF HIM.**

Preach the word! Be ready in season and out of season.

2 TIMOTHY 4:2

*S*everal years ago in England a man wrote to the editor of the *British Weekly*. He said he couldn't remember any sermons preached in church and he questioned whether they were all that important. "I have been attending a church service for the past 30 years and have heard probably 3,000 sermons," he wrote. "To my consternation I discovered that I cannot remember a single sermon!" Many readers responded in the Letters to the Editor column, but this letter settled the issue: "I have been married for 30 years. During that time I have eaten 32,850 meals—mostly of my wife's cooking. Suddenly, I have discovered that I cannot remember the menu of a single meal. And yet, I received nourishment from every single one of them. I have the distinct impression that without them, I would have starved to death long ago."

Don't worry if you can't remember the sermon. If you have a receptive heart, God's truth will slowly but surely become firmly implanted in your life. —D. J. D.

GOD'S WORD IS FOOD FOR OUR SOUL.
HELP YOURSELF TO LARGE PORTIONS.

*Be steadfast, immovable, always abounding in the work of the Lord,
knowing that your labor is not in vain.*

1 CORINTHIANS 15:58

An article in *Workstyle* magazine emphasized the importance of getting ready for a trip beforehand. It gave guidelines on carrying the right amount of clothing, selecting the kind you will need, and being prepared for variations in weather. It gave specific directions for packing a suitcase by rolling garments into "logs," folding sweaters a certain way, and properly packing shirts or dresses. The article suggested that a person who is going on a journey should spend quality time in preparation. If he does, he'll be ready to go.

There are some parallels in the Christian's preparation for the journey to heaven. It would be unwise, for example, to wait until the hour of departure to start thinking about the journey. We must get ready now. We need to spend quality time preparing for the day we meet the Lord. We can best do this by investing our life in doing God's will. Concluding his instruction on the resurrection, the apostle Paul advised believers to be "steadfast, immovable, always abounding in the work of the Lord" (1 Cor. 15:58). As we do, we will be packing for heaven.
—D. C. E.

HEAVEN IS A PREPARED PLACE FOR A PREPARED PEOPLE.

*Whoever of you does not forsake all that he has
cannot be My disciple.*

LUKE 14:33

According to legend, when Julius Caesar landed on the shores of Britain with his Roman legions, he took a bold and decisive step to ensure the success of his military venture. Ordering his men to march to the edge of the Cliffs of Dover, he commanded them to look down at the water below. To their amazement, they saw every ship in which they had crossed the channel engulfed in flames. Caesar had deliberately cut off any possibility of retreat. Now that his soldiers were unable to return to the continent there was nothing left for them to do but to advance and conquer! And that is exactly what they did.

A similar commitment is necessary for Christians. We must break all ties that weaken or interfere with wholehearted commitment to Christ. We must forsake all to follow Him (Luke 14:33). No person or thing should come before Him. Is any earthly attachment hindering our allegiance to Christ? If there is, we need to "burn some boats."
—M. R. D. II

**ONLY WHEN WE DIE TO ALL ABOUT US
DO WE LIVE TO GOD ABOVE US.**

He knows the way that I take;
when He has tested me, I shall come forth as gold.

JOB 23:10

While Michelangelo was working on St. Peter's Cathedral, he was criticized by some of the men who were working on the building. They didn't like what they saw and they told him so. The great artist responded, "Even if I were able to make my plans and ideas clear to you—which I am not—I am not obliged to do so. I must ask you to do your best to help me, and when the work is complete the conception will be better understood." History has confirmed that he was right. Those who found fault with his work were doing so out of ignorance. Not understanding what was in the mind of the artist, they couldn't see the whole picture and full design.

You may be going through the deep waters of trial, affliction, or adversity today and cannot understand what God is doing in your life. From our limited point of view, it often appears that everything is wrong and out of control. But rest assured that He knows what He's doing. —R. W. D.

**SOMETHING WONDERFUL OFTEN BEGINS
WITH SOMETHING DIFFICULT.**

Teach me to do Your will, for You are my God;
Your Spirit is good.

PSALM 143:10

For the last three years an architectural firm in Denver
Colorado, has had a "quiet time" for its employees. Sixty
minutes of silence are set aside each day at mid-morning for thinking
and planning. It has proven to be an essential feature for the staff of
twenty-five who work together in one large open room. One employee
said that at first the idea didn't sound very good to them. But now,
having discovered its benefits, they have become very protective of their
quiet time. They have found it to be an important aid in realizing one
of the firm's goals, which is to have an atmosphere of "integrity and
calmness."

What about us? Do we have enough of the right kind of quiet
time? Let's not use the excuse that we really can't afford the time to get
alone with God and be quiet. The truth is, we really can't afford to be
without it. —M. R. D. II

IF YOU WANT STRENGTH TO MEET THE DAY,
TAKE TIME ALONE TO PRAY.

As the elect of God, holy and beloved, put on tender mercies,
kindness, humility, meekness, longsuffering.

COLOSSIANS 3:12

An English nobleman, Sir Bartel Fere, served as governor of Bombay, India, in the 1860s. He was known by both family and acquaintances as "the helpful man." On one occasion when he was returning from a long trip, his wife sent a newly hired servant to meet him and help with his baggage. "How shall I know Sir Bartel?" asked the servant. The governor's wife responded, "Look for a tall gentleman helping somebody."

As Christians, we are commanded to "put on tender mercies, kindness, humility, meekness, longsuffering" (Col. 3:12). You may wonder what you can do for your Lord because you feel you have so few talents. Start by being a loving, sharing, and caring Christian to those in your family. Then spread the kindness around. Be known as one who is always "helping somebody." —P. R. V.

HOW BEAUTIFUL A DAY CAN BE WHEN KINDNESS TOUCHES IT!

He knows our frame;
He remembers that we are dust.

PSALM 103:14

A man doing some shopping in a grocery store was being closely followed by his small son. The boy was carrying a large basket, and the father was loading it with one item after another. He put in canned goods, sugar, flour, meat, and a variety of vegetables. A customer who was watching began to feel sorry for the youngster, thinking his load was becoming too heavy for him. Walking up behind him, she said quietly, "That's a big load for a little chap like you to carry, isn't it?" The boy turned to her as if surprised by her question. Then he smiled and said, "Oh, don't worry, my dad knows how much I can carry!"

Our heavenly Father also knows our load limit and understands precisely how much each of us can endure. Having made us, He thoroughly understands our individual weaknesses and is tenderly concerned about our frailties. At times we may feel we have reached the absolute limit of our endurance, but our heavenly Father will never allow our burdens to become greater than we can bear. He knows exactly how much we can carry! —H. G. B.

THE GOD WHO KNOWS OUR LOAD LIMIT
GRACIOUSLY LIMITS OUR LOAD.

*If anyone desires to come after Me, let him deny himself,
and take up his cross, and follow Me.*

MATTHEW 16:24

Perhaps one of the most effective advertisements ever written appeared in a London newspaper earlier in the 19th century. It read: "Men wanted for hazardous journey. Small wages, bitter cold, long months of complete darkness, constant danger. Safe return doubtful." The ad was placed by Sir Ernest Shackleton, the famous South Pole explorer. Commenting on the overwhelming response he received, Shackleton said, "It seemed as though all the men in Great Britain were determined to accompany us." They were evidently men of great courage, willing to undergo extreme sacrifice for a worthy cause.

Shackleton's advertisement reminds me of the words of Christ in Matthew 16:24, "If anyone desires to come after Me, let him deny himself, and take up his cross, and follow Me." He is also looking for those who will go with Him on a hazardous journey—the way of the cross. He wants only those who are willing to serve Him regardless of the cost. —R. W. D.

**WE ARE PARDONED FROM SIN;
WE ARE NOT EXCUSED FROM SERVICE.**

These words which I command you today shall be in your heart.
You shall teach them diligently to your children.

DEUTERONOMY 6:6–7

A little girl called out, "Mommy, you know that vase in the china cabinet—the one that's been handed down from generation to generation?" "Yes dear, I know which one you mean. What about it?" "Well Mommy, I'm sorry, but this generation just dropped it!"

Now, some earthly possessions have sentimental value, and to break them is a great loss. But how much more tragic it would be for a new generation to "drop it" spiritually—to fail to pass along the godly heritage they have received! That would be an eternal loss.

We must diligently instruct our children by word and example so they can provide a rich spiritual heritage for their children. Only then will God's truth not be lost from generation to generation. —R. W. D.

THE BEST SAFEGUARD FOR THE NEXT GENERATION
IS A GOOD EXAMPLE BY THIS GENERATION.

*God is faithful, who will not allow you
to be tempted beyond what you are able.*

1 CORINTHIANS 10:13

In July 1911, a stuntman named Bobby Leach went over Niagara Falls in a specially designed steel drum and lived to tell about it. Although he suffered minor injuries, he survived because he recognized the tremendous dangers involved in the feat, and because he had done everything he could to protect himself from harm. Several years after that incident, while skipping down a street in New Zealand, Bobby Leach slipped on an orange peeling, fell, and badly fractured his leg. He was taken to a hospital where he later died of complications from that fall. He received a greater injury walking down the street than he sustained in going over Niagara. He was not prepared for danger in what he assumed to be a safe situation.

Some great temptations that roar around us like the foaming cataract of Niagara will leave us unharmed, while a small, insignificant incident causes our downfall. Why? Simply because we become careless and do not recognize the potential danger in it. A victorious Christian is an alert Christian. —R. W. D.

A PREPARED CHRISTIAN IS A PRAYING CHRISTIAN.

I will run the course of Your commandments,
for You shall enlarge my heart.

PSALM 119:32

I was intrigued by an article that explained how a trained runner can keep on running. It detailed what happens in the body in a distance race. When the body begins to overheat, sweat glands release liquid to cool it. When it begins to run low on sugar, which is fuel for the muscles, a hormone from the pancreas tells the liver to release stored sugar into the bloodstream. As the legs and heart need more oxygen, the brain signals the heart to beat faster. Blood flow to the internal organs and upper body is shut down by 80 percent so that more blood gets to the legs and heart. Deep breathing brings in more air. Blood vessels in the legs dilate 400 percent to accommodate the increased flow of blood. All of this enables a person to run long distances.

Just as God has built into the body the capacity to keep running, so too He sustains us spiritually in the race of life. Through His indwelling Holy Spirit, He uses His Word, the church, Christian friends, prayers, and other means to give us the energy and endurance we need in our long-distance race toward Home. —D. C. E.

RUNNING WITH PATIENCE IS PERSEVERANCE IN THE "LONG RUN."

If then you were raised with Christ,
seek those things which are above, where Christ is.

COLOSSIANS 3:1

The graphic difference between an earthly minded person and a heavenly minded person can be seen in two Middle Eastern tombs. The first is the burial place of King Tut in Egypt. Inside, the walls are covered with precious metal and blue porcelain. The mummy of the king is enclosed in a beautifully inscribed, gold-covered sarcophagus. Although King Tut apparently believed in an afterlife, he thought of it in terms of this world's possessions, which he wanted to take with him. The other tomb, in Palestine, is a simple rock-hewn cave believed by many to be Jesus' burial site. Inside there is no gold, no earthly treasure, and no body. Jesus had no reason to store up this world's treasures. His goal was to fulfill all righteousness by doing His Father's will. His was a spiritual kingdom of truth and love.

When this life is over, all we can take with us are spiritual treasures. Everything else stays here. May we seek to be Christlike in thought, word, and deed so that we will live like "heavenly" people.
—P. R. V.

WISE IS THE PERSON WHO GEARS HIS GOALS TO HEAVENLY GAINS.

The darkness shall not hide from You;
the darkness and the light are both alike to You.

PSALM 139:12

The early American Indians had a unique practice of training young braves. On the night of a boy's thirteenth birthday, after learning hunting, scouting, and fishing skills, he was put to one final test. He was placed in a dense forest to spend the entire night alone. Until then, he had never been away from the security of the family and the tribe. But on this night, he was blindfolded and taken several miles away. When he took off the blindfold, he was in the middle of a thick woods and he was terrified! Every time a twig snapped, he visualized a wild animal ready to pounce. After what seemed like an eternity, dawn broke and the first rays of sunlight entered the interior of the forest. Looking around, the boy saw flowers, trees, and the outline of the path. Then, to his utter astonishment, he beheld the figure of a man standing just a few feet away, armed with a bow and arrow. It was his father. He had been there all night long.

We sometimes feel like that boy—alone, fearful, engulfed by darkness. But in the thickest gloom is the all-seeing eye of our Father God. We have no reason to fear. —D. J. D.

IN THE DARK OF THE NIGHT, GOD IS THE LIGHT.

October

He has done marvelous things;
His right hand and His holy arm have gained Him the victory.

PSALM 98:1

In his book *Vital Union with Christ*, A. T. Pierson wrote, "A veteran of Waterloo used to tell how the trained soldiers of the Duke of Wellington, the night before that decisive battle that turned the destinies of Europe, took the raw recruits and told them of the skill, the capacity, the courage of their great commander. They so inspired them with confidence in the Iron Duke that however the battle might seem to waver, the ultimate issue might be confidently expected to be victory. Those raw recruits went into battle expecting to win."

We serve One who is even greater, and we too are confident of victory. Sometimes the wickedness of this world seems to be succeeding. But we serve a Savior who triumphed over sin and death and secured the victory! We're on the winning side! —R. W. D.

**THERE ARE NO LOSERS WITH CHRIST
AND NO WINNERS WITH THE DEVIL.**

They sat down with him . . . and no one spoke a word to him,
for they saw that his grief was very great.

JOB 2:13

Once during Queen Victoria's reign, she heard that the wife of a common laborer had lost her baby. Having experienced deep sorrow herself, she felt moved to express her sympathy. So she called on the bereaved woman one day and spent some time with her. After she left, the neighbors asked what the queen had said. "Nothing," replied the grieving mother. "She simply put her hands on mine, and we silently wept together."

Do you know someone who has experienced great loss? Silent empathy may be the best comfort you can give. You do not need to worry about what to say. The most comforting people are those who simply give a hug or hold a hand and show they care. —H. G. B.

A HEARTFELT TEAR CAN SHOW SUCH LOVE
AS WORDS CAN NEVER DO.

The heavens declare the glory of God;
and the firmament shows His handiwork.

PSALM 19:1

Who can contemplate the magnificence of the universe without acknowledging the greatness of God? Consider these facts about the precise design of our amazing planet.

- The distance of the earth from the sun, approximately 93,000,000 miles, is just right to sustain life.
- The 23 1/2 degree tilt of the earth on its axis ensures seasonal changes, without which much of the earth would be desert.
- The balance of oxygen (21%) and nitrogen (78%) in the air we breathe is perfect for supporting life.
- An ozone layer in the atmosphere shelters our planet from deadly ultraviolet rays from the sun.

These all speak of a God of order, design, and greatness. Even more amazing is the fact that God has taken a personal interest in us. God cared so much that He sent His only Son to die for us. The great Creator became our Savior. How great is our God! — P. R. V.

ALL CREATION IS AN OUTSTRETCHED FINGER
POINTING TOWARD GOD.

You shall not bear false witness against your neighbor.

EXODUS 20:16

I read about a twelve-year-old boy who was a key witness in a crucial lawsuit. One of the lawyers had put him through a rigorous cross-examination and had been unable to shake his clear, damaging testimony. In a stern voice, the lawyer said, "Your father has been telling you how to testify, hasn't he?" "Yes," said the boy. "Now," said the lawyer with smug satisfaction, "just tell us what your father told you to say." "Well," replied the boy, "Father told me that the lawyers may try to tangle me; but if I would just be careful and tell the truth, I could say the same thing every time."

As Christians, that should be our approach in everything we say. Truth should be the hallmark of every Christian. We are to be models of honesty in a society marked by falsehood, rationalization, and devious attempts to avoid telling the truth. But for the child of God, honesty is more than the best policy, it should be the only policy. —P. R. V.

TRUTH DOES NOT NEED DEFENDERS
SO MUCH AS IT NEEDS WITNESSES.

Do not grow weary in doing good.

2 THESSALONIANS 3:13

God wants us to keep on doing what is right—persevering in His strength no matter what happens or how people respond.

- People can be unreasonable, illogical, and self-centered;
  love them anyway.
- If you do good, some will accuse you of selfish motives;
  do good anyway.
- The good you do today may be forgotten tomorrow;
  do good anyway.
- Honesty and frankness make you vulnerable;
  be honest anyway.
- Sinners don't always want to hear the gospel;
  witness lovingly anyway!

Applying these rules of "doing-anyway" in our lives will make us better, more victorious Christians. —H. G. B.

THE WORLD CROWNS SUCCESS, BUT GOD CROWNS FAITHFULNESS.

Watch and pray, lest you enter into temptation.

MARK 14:38

When we recognize the ugliness of temptations, we will be better able to resist them. Someone has written, "If only I could see my temptations as I see other people's, they wouldn't be a bit hard to fight. Other people's temptations look so ugly and foolish. But my own temptations come with a rosy light about them so that I don't see how hateful they are until afterward."

There are two ways to see temptations in their true colors. One is to pray about them and thus bring them into the clear light of God's presence. The other is to say, "How would this look if someone else yielded to it?" To the one being tempted, enticement to sin may be appealing. But if we yield, we start down a path of self-destruction.

If we know God's Word, which is the sword of the Spirit, and understand how to wield it, we can be victorious over Satan. So let's be strong in the Lord, filled with His Spirit, and quick to recognize the ugliness of sin. That's how to resist temptation. —R. W. D.

IF YOU WANT TO MASTER TEMPTATION, LET CHRIST MASTER YOU.

It is to your advantage not only to be doing what you began . . .
but now you also must complete the doing of it.

2 CORINTHIANS 8:10–11

An article in the newspaper told of a man in Vicenza, Italy, who got last-minute jitters on the day of his wedding and wanted to back out. Just a couple hours before the ceremony, he got an idea. Hurrying to a nearby town, he entered a house, faked a robbery, and left a trail of clues. He even let the owner of the house get a good look at him. Later, as he made his way to the church where the wedding was scheduled, police arrested him and charged him with attempted robbery. The article was headlined, "Idea to Stop Wedding Is Really a Steal."

It may be that right now you are being confronted with a similar situation. Perhaps you set out to do the will of God and to follow Him faithfully, only to find the path harder than you had anticipated. Or maybe you are wondering how you can avoid a commitment, detour around a difficult task, or obey only partially a direct teaching of God's Word. I'd encourage you to continue what you started. Joy will fill your heart and the Father will be pleased when you keep your commitments.
—P. R. V.

**THE BEST WAY TO KEEP GOOD INTENTIONS FROM DYING
IS TO EXECUTE THEM.**

Be anxious for nothing, but in everything by prayer and supplication,
with thanksgiving, let your requests be made known to God.

PHILIPPIANS 4:6

once read about an unusual woman who had learned the secret of victory over worry. Although a widow for years, she had successfully raised not only her own six children but twelve adopted ones as well. When a reporter asked how she managed to remain so calm and poised with her busy schedule, she said, "Oh, I'm in a partnership." "What kind of partnership?" he asked. She replied, "One day, a long time ago, I said, 'Lord, I'll do the work, and You do the worrying.' I haven't had a worry since."

What a wonderful partnership! Our daily duties and responsibilities won't be a burden if we let God do His part. When we give Him the "worrying," we become free from fear and anxiety. When we allow Him to be part of all we do, our weak efforts are supported by His divine power. When we are willing to do what He has assigned, we can present our need to Him and trust Him for His help. We can let Him do the worrying! —R. W. D.

IF WE WORRY, WE *CAN'T* TRUST; IF WE TRUST WE *WON'T* WORRY.

Be ye doers of the word, and not hearers only, deceiving yourselves.

JAMES 1:22

General George Patton of World War II fame was seldom at a loss for words. During a battle in North Africa, his troops and tanks were engaged in a successful counterattack of German forces under General Erwin Rommel. Patton is reported to have shouted in the thick of the battle, "I read your book Rommel! I read your book!" And that he did. In Rommel's book *Infantry Attacks*, the famed "Desert Fox" carefully detailed his military strategy. And Patton, having read it and knowing what to expect, planned his moves accordingly.

Satan has authored no book, but God has clearly outlined our enemy's tactics in His Holy Word. By studying God's Word we can understand our enemy and plan our defense. By being alert to Satan's tactics and submitting to God's will we can resist the evil one. Victory is ours! —D. J. D.

SATAN'S PLOYS ARE NO MATCH FOR THE SAVIOR'S POWER.

Then they crucified Him, and divided His garments.

MATTHEW 27:35

In 1968, Admiral Elmo Zumwalt, Jr., took command of the American naval forces in Vietnam. In an effort to reduce U.S. casualties, he ordered the waterways sprayed with the chemical defoliant Agent Orange. It was a move designed to push back the jungle and make it harder for North Vietnamese to ambush Navy river patrol boats at pointblank range. One of those boats was commanded by twenty-one-year-old Lt. Elmo Zumwalt III. The tragedy and irony of the story is that today he suffers from an usually fatal form of lymph cancer that both father and son believe was caused by his exposure to Agent Orange. Theirs is the heartbreaking story of a father who made a decision that unintentionally resulted in great suffering for his own son. Yet they both agree that it was the right decision to make.

Imagine how much greater was the heartbreak of God the Father! In conquering sin and death to provide salvation for us, He intentionally made a decision that resulted in immeasurable agony for His only begotten Son. It was a decision that brought unbearable pain and suffering; but it was the right decision. —M. R. D. II

**THE TRUEST MEASURE OF GOD'S LOVE
IS THAT HE LOVES WITHOUT MEASURE.**

Let each one examine his own work, and then he will have
rejoicing in himself alone, and not in another.

GALATIANS 6:4

Several years ago, an angry man rushed through the Rijks Museum in Amsterdam until he reached Rembrandt's famous painting *Nightwatch*. Then he took out a knife and slashed it repeatedly before he could be stopped. A short time later, a distraught, hostile man slipped into St. Peter's Cathedral in Rome with a hammer and began to smash Michelangelo's beautiful sculpture, *The Pieta*. Two cherished works of art were severely damaged. But what did officials do? Throw them out and forget about them? Absolutely not! Using the best experts, who worked with the utmost care and precision, they made every effort to restore the treasures.

Christians ought to have the same attitude toward a believer whose testimony has been damaged by sin. When one of God's children falls into sin and is marred, our first and only thought should be to restore, not to condemn. Tenderly and compassionately we must pray and work to bring that one back to spiritual wholeness and fellowship within the body of Christ. —D. C. E.

WE CAN'T EXPECT OTHERS TO SEE EYE TO EYE WITH US
IF WE LOOK DOWN ON THEM.

Above all these things put on love,
which is the bond of perfection.

COLOSSIANS 3:14

Several years ago I read the story of Sammy Morris, a devoted Christian from Africa who came to America to go to school. Although his pathway to service for Christ was not easy, his difficulties never deterred him. Perhaps this was because he had learned genuine humility. One incident that showed his heart was when he arrived at Taylor University in Upland, Indiana. He was asked by the school's president what room he wanted. Sammy replied, "If there is a room nobody wants, give it to me." Later the president commented, "I turned away, for my eyes were full of tears. I was asking myself whether I was willing to take what nobody else wanted."

Today we are bombarded with the philosophy of "I'm number one" and the concept of self-love—even in religious circles. We need to put on "humbleness of mind." Paul said, "Let this mind be in you which was also in Christ Jesus, who . . . made Himself of no reputation" (Phil. 2:5–7). If we do this, we can, like Sammy Morris, be willing to take what nobody else wants. That's genuine humility. That's the mind of Christ. —P. R. V.

THE SMALLER WE BECOME THE MORE ROOM GOD HAS TO WORK.

As you are partakers of the sufferings,
so also you will partake of the consolation.

2 CORINTHIANS 1:7

While riding on a train through a small town in Georgia, my friend E. Schuyler English observed a large sign painted on the side of a fix-it shop. It read, "We can mend everything but a broken heart." That may be a bit of an exaggeration, but it is also clever advertising.

That sign raises a vital question—is there anything that can mend a broken heart? When sadness darkens each day and grief overwhelms us, where do we turn for comfort and help? Can the human wisdom of friends, family, or business associates—as well-meaning as they may be— offer effective healing prescriptions? We soon discover that they don't have the answer.

There is One, however, who does mend broken hearts—"the Father of mercies and God of all comfort." If you struggle today beneath a crushing weight of sorrow, pour out your sorrows to the "God of all comfort." He alone can give relief to your aching soul. He alone can mend your broken heart.—P. R. V.

WHEN GOD ALLOWS EXTRAORDINARY TRIALS,
HE GIVES EXTRAORDINARY COMFORT.

*Wives, submit to your own husbands,
as is fitting in the Lord. Husbands, love your wives.*

COLOSSIANS 3:18–19

A 104-year-old California man and his 96-year-old wife recently celebrated eighty years of marriage. She had been a sixteen-year-old "child bride" in a marriage the families had arranged. They had no dating period—no chance to "fall in love" by today's standards. So many things were against them. Yet they raised five children, survived the Great Depression, and lived to see a day when nearly half of all marriages end in divorce.

How in the world did they do it? They stayed together on the basis of good old-fashioned values. For them, love meant commitment "till death us do part." What happened to those old values? Have we found better ideals, better principles of relationships, deeper insights, and better understanding? If so, why do so many people live with the regret of broken marriages, broken homes, broken families, and broken promises?

Maybe it's time to look again at the values that make marriages work—values such as mercy, kindness, humility, longsuffering, forbearance, and forgiveness (Col. 3:12–13). Do these sound old-fashioned? Perhaps, but they work! —M. R. D. II

A CHRISTIAN HOME IS ONE WHERE GOD IS A PERMANENT GUEST.

LORD, who may abide in Your tabernacle?
He who walks uprightly.

PSALM 15:1-2

Anger can cause us to do and say things we may deeply regret. George W. Martin tells the following true story: "I remember a fellow who once wrote a nasty letter to his father. Since we worked in the same office, I advised him not to send it because it was written in a fit of temper. But he sealed it and asked me to put it in the mail. Instead, I simply slipped it into my pocket and kept it until the next day. The following morning he arrived at the office looking very worried. 'George,' he said, 'I wish I had never sent that note to my dad yesterday. It hurts me deeply, and I know it will break his heart when he reads it. I'd give fifty dollars to get it back!' Taking the envelope from my pocket, I handed it to him and told him what I had done. He was so overjoyed that he actually wanted to pay me the fifty dollars!"

Nothing is ever gained by giving way to the dark passion of bitterness and anger. When someone wrongs us, we must learn to forgive and ask God to let the love of Christ fill our heart. It's the only way to keep from being hurt by bitterness, wrath, and anger. —H. G. B.

FORGIVENESS SAVES THE EXPENSE OF ANGER.

Remember those who rule over you,
who have spoken the word of God to you, whose faith follow.

HEBREWS 13:7

Just before winter sets in, geese from northern Canada begin their journey south, migrating to the lakes and ponds of North Carolina, Georgia, and Florida. Perhaps you have seen the majestic flight of those birds—whose wingspans can reach five to six-and-a-half feet—as they traverse the sky in their characteristic flight pattern. According to Lamar Dodd's *Mark Trail*, some authorities believe that "Canada geese fly in a V-formation to take advantage of the air currents stirred up by the birds flying ahead. The lead goose does most of the hard work, overcoming air resistance." The trailing birds benefit from the ones in front.

Think of all those who have gone before—some giving their lives—so we could hear about Christ. They were pioneers. And now perhaps God has placed us in a position where resistance to the gospel is strong. Our witness in that God-appointed spot can clear the way for others to follow. So let's keep flying! As we follow the faith of previous Christian stalwarts, we provide encouragement and help for fellow Christians who come later. —P. R. V.

IF YOU WANT YOUR INFLUENCE FOR JESUS TO LAST, PUT HIM FIRST.

*The men of Sodom were exceedingly wicked
and sinful against the LORD.*

GENESIS 13:13

There's an old story about a man who tried to save the city of Sodom from destruction by warning the citizens. But the people ignored him. One day someone asked, "Why bother everyone? You can't change them." "Maybe I can't," the man replied, "but I still shout and scream to prevent them from changing me!"

Lot was a righteous man (2 Pet. 2:7) who should have done some screaming. The record of his life reminds us of how our sense of moral indignation can be dulled by the world. There's much immorality in today's world—sex before marriage, homosexual behavior, taking the life of the unborn, and pornography. Out of our love for people and a deep concern about the influence of sin on society, we protest! Even if our screaming does little to change society, we do it anyway because we don't want society to change us—and we just may help others. —D. J. D.

**THOSE WHO CANNOT BE ANGRY AT EVIL
LACK ENTHUSIASM FOR GOOD.**

He built an altar there
and called on the name of the LORD.

GENESIS 26:25

In the early 1900s, a policeman was walking his beat in Chicago when he observed a man standing before a little mission. He had removed his hat, and the officer thought he was acting rather strangely. Thinking the man might be drunk or ill, the policeman approached him. He noticed that his eyes were closed, so he nudged him and said, "What's the matter, Mac? Are you sick?" The man looked up and smiled. "No, sir. My name is Billy Sunday. I was converted right here in this mission. I never pass this way without taking the opportunity, if possible, to stand quietly for a moment and whisper a prayer of thanksgiving."

In the Old Testament, altars were often erected as memorials of praise. They hallowed a certain spot where a devout worshiper had encountered God. That was true of the one built by Isaac recorded in Genesis 26. While we no longer follow this practice today, some places do hold a blessed spiritual significance for us. As we occasionally return to them, our hearts are lifted in praise to the Lord for His goodness.
—H. G. B.

LET PRAISE BE NOT AN INCIDENT BUT AN ATTITUDE OF LIFE.

*The heart of the wise teaches his mouth,
and adds learning to his lips.*

PROVERBS 16:23

Experts tell us that people often hide what they are trying to say behind a wall of words. This is a kind of double talk in which their words do not coincide with their feelings. Gerald Nierenberg, a New York lawyer, wrote a book about this problem called *Meta-Talk: Guide to Hidden Meanings in Conversation.* In it he gives 350 examples of verbal distortion. Another communications consultant says many people are afraid that honesty in speech will cost them friendships, love, or respect. So they either keep their lips zipped or say something other than what they mean. Additional factors that may impede straight talk are shyness, lack of self-worth, fear of displaying ignorance, fear of criticism, and fear of hurting someone's feelings.

Christians are not immune to this problem. Trying to be both loving and truthful is often extremely difficult. The Bible, however, provides a balanced and optimistic approach to this dilemma. Being honest with people may hurt, but if we speak kindly and with compassion we give them the support they need to face reality.
—M. R. D. II

GENTLE WORDS FALL LIGHTLY, BUT THEY HAVE GREAT WEIGHT.

*"Why do you call Me 'Lord, Lord,'
and not do the things which I say?"*

LUKE 6:46

Archibald Rutledge wrote that one day he met a man whose dog had just been killed in a forest fire. Heartbroken, the man explained to Rutledge how it happened. Because he worked out-of-doors, he often took his dog with him. That morning, he left the animal in a clearing and gave him a command to stay and watch his lunch bucket while he went into the forest. His faithful friend understood, for that's exactly what he did. Then a fire started in the woods, and soon the blaze spread to the spot where the dog had been left. But he didn't move. He stayed right where he was, in perfect obedience to his master's word. With tearful eyes, the dog's owner said, "I always had to be careful what I told him to do, because I knew he would do it."

If a dog can be expected to obey his master, how much more should we who know the Lord and have been redeemed be obedient to His commands! May you and I be so dependable in doing the Lord's will that our Master would be able to say of us, "I knew he would do it!"—R. W. D.

**THE COST OF OBEDIENCE IS NOTHING
COMPARED TO THE COST OF DISOBEDIENCE.**

Make me understand the way of Your precepts;
so shall I meditate on Your wonderful works.

PSALM 119:27

Martin Luther said he studied God's Word the same way he gathered apples. First he shook the whole tree, that the ripest fruit might fall. Then he shook each limb, each branch, and every twig. Finally he looked under every leaf. In other words, he began by reading the Bible as a whole, as he would any other volume. He then took time to shake every limb—studying the Scriptures more carefully, a book at a time. Next he would examine every branch and twig, giving attention to each chapter, paragraph, and sentence. At last he would look under each leaf by searching out the full meaning of the individual words. There are many ways to study God's Word, but Luther's is a good one.

The Bible is a life-giving book that directs, preserves, edifies, and quickens the saints of God. Meditating daily on its pages with a prayerful, teachable attitude will remove deadness from the heart and coldness from the spirit. As we read the precious treasury of God's thoughts with a reverent, inquiring mind, the Bible will come alive. We will find it practical and relevant to our needs. —H. G. B.

AS YOU PORE OVER GOD'S WORD,
HIS POWER WILL POUR THROUGH YOU.

Lay up for yourselves treasures in heaven, where neither moth nor rust destroys and where thieves do not break in and steal.

MATTHEW 6:20

The Lord Jesus is now in heaven, preparing a place for all who have put their trust in Him. That thought reminds me of these observations by an unknown writer: "I once had friends who were traveling abroad. Planning to build a new house upon their return, as they journeyed the dream of that new home was constantly in their minds. When they found a beautiful painting, statue, or vase, they purchased it and sent it on ahead to await their arrival. The same thing was done with rare and curious treasures, which afterward, when placed in their new home, could be linked with the happy memories of their trip." The writer then made this application: "I love to think that we, in our journey here on earth, are doing the same for our heavenly home. The kindly deed that made a rare picture in somebody's life, the little sacrifice that blossomed into joy, the helpful friendship—all these we shall find again. . . . Whatever of beauty, tenderness, faith, or love we can put into other's lives . . . will be among our treasures in heaven." —R. W. D.

THE WISE CHRISTIAN GEARS HIS GOALS TO HEAVENLY GAINS.

Behold, I stand at the door and knock. If anyone hears My voice
and opens the door, I will come in to him.

REVELATION 3:20

The early twentieth-century pastor Walter B. Hanson told of an acquaintance in the English countryside where he grew up. She was an old saint known as Granny Pood. Hanson was walking along the road one day when he met Granny. They chatted and he asked, "Where are you going?" She told him she was on her way to visit another woman who was old and poor and that she would probably stay to have tea with her. Because he knew the woman, Hanson said impulsively, "Well, I do not think you will find much tea there." Upon hearing that, Granny reached under her shawl and brought out a little paper package and replied, "I am taking the tea with me."

That's what our Lord does when we open our hearts fully to Him. He brings His provisions with Him—the infinite resources of His own person. Think of what it means to fellowship with Him. How inadequate our strength! But the One who comes to dwell within us brings grace and strength for every need. —P. R. V.

CHRIST IS NOT SIMPLY OUR PROVIDER, HE IS THE PROVISION.

The children of men put their trust
under the shadow of Your wings.

PSALM 36:7

Many years ago near the royal English residence on the Isle of Wright stood several homes for the poor and aged. A missionary, visiting some of the elderly people, asked a lady, "Does Queen Victoria ever call on you here?" "Oh, yes," was the answer, "Her Majesty frequently comes to see us." Then, wondering if the woman was a Christian, the missionary inquired, "What about the King of kings?" The lady immediately smiled and replied, "No, sir, He doesn't visit here—He lives here. That's why we're so richly blessed!"

As I read that story, I was reminded of the incident recorded in Mark 2 and what occurred when Jesus was visiting in a house at Capernaum. Attracted by His miracles and His message, many people came to hear God's Word (v. 2). His presence produced faith, a spirit of helpfulness, and salvation (vv. 3–12). We, too, can be blessed when Christ lives in our homes. Let's make sure He is the honored (and permanent) guest every hour of every day. —H. G. B.

CHRIST MAY RESIDE IN OUR HOME,
BUT DOES HE PRESIDE IN OUR HOME?

Though I bestow all my goods to feed the poor,
. . . but have not love, it profits me nothing.

1 CORINTHIANS 13:3

A small South American fish called "four eyes" knows how to make the best of two worlds. His secret is his large bulging eyes. The Creator designed them so that he can see above the water and below it at the same time. The fish does this by cruising along through the water with the upper half of his eyes above the surface. This top half has an air lens, and the bottom half has a water lens. Together, the two lenses outfit "four eyes" with a set of natural bifocals, allowing him to see both the upper world and the underworld.

In a sense, Christians must be like this little tropical fish. We should look up longingly into the idealism of heaven while looking down lovingly into the realism of earth. The heavenward look is to reflect a hunger and thirst for truth and righteousness, while the earthly look shows our compassion and love for the lost and suffering. Who is in a better position to know the best of both worlds than Christians? We have received both truth and love. — M. R. D. II

KEEP GOD'S TRUTH IN YOUR HEAD
AND HIS LOVE IN YOUR HEART.

*He who believes in the Son of God
has the witness in himself.*

1 JOHN 5:10

My friend Herb Tyler was visiting Bern, Switzerland and stopped at a cafe to order a cup of tea. When the French waitress brought it, she also offered some cream in a tiny pitcher with the Swiss emblem on the side. Herb asked her, "How much for this porcelain pitcher?" She replied, "You want to buy?" "Yes," said my friend. She responded in some amazement because, as she noted, "Americans don't buy." Then she showed what many tourists do. She made the motions of pouring out the cream and sneaking the pitcher into a pocket. To this, Herb said, "Not when we have Jesus Christ in our heart." The waitress asked, "Who is Jesus Christ?" A few minutes later she finished her work and sat down across the table from Herb, and he told her about Jesus. That day a French waitress in Bern, Switzerland, received Christ as her Savior.

As Christians, we are ambassadors for Christ, our King. Our behavior before the world, both in word and action, must therefore be above reproach. Integrity may be the key that opens the door for our witness for Christ.—P. R. V.

WHEN YOU GIVE YOUR WORD, KEEP IT.

Caleb . . . said, "Let us go up at once and take possession,
for we are well able to overcome it."

NUMBERS 13:30

A shoe salesman was sent to a remote part of the country. When he arrived, he was dismayed because everyone went around barefooted. So he wired the company, "No prospect for sales. People don't wear shoes here." Later another salesman went to the same territory. He too immediately sent word to the home office. But his telegram read, "Great potential! People don't wear shoes here!"

When Joshua and Caleb returned from Canaan they described a land flowing with milk and honey and opportunity. The other ten spies also saw a land flowing with milk and honey but they also saw obstacles standing in the way of conquering the land. How could two opinions based on the same facts be so different? The answer is simple. The majority view didn't take God into account, and that spelled insurmountable obstacles! The minority report, however, included God, and that spelled unlimited opportunity! —D. J. D.

YOU WON'T BE BLIND TO POSSIBILITIES
IF YOU KEEP YOUR EYES ON JESUS.

Let all those rejoice who put their trust in You.

PSALM 5:11

I was sitting in my rowboat on Pratt Lake about midnight, fishing for pike. The air was calm, and the surface of the lake was like glass. The moon, full and silvery, was reflected perfectly in the still water, and I marveled at the awesome sight. Then I whimsically cast a lure into the reflection, and it looked as if the moon had been shattered into a thousand pieces. Now, I would have been foolish to think that the moon itself had suddenly been shattered by some lunar explosion. All I had to do was look up into the sky to reassure myself that the moon was still there—shining brightly and unchanged.

Sometimes Christians confuse a temporary loss of the joy of their salvation with a loss of their salvation itself. Because of unconfessed sin, broken fellowship with God, or a decrease in their love for others, they do not feel the underlying joy in Christ they once knew. Because the feeling is gone, they conclude that their salvation is gone as well. But how wrong they are! Losing the feeling of being saved is like shattering the reflection of the moon. Just as the moon remains unchanged, so our salvation is still secure. —D. C. E.

OUR SALVATION IS BASED ON FAITH, NOT FEELING.

*Having then gifts differing according to the grace
that is given to us, let us use them.*

ROMANS 12:6

Gary Inrig in *A Call to Excellence* tells the following story.
"Bertoldo de Giovanni is a name even the most enthusiastic
lover of art is unlikely to recognize. . . . He was the pupil of Donatello,
the greatest sculptor of his time, and he was the teacher of Michelangelo,
the greatest sculptor of all time. Michelangelo was only fourteen years
old when he came to Bertoldo, but it was already obvious that he was
enormously gifted. Bertoldo was wise enough to realize that gifted people
are often tempted to coast rather than to grow, and therefore he kept trying
to pressure his young prodigy to work seriously at his art. One day he
came into the studio to find Michelangelo toying with a piece of sculpture
far beneath his abilities. Bertoldo grabbed a hammer, stomped across the
room, and smashed the work into tiny pieces, shouting this unforgettable
message, 'Michelangelo, talent is cheap, dedication is costly!'"

Likewise, each Christian has talents he can use in the Lord's work,
but they must be developed through dedication and commitment. Have
you discovered those special gifts God has given you? Then dedicate
them to Him. It's the first step toward using your gifts for His glory.
—D. C. E.

**YOUR LIFE IS GOD'S GIFT TO YOU:
WHAT YOU DO WITH IT IS YOUR GIFT TO GOD.**

It is God who arms me with strength,
and makes my way perfect.

PSALM 18:32

James Gray wrote about a tourist in Portugal who saw a fisherman's wife at the water's edge holding a small child by the hand. Just beyond where they were walking was a sharp drop off. Still the mother kept leading the boy toward the brink. The frightened youngster clung to her, but with affectionate words she led him to the same spot again and again. Finally, encouraged by her reassurances, he toddled along the edge by himself. Gray said, "The traveler trembled at the risk, . . . a few feet farther the water deepened dangerously. But there was no real cause for alarm. The mother's eye was on the boy, and her hand was ready to catch him before he went too far. 'What are you doing?' the traveler asked. 'Drawing out his fear,' the woman answered."

If God asks us to walk on dangerous paths, we can count on His presence and unfailing help. As we cling by faith to His promises, we will find that His unfailing presence will "draw out" our fear. —H. G. B.

FAITH LOOKS BEYOND THE SHADOW TO SEE THE SAVIOR.

*Through one Man's righteous act the free gift came to all men,
resulting in justification of life.*

ROMANS 5:18

The final draft of the Emancipation Proclamation was taken to Abraham Lincoln at noon on January 1, 1863. Twice the president picked up his pen to sign it, and twice he laid it down. Turning to Secretary of State William Seward, he said, "I have been shaking hands since 9:00 o'clock this morning, and my right arm is almost paralyzed. If my name ever goes into history, it will be for this act, and my whole soul is in it. If my hand trembles when I sign the proclamation, all who examine the document hereafter will say, 'He hesitated.'" The president then took up the pen again and slowly but firmly wrote, "Abraham Lincoln." That historic act endeared Lincoln to the world as the Great Emancipator.

One greater than Lincoln and with even surer resolve brought freedom to the human race. Jesus signed our liberty with His own blood by dying on the cross to release us from the awful slavery of sin. Having trusted the Savior, we have been set free from sin's awful condemnation. Now by His Spirit we have the power to turn from sin and live for Him. That's the only way to honor Christ—our Great Emancipator. —D. J. D.

**THE EMPTY CROSS AND THE EMPTY TOMB
SPELL A FULL SALVATION.**

November

As a father pities his children,
so the LORD pities those who fear Him.

PSALM 103:13

A. Parnell Bailey visited an orange grove where an irrigation pump had broken down. The season was unusually dry and some of the trees were beginning to die for lack of water. The man giving the tour then took Bailey to his own orchard where irrigation was used sparingly. "These trees could go without rain for another two weeks," he said. "You see, when they were young, I frequently kept water from them. This hardship caused them to send their roots deeper into the soil in search of moisture. Now mine are the deepest-rooted trees in the area. While others are being scorched by the sun, these are finding moisture at a greater depth."

Children actually want loving discipline. If they don't receive it, they can feel aimless and insecure. Perhaps they'll thrive for a time, but in life's droughts they will wither and die. Every parent is challenged by the question, "How much freedom should I give my children?" A proper balance between too much and too little is difficult to maintain and requires great wisdom and guidance from our heavenly Father. —D. J. D.

THE SUREST WAY TO MAKE LIFE HARD FOR YOUR CHILDREN
IS TO MAKE IT SOFT FOR THEM.

Where can I go from Your Spirit?
Or where can I flee from Your presence?

PSALM 139:7

I read about an interesting map that is on display in the British Museum in London. It's an old mariner's chart, drawn in 1525, outlining the North American coastline and adjacent waters. The cartographer made some intriguing notations on areas of the map that represented regions not yet explored. He wrote: "Here be giants," "Here be fiery scorpions," and "Here be dragons." Eventually, the map came into the possession of Sir John Franklin, a British explorer in the early 1800's. Scratching out the fearful inscriptions, he wrote these words across the map: "HERE IS GOD."

We Christians sometimes respond to "the unknown" like that ancient mariner. As we pass through difficult and frightening situations, we may feel as though we are being threatened by the "giants" of fear, the "scorpions" of pain, or the "dragons" of discouragement. But God's children find great comfort and courage in knowing that wherever they go and in whatever situation they may find themselves, God is with them. Wherever we are, we can joyfully exclaim, "HERE IS GOD!"—R. W. D.

FOR THE CHRISTIAN, NO DANGER
CAN COME SO NEAR THAT GOD IS NOT NEARER.

*When we were enemies we were reconciled to God
through the death of His Son.*

ROMANS 5:10

During the seventeenth century, Oliver Cromwell, Lord Protector of England, sentenced a soldier to be shot for his crimes. The execution was to take place at the ringing of the evening curfew bell. However, the bell did not sound. The soldier's fiancee had climbed into the belfry and clung to the great clapper of the bell to prevent it from striking. When she was summoned by Cromwell to account for her actions, she wept as she showed him her bruised and bleeding hands. Cromwell's heart was touched and he said, "Your lover shall live because of your sacrifice. Curfew shall not ring tonight!"

Like that condemned man, we are all rebels against God under a sentence of death. But He loved us so much that He sent His Son, the Lord Jesus, to intervene in our behalf. He has saved us at great cost to Himself. If skeptics had questioned Jesus after His resurrection, all He would have had to do is show them His hands—His bruised, nail-pierced hands. They are ample proof that He has given Himself for mankind.—H. G. B.

CHOOSING CHRIST CHANGES LIFE FOREVERMORE.

Your word is a lamp to my feet and a light to my path.

PSALM 119:105

When the western United States was being settled, roads were often just wagon tracks. These rough trails posed serious problems for those who journeyed on them. On one of these winding paths was posted a sign which read: "Avoid this rut or you'll be in it for the next twenty-five miles!"

In a similar way, we must be careful to steer clear of sinful attitudes and deeds, because once we get into these "ruts" we may be trapped by them for many years. Negative thoughts may seem harmless, but if we do not check them daily and replace them with forgiveness and loving acts, we soon become critical in our whole outlook on life. Nurturing godly habits takes work, especially if old patterns of behavior must be uprooted.

But as we yield to the Holy Spirit's control and fill our minds with the truths of Scripture, we will form good character traits that will help us make our way successfully through the wilderness of this world. —H. G. B.

**A BAD HABIT IS LIKE A COMFORTABLE BED—
EASY TO GET INTO BUT HARD TO GET OUT OF!**

Blessed are those who hunger and thirst for righteousness,
for they shall be filled.

MATTHEW 5:6

A devoted follower of Socrates asked him the best way to acquire knowledge. Socrates responded by leading him to a river and plunging him beneath the surface. The man struggled to free himself, but Socrates kept his head submerged. Finally, after much effort, the man was able to break loose and emerge from the water. Socrates then asked, "When you thought you were drowning, what one thing did you want most of all?" Still gasping for breath, the man exclaimed, "I wanted air!" The philosopher wisely commented, "When you want knowledge as much as you wanted air, then you will get it!"

The same is true with our desire for righteousness. When we trust Christ, God declares us righteous in His sight. But that doesn't mean we are perfect. We need to grow daily in the grace and knowledge of our Lord and Savior Jesus Christ (2 Pet. 3:18). And this can happen only if we have an intense desire to grow. It should be our highest aspiration to be like Christ every day. —R. W. D.

SANCTIFICATION REQUIRES CONSECRATION WITHOUT RESERVATION.

*We are His workmanship,
created in Christ Jesus for good works.*

EPHESIANS 2:10

Several centuries ago, a Japanese emperor commissioned an artist to paint a bird. A number of months passed, then several years, and still no painting was brought to the palace. Finally the emperor became so exasperated that he went to the artist's home to demand an explanation. Instead of making excuses, the artist placed a blank canvas on the easel. In less than an hour, he completed a painting that was to become a brilliant masterpiece. When the emperor asked the reason for the delay, the artist showed him armloads of drawings of feathers, wings, heads, and feet. Then he explained that all of this research and study had been necessary before he could complete the painting.

In a sense Christians are similar to that piece of art. We are "sealed with the Holy Spirit of promise" (Eph. 1:13), and predestined by God "to be conformed to the image of His Son" (Rom. 8:29). But this process takes time. The "artist" is the Holy Spirit—sent by the Lord Jesus at Pentecost to indwell believers. Slowly but surely He leads us to spiritual growth and maturity. Our transformation requires years of patience and will not be finished until we enter the presence of our King. —D. C. E.

**THE WORK CHRIST ACCOMPLISHED FOR US,
HIS SPIRIT COMPLETES IN US.**

What is desired in a man is kindness.

PROVERBS 19:22

Marion F. Ash and an elderly gentleman were painting a farmhouse on a hot summer day. They had just refreshed themselves with a cold drink of water and were returning to their ladders when a small boy with only one arm came riding toward them on his bike. He stopped and said, "I live down the road a ways. Ma sent me to see if you needed some drinking water. If you do, I can go back and fetch it in a glass canning jar." Mr. Ash was about to decline the offer, but his older companion said, "You sure came in the nick of time, Sonny. A good drink of water would do wonders for both of us." The youngster grinned and called out, "I'll be right back. I bet you think you're lucky that I came along!" The elderly man replied, "You can say that again! Now our worries are over. We've got another man on the job." Commenting on this incident, Mr. Ash wrote, "With a few well-chosen words my friend had transformed a young, handicapped lad into a confident human being."

The world needs people who affirm the worth of others by acts of kindness and words of encouragement. This poor old world needs the wealth of positive attitudes and hopeful persuasion. —H. V. L.

KIND WORDS ARE MUSIC TO A HURTING HEART.

Lead me in Your truth and teach me,
for You are the God of my salvation.

PSALM 25:5

During World War II, the King of England ordered an evacuation of children from the bomb-torn areas of London. Since many of the youngsters had never been away from home, they were anxious and upset. A mother and father had just put their young son and daughter aboard a crowded train and said good-bye. No sooner had it left the station than the little girl began to cry. She told her brother she was scared because she didn't know where they were going. Brushing his own tears away, he put his arm around his sister to comfort her. "I don't know where we are going either," he said, "but the King knows, so don't worry!"

Many of us are like that little girl—fearful because we often feel alone and uprooted in this dark and dangerous world. The emergencies and problems we meet each day can be faced with calmness if we simply trust God's leading. We may not always understand where God is taking us, but we are assured that the King knows! —H. G. B.

WHEN YOU CAN'T SEE THE ROAD AHEAD,
HOLD TIGHT TO THE HAND OF THE ONE WHO CAN.

"If he sins against you seven times in a day, and seven times in a day returns to you, saying, 'I repent,' you shall forgive him."

LUKE 17:4

If you play golf, you know how important it is to hit the ball at just the right spot on the club face. And if you have kept up with the latest advancements in golf equipment, you also know that it is becoming easier to do just that. A golf pro recently described the newest drivers and irons as being very "forgiving." He explained that the improved metal-head woods, featherweight clubs, and hollow-back irons have expanded what is often referred to as the "sweet spot" on the club. He said that now it is possible to hit the ball on the heel or the toe of the club and still get good distance.

The idea of a golf club that has a large and forgiving "sweet spot" reminds me of how Christians should respond to one another. Instead of being like the old, unforgiving club that required near perfect performance, we should be like the new club that is generous with the faults of the golfer. We should have a large "sweet spot" that provides plenty of room to forgive any repentant brother or sister in Christ.
—M. R. D. II

WE CAN STOP FORGIVING OTHERS WHEN CHRIST STOPS FORGIVING US.

You will keep him in perfect peace, whose mind is stayed on You,
because he trusts in You.

ISAIAH 26:3

A contest was held in which artists were invited to paint a picture of perfect peace. The judges eventually narrowed the number of competitors to two. The first had created a scene of a quiet mountain lake. The second depicted a thundering waterfall with the branch of a birch tree bending over the foam. On the fork of that limb, wet with spray, a robin sat undisturbed on her nest. The first picture spoke of tranquility, but the second won the prize because it showed in dramatic detail that absolute calmness can be found in the midst of turbulent surroundings. Yes, it is easy to remain unruffled when everything is quiet and serene. But to rest while the storm is raging—that is "perfect peace."

As you face the trials and testings of life, turn all your anxieties over to the Lord. Center your thoughts on Him and the precious promises of His Word, and you'll experience a peace that passes all understanding. —H. G. B.

THOSE WHO PLACE THEMSELVES IN THE CARE OF GOD
EXPERIENCE THE PEACE OF GOD.

Do not lie to one another,
since you have put off the old man with his deeds.

COLOSSIANS 3:9

*D*r. Madison Sarratt taught mathematics at Vanderbilt University for many years. Before giving a test, the professor would admonish his class something like this: "Today I am giving two examinations—one in trigonometry and the other in honesty. I hope you will pass them both. If you must fail one, fail trigonometry. There are many good people in the world who can't pass trig, but there are no good people in the world who cannot pass the examination of honesty."

In many ways, all of us are taking the test of truthfulness each day. For instance, what do we do at the checkout counter when the clerk gives us too much change by mistake? It's so easy to say nothing. Besides, it's the cashier's error, not ours! And what about our conversation with others? It's so easy to color the facts or express half-truths to protect ourselves or to make an impression. Our integrity is constantly being tested. How do we score? Do we pass the exam? —D. J. D.

NO ONE WILL KNOW YOU ARE HONEST
UNLESS YOU GIVE OUT SAMPLES.

Do not be wise in your own eyes;
fear the LORD and depart from evil.

PROVERBS 3:7

Bernie May of Wycliffe Bible Translators wrote, "As an airplane pilot, from the first time I sat in the beginner's seat beside my instructor I was taught to 'trust' my instruments. 'Your instincts will fool you,' my instructor rightly told me. 'You must learn that even though you may feel you are flying south, if your compass says you are flying east, you'd better believe it.' Often when a plane is surrounded by swirling mist and being buffeted by strong winds, you may feel you are in a dive and be tempted to pull back on the controls. But if your instruments say you are flying level—or even climbing— you'd better believe them. To pull back on the controls might put you into a steep climb, which would cause the plane to stall, drop off in a spin, and leave you out of control."

Just as a pilot must learn to trust his instruments, we must learn to trust God. Our feelings lie; our vision is shortsighted. But as we stay close to Him and acknowledge His direction, we will begin to depend solely on His guidance. —D. C. E.

**IT IS BETTER TO WALK IN THE DARK WITH GOD
THAN TO GO ALONE IN THE LIGHT.**

Lord, teach us to pray.

LUKE 11:1

James Francis has given a concise explanation of The Lord's Prayer recorded in Matthew 6:9–13. He notes that it begins with worship and ends with intercession: "When we are told to pray, 'Our Father in heaven,' we are admonished to come simply as a child addressing his Father. When we exclaim, 'Hallowed be Your name,' it is as a worshiper addressing his God. 'Your kingdom come' reminds us that we petition the throne as a citizen who approaches his King. 'Your will be done on earth as it is in heaven' emphasizes that we come as a servant speaking to his Master. 'Give us this day our daily bread' pictures us as a beggar approaching his Benefactor. 'And forgive us our debts, as we forgive our debtors' is the plea of a sinner seeking pardon from his Savior. 'And do not lead us into temptation' depicts a pilgrim beseeching his Guide for safe, providential direction. 'But deliver us from the evil one' is the cry of one . . . who seeks help from his great Defender."

As we meditate on the deep significance of our Lord's instructions about prayer, our own prayers will become more effective. —H. G. B.

**SOMETHING HAPPENS WHEN WE PRAY—
SIN, DISEASE, AND FEAR GIVE WAY.**

Christ also suffered for us, leaving us an example,
that you should follow His steps.

1 PETER 2:21

The more we get to know Jesus, the more we realize how far short we fall from His perfection. We are also made aware of those qualities that should be reproduced in our lives through the power of the Holy Spirit within us.

David Gregg described a perfect illustration of these truths: "A visitor going into the studio of a great painter found on his easel some very fine gems, brilliant and sparkling. Asked why he kept them there, the painter replied, 'I keep them there to tone up my eyes. When I am working in pigments, unconsciously the sense of color becomes weakened. By having these pure colors before me to refresh my eyes, the sense of color is brought up again, just as the musician by his tuning fork brings his strings up to concert pitch.'" Gregg then made this application: "For right living we need clear conceptions of the perfect One. We need to be toned up. We need to be reminded constantly of the high and holy life of the perfect Man, Christ Jesus." —R. W. D.

TO HAVE AN UPRIGHT LIFE, LEAN ON JESUS.

*Do not worry about tomorrow,
for tomorrow will worry about its own things.*

MATTHEW 6:34

Did you hear about the clock that had a nervous breakdown? At first everything was fine—it was keeping good time and operating in excellent fashion. But then it started to think about how many ticks would go through its mechanism before it died of old age. Two ticks a second would add up to 120 ticks a minute, 7,200 per hour, 172,800 per day, 1,209,600 per week, and 62,899,200 ticks for the year. Troubled by these staggering statistics, the poor clock collapsed from nervous exhaustion. The owner took it to a clock doctor who probed until he learned what was worrying the timepiece. "I have to tick so much," said the clock. "But just a minute," replied the doctor, "how many ticks do you have to produce at a time?" "Oh, I operate one tick at a time," responded the clock.

A fanciful story? Yes, but many of us think that way. We borrow trouble from tomorrow rather than trusting God for each day. Faith in the ability of our Heavenly Father to supply every need and meet every emergency will enable us to live triumphantly. We can confidently place tomorrow in His hands. —P. R. V.

**PUT YOUR CARES IN GOD'S HANDS.
HE'LL PUT PEACE IN YOUR HEART.**

So we built the wall, and the entire wall was joined together
up to half its height, for the people had a mind to work.

NEHEMIAH 4:6

A poor, hungry young man stood idly on a bridge watching some fishermen. Seeing one of them with a basket full of fish by his side, he said, "If I had a catch like that, I'd be happy. I'd sell it and buy some food and clothes." "I'll give you that many fish if you do a small favor for me," said the fisherman. "What do you want me to do?" came the reply. "Just tend this line awhile. I've got some business down the street." Gladly the young man accepted the offer. After the man left, the trout and bass continued snapping greedily at the baited hook. Soon he lost all his depression in the excitement of pulling in a large number of fish. When the angler returned, he said to the young man, "I'll keep my promise to you by giving you everything you've caught. And I hope you've learned a lesson. You mustn't waste time daydreaming and merely wishing for things. Instead, get busy and cast in a line for yourself!"

When we give ourselves wholeheartedly to the task at hand, we can accomplish outstanding results. —H. G. B.

The father of success is WORK;
the mother of achievement is AMBITION.

This is a faithful saying and worthy of all acceptance, that Christ Jesus came into the world to save sinners, of whom I am chief.

1 TIMOTHY 1:15

Years ago a drunken man in Chicago headed toward Lake Michigan to drown himself. As he stumbled along in front of the Pacific Garden Mission, someone helped him through the open door. The man collapsed in front of the preacher and fell asleep. The superintendent of the mission cared for him, gave him a bed, and the next day explained the gospel to him. That day Harry Monroe was transformed by the grace of God. Later he was to preach the gospel from that same platform where once he had slept in a drunken stupor. Mr. Monroe eventually became superintendent of the mission, and when he died it took all day for people to pay their respects. A newspaper editorial described him as one of Chicago's most useful men.

What made the difference? Someone reached out in love to a penniless derelict. Like Christ, he looked beyond the wreckage produced by sin and saw a person of great potential and worth. —D. J. D.

GOD SAVES US, NOT FOR WHAT WE ARE
BUT FOR WHAT HE CAN MAKE OF US.

And Abraham called the name of the place,
"The-LORD-Will-Provide."

GENESIS 22:14

A young bride planned to entertain some friends but lacked some of the things she would need. So she went to a neighbor to borrow them. After giving the items to her, the neighbor asked, "Is that all you want?" "Yes, I think so," the young woman answered. Then her neighbor, who was an experienced hostess, handed her some other items and said, "But you will also need some of this, and that, and some more of these." Later the young woman remarked, "I was so thankful I went to someone who knew exactly what I needed and was willing to supply it."

How well that describes God! Through the sacrifice of His Son, He has given us salvation. But that's not all. He also provides power through the Holy Spirit so that we can do His will. God sees beforehand what our needs are, and He provides for them. He is our *Jehovah-Jireh*—the Lord who provides! —P. R. V.

WHERE GOD GUIDES, HE PROVIDES.

As newborn babes, desire the pure milk of the word,
that you may grow thereby.

1 PETER 2:2

Several years ago the telephone company put an advertisement in its phone book promoting the use of the yellow pages. The ad said:

BORN TO BE BATTERED

. . . the lovin' phone call book.

- UNDERLINE IT
- CIRCLE THINGS
- WRITE IN THE MARGINS
- TURN DOWN PAGE CORNERS

The more you use it, the more valuable it gets to be.

The Bible also becomes more valuable to us the more we use it. Because "the Word of the Lord endures forever," we must become familiar with divine truth. We should underline some things and circle others. Important observations and key ideas should be jotted in the margins. Let's make our Bibles an important part of our lives. The Bible that is studied is the best Bible! —D. C. E.

A BIBLE THAT IS FALLING APART
USUALLY BELONGS TO A PERSON WHO ISN'T.

With the lute I will praise You—
and Your faithfulness, O my God!

PSALM 71:22

In his book *Standing Out*, Charles Swindoll wrote, "The splinter in my thumb this morning brings back pleasant memories of yesterday's diversion. Cranking up the old radial-arm saw in my garage, I wound up with two perky cedar window-box planters. I plunged into the project with the zeal of a paratrooper, ecstatic over the airborne sawdust, delighting over every angle, every nail, every hammer blow, even the feel of the wood and the scream of the saw. I caught myself thinking about nothing but the next cut and its proper measurement, the exhilaration of accomplishment, the sheer joy of doing something totally opposite of my career and completely different from my calling."

When we get cranky and hard to live with, we probably need some meaningful diversion from life's routine. Sir William Osler wrote, "No man is really happy or safe without a hobby, and it makes precious little difference what it may be—botany, beetles, or butterflies, fishing, mountaineering, or antiques." Are you getting increasingly irritable and finding it hard to relax? Perhaps it's time for a hobby! —D. C. E.

MANY PEOPLE ARE TOO BUSY MAKING A LIVING
TO MAKE LIFE WORTH LIVING.

He who says he abides in Him
ought himself also to walk just as He walked.

1 JOHN 2:6

A senior executive of a large bank in New York City told how he had risen to a place of prominence and influence. At first he served as an office boy. Then one day the president of the company called him aside and said, "I want you to come into my office and work with me each day." The young man replied, "But what could I do to help you, sir? I don't know anything about finances." "Never mind that. You will learn faster what I want to teach you if you just stay by my side and keep your eyes and ears open." "That was the most significant experience of my life," said the executive. "Being with that wise man made me just like him. I began to do things the way he did, and that accounts for what I am today."

In a far deeper sense, we can be transformed by having a close fellowship with the Lord Jesus. Through meditation, prayer, and obedience to Him, we will gradually take on those qualities that characterize the Savior. —H. G. B.

**CHRISTIANITY IS NOT JUST CHRIST IN YOU,
BUT CHRIST LIVING THROUGH YOU.**

Your righteousness is an everlasting righteousness,
and Your law is truth.

PSALM 119:142

I love the story in *National Geographic* about Carl Sharsmith, an eighty-one-year-old guide in Yosemite National Park. "Carl was back at his tent quarters after a long afternoon with tourists. His nose was flaked white and red with sunburn; his eyes were watery, partly from age but also from hearing again an old question after a half century of summers in California's Yosemite National Park. A lady tourist had hit him with a question where it hurt: 'I've only got an hour to spend at Yosemite,' she declared. 'What should I do? Where should I go?' The old ranger finally found voice to reply. 'Ah, lady . . . only an hour.' He repeated it slowly. 'I suppose that if I had only an hour to spend at Yosemite, I'd just walk over there by the river and sit down and cry.'"

That story reminds me of the awesome wonder of spending time in God's Word. A whole lifetime is not long enough to appreciate fully the beauty and learning and value of the Bible. That's why we must take time to study its truths and make them real in our lives. —D. C. E.

THE DEEP TRUTHS OF THE WORD ARE BEST MINED
WITH THE SPADE OF MEDITATION.

Do not be conformed to this world,
but be transformed by the renewing of your mind.

ROMANS 12:2

A young woman who was greatly troubled went to a Scottish preacher, asking how she could resolve the question of her own desires when they seemed to contradict the will of God. The minister took out a slip of paper and wrote two words on it. Then he handed it to her with the request that she sit down for ten minutes, ponder the words, cross out one of them, and bring the slip back to him. The woman sat down and looked at the slip. It had two words on it, "No" and "Lord." Which should she cross out? It did not take her long to see that if she was saying no, she could not say Lord, and if she wanted to call Christ Lord, she could not say no.

Herein lies the secret of discerning God's will for our lives. From the limitless options before us, we cannot know God's choice until we put ourselves unconditionally at His disposal. Once the question of being yielded is settled, we can take the second step—bringing our behavior in line with the renewing of our minds. And that renewing occurs only when we pattern our thinking after the principles of God's Word. —D. J. D.

GOD GIVES HIS BEST TO THOSE WHO LEAVE THE CHOICE WITH HIM.

The Son of Man did not come to be served,
but to serve, and to give His life a ransom for many.

MARK 10:45

At an organ recital many years ago, the man who pumped the bellows suddenly became ill. Immediately a famous composer who was present in the organ loft stepped forward and took his place so that the concert could go on. After the performance, a friend found out what had happened and criticized the composer for stooping to do such "commonplace" work. "Commonplace?" replied the composer. "I love music so much that nothing I can do for it seems commonplace."

That same spirit should motivate us in our service for the Lord. To be "somebody" in the kingdom of God, we must be willing to start at the bottom and let God promote us. Ambition is a commendable trait and is vital to being successful in life. But in the Lord's work it must be seen in the context of choosing the lowest place rather than the position of prominence. Instead of looking for a place of significance, let's look for a place of service. —D. J. D.

WE MUST BE BIG ENOUGH TO BECOME SMALL ENOUGH
FOR GOD TO USE US.

*The sheep hear his voice; and he calls his own sheep
by name and leads them out.*

JOHN 10:3

Marvin Rosenthal, writing in *Israel, My Glory*, tells about a mother who was asked by a census taker how many children she had. She responded, "Well, there's Billy and Harry and Martha and—" "Never mind the names," the man interrupted. "Just give me the number!" The mother, becoming indignant, replied, "They haven't got numbers, they've all got names."

That's the way it is in our relationship with the Lord. Paul, writing to Timothy, gave the assuring word that "the Lord knows those who are His" (2 Tim. 2:19). And Jesus said, "I am the good shepherd; and I know My sheep" (John 10:14). We're not just numbers to Him. He calls us by name! —R. W. D.

GOD KNOWS EACH WINDING PATH I TAKE,
AND EVERY SORROW, PAIN, AND ACHE.

The fear of the LORD
is the beginning of knowledge.

PROVERBS 1:7

Several years ago, Jack Eckerd, founder of the Eckerd drugstore chain, committed his life to Christ. Shortly afterward as he walked through one of his stores, he noticed the magazine racks with their glossy copies of *Playboy* and *Penthouse*. Although Eckerd was retired from active management, he called the president of the company and urged him to get rid of those pornographic magazines. The president protested because substantial profits were gained from their sales. Being the largest stockholder, Eckerd himself stood to lose a lot of money by such a decision. But he remained firm in his objection, and he prevailed. The offensive magazines were removed from all 1,700 drugstores. When he was asked what motivated him to take this action, Eckerd replied, "God wouldn't let me off the hook!"

Living under the lordship of Jesus Christ must make a difference in the everyday decisions of life. We must be willing to pay the price of discipleship. Unless Jesus makes a difference in how we live, we have no right to call Him Lord. Remember, if Christ isn't Lord of all, He is not Lord at all. —D. J. D.

**THERE IS ONLY ONE WAY TO LIVE FOR CHRIST
AND THAT IS DAY BY DAY.**

*Let us do good to all, especially to those
who are of the household of faith.*

GALATIANS 6:10

*S*everal years ago an article appeared in *Time* magazine about
a doctor who lived through the terrible bombing of Hiroshima.
When the blast occurred, Dr. Fumio Shigeto was waiting for a streetcar
only a mile away, but he was sheltered by the corner of a concrete
building. Within seconds after the explosion, his ears were filled with
the screams of victims all around him. Not knowing what had happened,
he stood there for a moment bewildered—one doctor wondering how
he could ever handle this "mountain" of patients. Then, still somewhat
stunned, Dr. Shigeto knelt, opened his black bag, and began treating the
person lying at his feet.

When you are faced with the distressing spiritual needs of a
lost world, don't despair. Do good to those around you. Pray and give
sacrificially to missions. All God asks is that you do what you can do.
—M. R. D. II

DO WHAT YOU CAN WHERE YOU ARE WITH WHAT YOU HAVE.

Direct my steps by Your word,
and let no iniquity have dominion over me.

PSALM 119:133

When my wife and I are preparing for a trip, one of the first things we do is get out the road atlas. We study it intensely to learn the best routes, determine the number of miles we'll have to travel, pick out interesting places to visit, decide how far we can get in a day, and estimate expenses. On the journey, the atlas is our constant companion, and we consult it many times a day. We couldn't get along without it.

Like the highway traveler, we as Christians are on a long and sometimes hazardous journey. We face many decisions and will have many needs on our pilgrimage to paradise. The Bible has been given to us to help us make those decisions and to meet those needs. It should be our constant companion—studied diligently and consulted often along the way. We can't do without it. —D. C. E.

THE BIBLE IS LIKE A COMPASS—
IT ALWAYS POINTS IN THE RIGHT DIRECTION.

Greater love has no one than this,
than to lay down one's life for his friends.

JOHN 15:13

everal years ago studies were conducted among former American prisoners of war to determine what methods used by the enemy had been most effective in breaking their spirit. The findings revealed that they did not break down from physical deprivation and torture as quickly as they did from solitary confinement or from disrupted friendships caused by frequent changing of personnel. Attempts to get the prisoners divided in their attitudes toward one another proved to be the most successful method of discouraging them. It was further learned that the soldiers were not sustained primarily by faith in their country or by the rightness of the cause for which they fought. They drew their greatest strength from the close attachments they had formed to the small military units to which they belonged.

Likewise, our personal relationship to God, vital as that is, is not sufficient to produce spiritual maturity and endurance. Social relationships within a unified, Spirit-filled body of believers are essential for growth and for maintaining our individual faithfulness to the Savior. —M. R. D. II

GOD IN HIS WISDOM HAS GROUPED US FOR GRACE.

All Scripture is given by inspiration of God, and is profitable
for doctrine, for reproof, for correction, for instruction in righteousness.

2 TIMOTHY 3:16

W. A. Criswell, in his book *The Bible for Today's World*, wrote, "Washington, D.C., is the home of the Bureau of Standards. Every weight and every measure that is used in the United States is a copy of the standard that is kept inviolate by the Bureau in Washington. In that Bureau there is a perfect inch, a perfect foot, a perfect yard, a perfect gallon, a perfect pint, a perfect millimeter, a perfect milligram. Every weight and measure that we have finds its standard in that Bureau in Washington, and all are judged by that standard."

Every person has a conscience, but because of sin it is not completely trustworthy. Now, if our conscience condemns us but is unreliable to guide us, what we need is a perfect, unchanging standard to guide our conscience. What the Bureau of Standards is to weights and measures, God's Word is to our conscience. It shows us His perfect will. Forever settled in heaven, God's Word is our perfect standard! —R. W. D.

AN IMPERFECT CONSCIENCE NEEDS A PERFECT GUIDE.

December

Come to Me, all you who labor and are heavy laden,
and I will give you rest.

MATTHEW 11:28

From nature we can learn a lesson about the importance of rest. Built into the life of every tree are stages of dormancy. In his book *As a Tree Grows*, W. Phillip Keller points out that in northern climates the dormant phase is in the winter, and in the tropical regions it is during the hot, dry season. "It is important to understand," says Keller, "that dormancy is not death. A tree may appear to be dead, it is true. The leaves of deciduous trees will be all stripped off in the fall, leaving a stark skeleton. The tree is nevertheless very much alive—but at rest." He added that this dormancy is immediately followed by a period of active growth. The dormant phase is a rebuilding and reconditioning for the upsurge of vigorous activity ahead.

Some Christians think that inactivity is a waste of time. They see the occasional lulls that come into life as being unproductive. But that is not necessarily the case. Notice what Christ did for His disciples after they had finished a strenuous period of evangelistic activity. He led them into the wilderness to rest so they could be restored for further service.

—D. C. E.

TIME IN CHRIST'S SERVICE REQUIRES TIME OUT FOR RENEWAL.

Cleanse me from secret faults.
Keep back Your servant also from presumptuous sins.

PSALM 19:12–13

An incident from the early days of computer technology illustrates how a small problem can lead to big complications. It was 1945, and the U.S. Navy was working hard to get the first digital computer into operation. All of a sudden the room-sized machine broke down completely. A preliminary investigation into the problem left the technicians baffled. Finally, after a more thorough search, one of the scientists discovered the cause of the breakdown. Deep inside the computer, a moth had crawled between two electrical contact points and was stuck. The circuit could not be closed. As soon as the moth was removed, the machine began running again.

How about it? Has some "little" sin come between you and God to disrupt your fellowship with Him? Ask the Holy Spirit to help you identify it. Then get rid of it. When fellowship is restored, you'll be glad you took the time to get the "bugs" out of the system. —D. C. E.

GOD'S SPIRIT IS YOUR POWER SOURCE.
DON'T LET SIN BREAK THE CONNECTION.

You comprehend my path and my lying down,
and are acquainted with all my ways.

PSALM 139:3

Have you ever thought about the remarkable, intricate design of some of the world's little creatures? An example is the honey bee. That tiny insect organizes a virtual city by building 10,000 cells for honey, 12,000 cells for larvae, and an inner sanctum for the queen. He can also sense a dangerous rise in temperature in the hive and organize the other bees to stand at the entrances and fan their wings to keep the honey cool. In addition, one little honey bee can patrol twenty square miles of a field in its search for flowers.

If God has taken such care to build these capabilities into a tiny bee, how much more He has done for us—the crown of creation! In Psalm 139, David has given us a clear picture of God's hand in the affairs of mankind. Our Heavenly Father is "acquainted with all my ways," said the psalmist. In addition, He knows our every thought, He has placed His protecting restraints around us, and His loving hand is upon us. No wonder the writer exclaimed, "Such knowledge is too wonderful for me!"
—P. R. V.

THOSE WHO SEE GOD'S HAND IN EVERYTHING
CAN LEAVE EVERYTHING IN HIS HAND.

For you died, and your life is hidden with Christ in God.

COLOSSIANS 3:3

One of the seven astronauts who lost their lives in the tragic explosion of the space shuttle *Challenger* was Christa McAuliffe. She had been selected from among many applicants to be the first teacher in space. Her enthusiasm, vision, and commitment to both education and the space program captured the imagination of many educators and students. For that reason her death was taken very personally by many. I remember hearing memorial statements that showed the extent to which others identified with her. One teacher said, "When Christa stepped onto that shuttle, we stepped on with her. And when she died, a part of us died too."

These comments about Christa remind me of the Christian's identification with Christ. In a much deeper and far more profound sense, we can say, "When He was lifted up on that cross, we were there with Him. When He died, we died!" It was because of His love for us that He allowed Himself to be crucified. But our confession of faith must be more than a memorial statement. It must show that we have put away our old life of sin and have set our mind on things above. —M. R. D. II

THE CROSS IS MORE THAN A MEMORIAL.
IT IS THE GREATEST MEASURE OF LOVE.

My voice You shall hear in the morning, O LORD;
in the morning I will direct it to You.

PSALM 5:3

Ray Ortlund, in *The Best Half of Life*, wrote, "I like to start out the morning covering the whole day by prayer. After a time of praise and confession, I take out my appointment book and pray through the hours. I pray for everyone I am scheduled to see. I ask that I might be helpful to them, but also open to what they may have for me. I pray for the unscheduled ones I will bump into. I've found that if I pray over my interruptions and get them squarely under God's sovereign control, they don't irritate me. I realize they are part of God's plan. So, pray over your day. Pray about every phone conversation; pray about your lunchtime. The lunch hours are important to use for God. Pray over evening; pray and think about the time you'll be with those you love the most. Pray through the day before you experience it. Then relax. Whatever comes—you've got it covered."

Each day presents trying circumstances, unique challenges, and exciting opportunities. So before we begin our activities, let's turn the day over to God. Then, whatever happens, we've got it covered! —D. C. E.

MORNING PRAYERS LEAD TO EVENING PRAISE.

I have come that they may have life,
and that they may have it more abundantly.

JOHN 10:10

An elderly couple had no means of support except a weekly gift of money from a man in their church. One Sunday the couple's benefactor, who lived quite far away, wanted to remain in the area for the afternoon service. So he said to the old couple, "Would you mind if I joined you for dinner after the morning service?" Immediately the couple thought of the half loaf of stale bread, a bit of butter, and some cheese that was the entire contents of their cupboard. How could this friend dine with them, they thought? But the man interrupted their worries by adding, "I have brought a basket of things with me and there will be plenty for the three of us." When he arrived at the poor, bare cottage, he unpacked the basket. Soon the three of them were gathered around a table that was spread with fried chicken, sliced ham, and apple pie. The man had not only come to dine with them, but he had also brought the feast.

What a picture of Jesus' relationship with us! He desires to fellowship with us, and by His power He provides us with all that we need. We have nothing to offer, but into our spiritual poverty He brings all the riches of His grace. —P. R. V.

GRACE IS EVERYTHING FOR THOSE WHO DON'T DESERVE ANYTHING.

I drew them with gentle cords, with bands of love.

HOSEA 11:4

The naturalist S. L. Bastian tells of a certain kind of spider that builds its nest in the branch of a small tree or bush. In this delicate enclosure the baby spiders are hatched. If the nest is disturbed in any way, the little spiders will all rush out in fright. At once the mother goes to their side. She is alerted to their potential danger in a most unique manner. Each of the young ones has a thin silky strand attached to it, and all of these threads are joined to the body of the mother. When the babies are threatened by an enemy, they naturally scurry off, giving their lines a sharp tug. This is instantly felt by the adult spider. Within seconds she pulls them back to the nest where they are protected from harm.

We, too, are linked to God with eternal cords that cannot be broken. When danger affects us in our daily walk, our Savior's attention is drawn to us in a special way because of the "bands of love" between Him and us. He does not leave us to shift for ourselves. What a comfort it is to know that we are forever bound to the Lord by the gentle cords of His eternal love! —H. G. B.

HOW BLESSED TO BE BOUND BY THE CORDS OF GOD'S LOVE.

Present yourselves to God as being alive from the dead,
and your members as instruments of righteousness to God.

ROMANS 6:13

My friend Jeff Callender told me this story about his daughter. "During the Christmas season when our daughter was three years old, the number of presents under the tree slowly increased as The Day approached. Caught up in the spirit and excitement of gifts and giving as only three-year-olds can be, one morning she was picking up, examining, shaking, and guessing what was inside every package. Then, in a burst of inspiration, she picked up a big red bow that had fallen off one present and held it on the top of her head. She looked up at me with twinkling eyes and beamed a smile as she said, 'Look at me, Daddy! I'm a present!'"

Christmas is the time when we commemorate God's greatest gift to mankind—His Son Jesus Christ. As we contemplate the love that prompted such giving, may our response be one of yielding our lives to Him for His glory. Let's echo the words of that little girl, "Look at me, Father! I'm a present!" —R. W. D.

GIVE GOD YOUR LIFE; HE CAN DO MORE WITH IT THAN YOU CAN.

Confess your trespasses to one another,
and pray for one another, that you may be healed.

JAMES 5:16

While waiting for the teller at a bank counter in Liverpool, England, evangelist Charles Alexander picked up a pen and began to write on a pad of paper. Two words had gripped his heart: "Pray Through." So he wrote them over and over until the paper was filled from top to bottom. When the teller returned to the window, the preacher transacted his business and left. The next day, a friend visited Alexander to tell him a striking story. A businessman had come into the bank shortly after Alexander had left. He was discouraged and weighed down with financial troubles. As he began to do his banking at the same counter, he noticed the pad with its long columns of "Pray Through." When he learned from the teller that Charles Alexander had printed those words, he exclaimed, "That is the very message I need! I have tried to worry through in my own strength, and have only mentioned my troubles to God. Now, I am going to pray through until I get light."

Our heavenly Father waits to hear fervent, earnest, persistent prayer from us rather than feeble, apathetic requests. When troubles surround us, let's determine to "pray through." —P. R. V.

IF YOU ARE A STRANGER TO PRAYER, YOU ARE A STRANGER TO POWER.

*And what does the LORD require of you but to do justly, to love mercy,
and to walk humbly with your God?*

MICAH 6:8

On a visit to America, Princess Diana went into a department store and saw a red-and-black polka-dot silk scarf. "This is very smart looking," she said to an aide, and then instructed her to buy the $8 item. Immediately after Diana's purchase, some men from the British Embassy rushed up to the counter to buy a scarf just like it—presumably for their wives. The wife of a store executive also bought one for her daughter, noting, "She'll be thrilled!" Later, when the store was reopened to the public, a swarm of women raced to the red-and-black, polka-dot scarves, as if guided by radar.

Oh, that we would be as quick to take our cues from the Lord as those people did from royalty! How spiritually enriched we would be if we studied Christ's words and actions and carefully considered His values and choices rather than looking to the world for direction. We must remain free from the deception of the ungodly, choosing instead to follow our divine Guide. —M. R. D. II

YOU ARE EITHER LEAVING YOUR MARK ON THE WORLD,
OR THE WORLD IS LEAVING ITS MARK ON YOU.

*I will praise You with uprightness of heart,
when I learn Your righteous judgments.*

PSALM 119:7

*D*id you know that half of the books of the Bible can be read in less than forty-five minutes each, and many of them in less than twenty? It has been demonstrated that the entire Old and New Testaments can be read aloud in less than seventy-one hours. I heard of one woman who read all sixty-six books of the Bible 143 times! At the age of eighty-five she was still meditating on its precepts by reading through the Scriptures at least four times a year.

A believer who wants to please God will look into His Word for instruction. He will study it carefully, meditate on its principles, and heed its counsels. As he follows its directions, he can avoid bungling and be assured of blessing. Don't go it alone. Go by the Book! —H. G. B.

APPLY YOURSELF WHOLLY TO THE SCRIPTURES
AND THE SCRIPTURES WHOLLY TO YOURSELF.

As the deer pants for the water brooks,
So pants my soul for You, O God.

PSALM 42:1

In his book *Three Deadly Foes*, Henry Durbanville drew a parallel between the Jewish tabernacle in the Old Testament and man. He pointed out that the tabernacle had three sections: the outer court, the holy place, and the holy of holies. Every Israelite was free to enter the outer court, only a select few could go into the holy place, and the high priest had exclusive access into the innermost holy of holies. The author explained that this "is a picture of our individual lives. There is a fringe of our life that is open to the world; a few are permitted to enter the inner chamber; but there is another chamber into which no human eye can see—the innermost shrine of personality. There is in that place a hunger of the soul and a quest of the heart that will not be satisfied with anything that earth can give."

No matter how a person might be blessed with friends and the things of this world, he can never find lasting fulfillment apart from God. Man, created in God's image yet damaged by sin, has an inner void that only God can fill. —R. W. D.

MAN'S SOUL FINDS NO REST UNTIL IT RESTS IN GOD.

DECEMBER 13

*Let each one give as he purposes in his heart,
not grudgingly . . . for God loves a cheerful giver.*

2 CORINTHIANS 9:7

According to an oriental legend, some farmers decided they should keep only their small potatoes for seed. That way they could enjoy the large ones for their meals. So that's what they did—they ate the big ones and planted the little ones. As the years passed, the practice was continued. But eventually the farmers began to notice something unusual at harvest time. Although the small seed potatoes produced a crop, the new potatoes were gradually reduced to the size of marbles. These farmers had learned a costly lesson. They could not expect to grow a crop of large potatoes if they ate the best ones and used the small leftovers for seed.

In God's field of service the generosity or stinginess of our planting will be revealed in the kind of yield we receive at harvest time. Let's think about how this affects the use of the money, the skills, and the talents God has given us. If we invest only a little of ourselves in using these gifts and keep the rest for selfish reasons, our fruitfulness as believers will be meager at best. Let's be sure we are "planting the big potatoes." —P. R. V.

IF WE SOW SPARINGLY WE CANNOT EXPECT TO REAP BOUNTIFULLY.

Delight yourself also in the LORD,
and He shall give you the desires of your heart.

PSALM 37:4

In his book *God's Psychiatry*, Charles L. Allen tells this story: "As World War II was drawing to a close, the Allied armies gathered up many hungry orphans. They were placed in camps where they were well-fed. Despite excellent care, they slept poorly. They seemed nervous and afraid. Finally, a psychologist came up with the solution. Each child was given a piece of bread to hold after he was put to bed. . . . This particular piece of bread was just to be held—not eaten. The piece of bread produced wonderful results. The children went to bed knowing instinctively they would have food to eat the next day. That guarantee gave the children a restful and contented sleep."

Sometimes we think we need more than we have. We substitute desire for need and need for desire. God has promised that if we delight ourselves in Him, He will give us the desires of our heart (Ps. 37:4). This is not an unconditional promise. We must first delight ourselves in Him. Then our desires will be in line with what He desires to give us—and that will bring us true contentment. —D. J. D.

**CONTENTMENT COMES NOT SO MUCH FROM GREATER WEALTH
AS FROM FEWER WANTS.**

*The shepherds returned, glorifying and praising God
for all the things that they had heard and seen.*

LUKE 2:20

In his portrayal of the nativity scene, Rembrandt focused attention entirely on the Babe in the manger. He did this by painting a shaft of light so that it falls exclusively on the Christ-child. Although he included other figures, they are shrouded in shadows. Rembrandt wanted nothing to detract from the significance of that baby—who was God in the flesh. He wanted Christ to be the sole object of adoration.

Luke's gospel gives us a similar picture of Jesus' birth. He is the focus of everyone's attention.

- The shepherds looked upon the baby Jesus and returned "glorifying and praising God" (2:20).
- The devout Simeon, taking the infant into his arms, referred to Him as a "light to bring revelation to the Gentiles" (2:32).
- The prophetess Anna "spoke of Him to all those who looked for redemption in Jerusalem" (2:38).
- The wisemen said, "We have seen His star in the East and have come to worship Him" (Mt. 2:2).

Come let us praise and adore Him, Jesus Christ the Lord.—H. G. B.

GOD'S HIGHEST GIFT AWAKENS MAN'S DEEPEST GRATITUDE.

If one member suffers, all the members suffer with it;
or if one member is honored, all the members rejoice with it.

1 CORINTHIANS 12:26

*D*uring a rehearsal at the Metropolitan Opera House in New York City, Toscanini, the famed maestro, offered some constructive criticism to a featured soloist. She was too proud to accept his help, however, and expressed her resentment by exclaiming in anger, "I am the star of this performance!" Toscanini responded wisely and firmly. "Madame," he said, "in this performance there are no stars."

Even though each Christian has his own unique traits and his own individual duties, taken together we comprise one body. We can make no advances with only solo work. All of us, from the greatest to the humblest, should work together in harmony and devotion. The Lord isn't looking for soloists to be stars; He needs workers who are willing to be servants. God's work calls for teamwork! —R. W. D.

EVERY MEMBER OF A CHURCH CARING
MEANS EVERY MEMBER SHARING.

"Wherever this gospel is preached in the whole world, what this woman has done will also be told as a memorial to her."

MARK 14:9

In Yorkshire, England, during the early 1800's, two sons were born to a family named Taylor. The older one set out to make a name for himself by entering Parliament and gaining public prestige. But the younger son chose to give his life to Christ. He later recalled, "Well do I remember, as in unreserved consecration I put myself, my life, my friends, my all, upon the altar. I felt I was in the presence of God, entering into covenant with the Almighty." With that commitment, Hudson Taylor turned his face toward China and obscurity. As a result, he is known and honored on every continent as a faithful missionary and the founder of the China Inland Mission (now known as Overseas Missionary Fellowship). For the other son, however, there is no lasting monument. He became known simply as "the brother of Hudson Taylor."

You may ask, "Is everyone who yields his life in devotion to the Lord revered like Hudson Taylor?" I'm afraid not. But regardless of any recognition here on earth, every dedicated believer will one day be rewarded by God Himself. That will be a remembrance without equal.

—P. R. V.

GOD'S HALL OF FAME IS FOR ETERNITY!

If you keep My commandments, you will abide in My love.

JOHN 15:9

A man who lived in northern Michigan went for a walk in a densely forested area. The trees were so thick and the woods so immense that a person could easily get lost. So when darkness began to settle in, the man decided it was time to head for home. Since he was used to being in the woods, and because he felt he had a keen sense of direction, he didn't bother to look at his compass. After walking for a long time, however, he decided he'd better make sure that he was going in the right direction, so he checked his compass. He was surprised to find it indicating that he was going west—not east as he had thought. But the man was so sure of his own sense of direction that he concluded there must be something wrong with the compass. He was about to throw it away in disgust when this thought came to him: My compass has never lied to me yet—maybe I should believe it. Well, the story has a happy ending. He found his way out of the woods and arrived home safely because he trusted his compass and didn't rely on himself.

Like that compass, God's instructions are always trustworthy. He will never lead us astray. —R. W. D.

THE BIBLE ALWAYS POINTS THE BELIEVER IN THE RIGHT DIRECTION.

If anyone ministers, let him do it as with the ability which God supplies, that in all things God may be glorified through Jesus Christ.

1 PETER 4:11

In her book *Today's Good Word*, Ethel B. Sutton told the story of a young British soldier who was blinded in battle. He was a trained musician, so after he recovered from his injury he spent much of his time playing the piano for the wounded in a London hospital. He sometimes wondered if anyone was paying attention to his music, for he often heard the tramping of feet through the corridors as visitors came and went. But he never let this distract him. He always put his best effort into his playing, hoping his music would encourage others. One day when he paused to rest, he heard somebody nearby heartily clapping his hands. Turning his sightless eyes in that direction, he asked, "Who are you?" "I am your King!" was the reply. The British monarch was visiting the wounded. Without realizing it, the young man had been using his talent to entertain royalty.

God has given each of us talents He wants us to use in His service. We may not understand why He asks us to serve in a particular place, nor do we know all the results of our labors. But we should remember that our Sovereign Lord is always observing our faithful endeavors. —H. G. B.

OUR TALENTS ARE NOT TO BE LAID UP FOR SELF,
BUT LAID OUT IN SERVICE.

A man's heart plans his way,
but the LORD directs his steps.

PROVERBS 16:9

It was Christmas Eve in Oberndorf, Austria, in 1818. Joseph Mohr, the vicar of the church, had written a new song for the Christmas Eve service and the organist Franz Gruber had set it to music. But the organ in the village church broke down. So Gruber grabbed a guitar and accompanied Mohr in the first-ever rendition of "Silent Night."

The story doesn't end there, however. When a man came to fix the organ, Gruber tested it by playing the new song. The repairman liked the song so much that he took a copy of it back to his own village. There, four daughters of a village glove-maker learned the song and began singing it in concerts all over the region. Because of that faulty organ, this new Christmas song blessed people all over Austria—and eventually the world.

When things break or when plans change, how should we respond? Often we fret and worry because we don't have the control we would like to have. That's when we need to step back, trust God, and wait to see how He is going to use the situation for His glory. —J. D. B.

IN THE DRAMA OF LIFE,
GOD IS THE DIRECTOR BEHIND THE SCENES.

He knows our frame.

PSALM 103:14

In the early days of the automobile, a Model-T Ford stalled in the middle of the road. The driver couldn't get it started no matter how hard he cranked or how much he tried to adjust the spark. Just then a chauffeured limousine pulled up behind him, and a wiry, energetic man stepped out from the back seat and offered his assistance. After looking under the hood and tinkering with something for a few moments, the stranger said, "Now try it!" Immediately the engine leaped to life and purred like a kitten. Extending his hand to the driver, the well-dressed man identified himself as Henry Ford. "I designed and built these cars," he said, "so I know what to do when something goes wrong."

In Psalm 139, David said that God, who created us and has planned our lives, understands us completely. He knows when we sit down and when we rise up, and He knows our thoughts even before they come into our minds. We can turn to Him with confidence when nothing seems to be going right. He knows the difficulty of our situation and exactly what we need. How comforting to know that God understands! —H. G. B.

THE ONE WHO MADE YOU IS THE ONE WHO CAN MEND YOU.

Whoever desires to save his life will lose it,
but whoever loses his life for My sake will find it.

MATTHEW 16:25

The goal of many professional athletes can be summed up in Vince Lombardi's comment, "Winning isn't everything—it's the only thing!" A ball club can outplay its opponents for most of a game, but, according to this view, if they lose in the final minutes their earlier efforts mean little. Winning is what counts. Another perspective is reflected in a slogan I saw as a boy in school. A large poster on the gymnasium wall read, "When all of life is over and the great Judge calls your name, it'll matter not whether you won or lost, but how you played the game."

A third approach is more in keeping with the Christian outlook in the game of life. Wanting to achieve and to win is not wrong. But when it comes to real success, we may need to experience some losses in order to gain God's approval. It won't be easy to sacrifice time, money, and friends to serve Christ. But if we do it willingly out of love for Him, we'll discover that winning the approval of men now isn't worthy of being compared with the glory of winning the praise of God later. —M. R. D. II

THERE ARE NO LOSERS WITH CHRIST
AND NO WINNERS WITH THE DEVIL.

Let each of you look out not only for his own interests,
but also for the interests of others.

PHILIPPIANS 2:4

A young actor was on his first date with a lovely girl he wanted to impress. All through dinner he talked about himself. He told her about his career, bragged about the favorable comments he had received from several big-name people, and spoke glowingly about his prospects for lead roles. When the dessert came, he finally said, "Ah, my dear. Enough about me. Now let's talk about you. What did you think of me in my last role?" Understandably, the young woman dropped him like a hot potato.

Self-centeredness runs contrary to the example set by our Lord Jesus. He left heaven to live in poverty, to endure rejection, and to die like a criminal on a Roman cross. When we reflect on His example, we can't help but see that Christianity and self-centeredness don't mix. Let's check up on ourselves. Whom do we resemble the most—that young actor or the Lord Jesus? —H. V. L.

A PERSON ALL WRAPPED UP IN HIMSELF
MAKES A VERY SMALL PACKAGE.

*"My soul magnifies the Lord,
and my spirit has rejoiced in God my Savior."*

LUKE 1:46-47

A Baltimore congregation found the answer to its financial troubles on a church wall. And it had been "hiding" there for more than twenty-five years! Someone finally recognized a piece of art hanging in the chapel as a valuable woodblock print by Albrecht Dürer, dated 1493. The work shows the angel telling Mary she would give birth to God's Son.

Some members just couldn't believe they had underestimated the value of the old masterpiece, saying in effect, "If it were real, why would it be here?"

What about us? Are we underestimating the value of the event depicted on that woodblock print? Jesus isn't hiding. The truth that God came to earth in human form is plainly announced in His Word. It is reflected in our art and in our hymnbooks. But the significance of Christ's birth is still neglected. Let's not get so wrapped up in activities and programs that we miss the immeasurable worth of knowing who that Baby was. —M. R. D. II

CHRIST'S BIRTH BROUGHT THE INFINITE GOD TO FINITE MAN.

*That was the true Light which gives light
to every man coming into the world.*

JOHN 1:9

An artist was painting a winter scene. Snow covered the ground and blanketed the pine boughs. Night was falling, and the landscape was enveloped in semi-darkness. A log cabin was barely visible in the shadows. The whole scene was one of gloom. Then the artist, using some of the yellow tints, with a few skillful strokes of his brush put into one of the cabin windows the cheerful glow of a lamp. And that lone light, its golden rays reflecting on the snow, completely transformed the impression given by the painting. In contrast to the cold darkness of the surrounding forest, that light in the window created a warm feeling of love and security.

What happened on that canvas is a striking portrayal of one of the most dramatic events of all history. When the Christ-child was born in Bethlehem's stable, a Light was placed in the window of this sin-darkened world. He is truly a Light in the darkness! Yes, He is "the true Light which gives light to every man who comes into the world" (John 1:9).
—R. W. D.

**CHRIST WAS BORN HERE BELOW
THAT WE MIGHT BE BORN FROM ABOVE.**

Christ Jesus came into the world to save sinners,
of whom I am chief.

1 TIMOTHY 1:15

When Martin Luther entered the monastery at Erfurt, Germany, he gave himself wholly to prayers, fastings, watchings, labors—all in a gigantic effort to gain peace from the guilt of his sins. But it was the simple testimony of the dean of the theological faculty, John Staupitz, that brought light to his troubled soul. He urged Luther to look away from his deceitful thoughts and evil impulses, and to cast himself wholly in the Redeemer's arms. "Trust the righteousness of His life and the atonement of His death," he said. Luther did that and found peace. But a short time later he lost the joy of his salvation. "Oh, my sin, my sin, my sin!" he lamented. With utmost kindness the dean replied, "Well, would you only be a sinner in appearance and also have a Savior only in appearance?" Then he added, "Know that Jesus Christ is Savior even of those who are great, real sinners, and deserving of utter condemnation."

If you are prone to look at your own sinfulness, you'll live in constant turmoil. Affirm your faith by thanking Jesus that He is a real Savior for real sinners. —D. J. D.

THERE ARE NONE SO GOOD THAT THEY CAN SAVE THEMSELVES.

Put on the Lord Jesus Christ,
and make no provision for the flesh, to fulfill its lusts.

ROMANS 13:14

The story is told of a man who liked to hunt pheasants. He thought he could do better if he had a dog to help him, so he bought one. However, he was disappointed when he discovered that the dog was interested only in chasing rabbits. The man had acquired a hound dog when what he needed was a bird dog. So instead of hunting pheasants, as he really wanted to, the man spent his time doing what his dog preferred. Finally the hunter decided he had better leave the dog at home.

The hunter solved his problem by taking decisive action. He equipped himself for pheasant hunting and went out without the distracting dog. That's what we must do in the spiritual realm. As we prepare for each day, let's choose to obey the injunction, "Put on the Lord Jesus Christ, and make no provision for the flesh, to fulfill its lusts." When we yield to Christ, rely on His strength, and put Him first, we will reject the evil impulses that arise from the law of sin in our members. That's how we "leave the dog at home." —R. W. D.

IF YOUR CHRISTIAN LIFE IS A DRAG,
WORLDLY WEIGHTS MAY BE KEEPING YOU DOWN.

*I would rather be a doorkeeper in the house of my God
than dwell in the tents of wickedness.*

PSALM 84:10

The United Press International carried this interesting story: "For several years a fourteen-inch statue was used as a doorstop in the home of Leo Carey of Green Township, Ohio. It was not until his estate was appraised that someone recognized the item as a replica in miniature by Rodin of his classic sculpture *The Thinker*, a masterpiece created in the nineteenth century. When art dealers evaluated the find, they estimated its worth at $16,000."

If you are serving the Savior in an area you feel is insignificant, unnoticed, and perhaps unappreciated, remember that you are of great worth to the Lord, who gives "grace to the humble." Let Psalm 84:10 be your rejoicing watchword: "I would rather be a doorkeeper in the house of my God than dwell in the tents of wickedness." —H. G. B.

DOING THE BEST WE CAN IS PART OF GOD'S PLAN.

The LORD is my rock and my fortress and my deliverer;
my God, my strength, in whom I will trust.

PSALM 18:2

The *Detroit News* carried an article about another kind of shield that I find amazing. It is the vast magnetic field that surrounds the earth. Generated by the sun, it is so large that Pioneer 10, which has traveled more than twenty-three trillion miles, has not yet passed out of its protective influence. Called the "heliosphere," this magnetic force shelters our entire solar system from harmful cosmic rays. Without it, life on earth would end.

Reading about our solar system's heliosphere made me think of the greatest protective shield of all—God Himself. David wrote, "The Lord is . . . my shield and . . . my stronghold." He knew that the Lord could keep him secure in a hostile world. We too can know that same confidence. Even though Satan may attack us and evil may surround us, the Lord is our protector. He guards our way and keeps us safe as we walk in obedience to His will. —D. C. E.

GOD IS OUR PERFECT SECURITY IN LIFE'S STORMS.

I press on, that I may lay hold of that
for which Christ Jesus has also laid hold of me.

PHILIPPIANS 3:12

After Calvin Coolidge, the thirtieth president of the United States, issued his famous "I do not choose to run" statement, he was besieged by reporters wanting details. One persistent journalist kept pressing Mr. Coolidge. "Exactly why don't you want to be president again?" he queried. Coolidge looked him squarely in the eye. "Because," he replied, "there's no chance for advancement!"

When a goal is reached, the anticipation associated with it is gone. This must never happen in the Christian life. For the apostle, the goal of being perfected required of him singleness of mind, oneness of purpose, and the bending of all his powers to knowing Christ's presence in life's varied experiences, whether prosperity or adversity. He was seeking to be fully conformed to his Lord, and this would take a lifetime. In the life of a growing Christian there's always room for advancement. —D. J. D.

WHEN GROWTH STOPS, DECAY BEGINS.

Your hand shall lead me,
and Your right hand shall hold me.

PSALM 139:10

While making a brief Christmas address to the people of the British Empire in 1939, King George VI spoke of his faith in God's leading. World War II had begun, and Great Britain faced the onslaughts of Hitler's reckless military barrage. As the King spoke to the people on that Christmas day, he concluded his remarks with these lines written by Minnie Louise Haskins some 30 years earlier: "And I said to the man who stood at the gate of the year: 'Give me a light that I may tread safely into the unknown.' And he replied: 'Go out into the darkness and put your hand into the Hand of God. That shall be to you better than light and safer than a known way.'"

Each of us today faces a future whose trademark is change overlaid with varying and perhaps foreboding circumstances. But we don't have to fear. We have Someone to guide us even in the darkest night. God's presence enables us to face tomorrow with complete confidence. Put your hand in His hand. —P. R. V.

WHEN YOU SEE GOD'S HAND IN EVERYTHING,
YOU CAN LEAVE EVERYTHING IN HIS HAND.

OUR DAILY BREAD

Enjoy it everyday!

You can continue to make *Our Daily Bread* part of your regular time with God. Every month, you can receive a new booklet of devotional articles. Each day's topic is timely and the Bible teaching is reliable—just like the articles you've enjoyed in this book.

To receive *Our Daily Bread* each month at home, with no cost or obligation, just write to us at the address below, or visit us at **www.odb.org/guide** to order online.

As part of the *Our Daily Bread* family, you'll also get opportunities to receive Bible-study guides and booklets on a variety of topics, including creation, the church, and how to live the Christian life.

To order your copy of Our Daily Bread, write to us at:

RADIO BIBLE CLASS — FOUNDED 1938

USA: PO Box 2222, Grand Rapids, MI 49501-2222
CANADA: Box 1622, Windsor, ON N9A 6Z7

Notes

Prayers

Notes

Prayers

Notes

Prayers

Prayers